ROUTLEDGE LIBRARY EDITIONS: EDUCATION

EVERYDAY IMAGINING AND EDUCATION

T0316371

EVERYDAY IMAGINING AND EDUCATION

MARGARET B. SUTHERLAND

Volume 158

Routledge
Taylor & Francis Group
LONDON AND NEW YORK

First published in 1971

This edition first published in 2012
by Routledge
2 Park Square, Milton Park, Abingdon, Oxfordshire OX14 4RN

Simultaneously published in the USA and Canada
by Routledge
711 Third Avenue, New York, NY 10017

First issued in paperback 2014

Routledge is an imprint of the Taylor & Francis Group, an informa business

British Library Cataloguing in Publication Data
A catalogue record for this book is available from the British Library

ISBN 13: 978 0 415 69969 3 (Volume 158)
ISBN 13: 978-1-138-00761-1 (pbk)

Publisher's Note
The publisher has gone to great lengths to ensure the quality of this reprint but
points out that some imperfections in the original copies may be apparent.

Disclaimer
The publisher has made every effort to trace copyright holders and would
welcome correspondence from those they have been unable to trace.

Margaret B. Sutherland

Everyday imagining and education

Routledge & Kegan Paul

London

First Published 1971
by Routledge & Kegan Paul Ltd
Broadway House,
68–74 Carter Lane,
London EC4V 5EL
Printed in Great Britain by
Ebenezer Baylis and Son, Limited
The Trinity Press, Worcester, and London
and set in 10 point Times 1 point leaded.

ISBN 0 7100 6995 2

Contents

Foreword

So much has been written about imagination from so many points of view that it seems possibly unnecessary to write more. But in many present and past discussions of imagination there has been, I think, an excessive amount of attention to the more unusual kinds of imagining and to the performance of people who are specially gifted. It is very easy to become concerned about the ability to produce masterpieces and to make new inventions or produce new theories; these are indeed important for the whole of society. Yet it is equally important to consider the kind of imaginative thinking which goes on constantly without producing such effects, for it is certainly important in the life of the individual.

Some people of course are concerned about this everyday imagining, and especially concerned about its effects on children when television or books stimulate it; but there is often a lack of co-ordination between their thinking and expert opinion or research. There is also at times a lack of communication between psychologists and educators who are interested in imagination, or between teachers of English and other educators or psychologists. It seems worth while therefore to try to consider together some educational theories, some psychological studies and some general opinions about imagination. Clearly it is not possible, in one book, to do each aspect full justice; those who are especially interested in literary studies of imagination or artistic creativeness will certainly feel that that side has been inadequately represented here; but then it has been very fully written about already. In the same way, specialists of other kinds will probably feel that their own fields have received too little attention; and from the philosophers' point of view there is a deplorable absence of discussion of the precise meaning of some of the terms used. But the book's purpose is not to treat each aspect exhaustively; it is to bring together opinions and information about the everyday activity of imagining. I hope that this will provide new interest, both for people who enjoy imagining and for teachers and parents who are concerned about children's imagination and who do not altogether accept some of the commonly accepted opinions and prejudices.

In this study I have drawn on work produced at widely separated points in time; this seemed worth doing, since it is easy to overlook the fact that imagination has been a study of considerable interest to many people for centuries. While past opinions have not the advantages of carefully controlled scientific studies, imagining is a kind of activity for which—as I have indicated at various stages—we must ultimately find evidence in individuals' accounts of their own experience. Reports by people living at different times are therefore useful and interesting. I have also introduced some speculative comment and personal opinion; I trust that it is sufficiently clear from the context when I am doing this and when I am reporting statements by other people or the results of controlled observations and surveys.

Chapter 1

Imagination: definitions and problems

Imagination is a word which we keep using without thinking very much about it; we use it with varying degrees of approval; we admire someone for being imaginative, we wish we had the imagination of a popular story-teller; we wish some people would stop imagining things, we worry about books, films, advertisements which over-stimulate the imagination; we claim that we can't imagine, we talk of encouraging children's imagination, we say that the child lives in a world of imagination. It is in fact one of those useful but misleading words which can fit without any perceptible jarring into a good many contexts.

Possibly, though, there are some classes of people who avoid using the word precisely because of its versatility; in the study of psycho-logy, for example, it went into eclipse for some years. Textbooks of psychology tended to dismiss imagination briefly, if they gave it a mention at all; it seemed to belong to a discredited, old-fashioned kind of psychology, possibly even to a faculty psychology; it was better to refer to fantasy, possibly to unconscious fantasy, if this kind of activity had to be mentioned. In more recent times, some psychological discussions seem to re-introduce the familiar activity under the name of creativity; except that creativity contrives to be distinct from creativeness and not to be quite the same thing as imagination. Creativity also enjoys, in some circles, a high degree of esteem as a rather better form of intelligence; possibly imagination may find renewed popularity as well.

In philosophical discussions also imagination has in the past enjoyed a considerable popularity as a topic for discussion; but philosophers often thought it a rather lowly form of activity. For some it has been associated with mere images of sense impressions; for others it has been associated with memory; but in itself it has tended to be regarded as an unsatisfactory form of mental activity, certainly inferior to rational thought.

There have been, on the other side, innumerable discussions of poetic imagination and the qualities which distinguish it; in these, imagination enjoys high prestige, but possibly because of this it tends to be considered a rare gift belonging only to exceptional people.

All this would certainly seem to indicate that imagination of some sort is in various human activities and that education should therefore be concerned with it. But in educational discussions it has an elusive value; it may be dismissed with faint praise and completely overshadowed by talk about concept formation or the development of skills; or it is included in those major global aims of education—like the development of morality, good citizenship, personality. 'Fostering imagination' is one of the things which we piously hope education does; but it is perhaps so obvious as to escape detailed study and careful prescription of method. It is not really desirable in education to make use of terms which are quite so widely used in so many contexts (though a great deal of educational discussion does centre on such semantic omnibuses, as someone has described them, conveying a variety of meanings to a number of different destinations). If education is concerned with imagination, if we are going to foster children's imagination, we should know more precisely what it is we are fostering—and of course whether it can be fostered. If imagining is a dangerous activity, we must know why, and must try to guard against it. So we must consider what is meant by 'imagination'.

What meanings are attributed to this word? We can find them in two contexts: (1) in past discussions and writings—the traditional views; (2) in contemporary discussions and conversations—the 'everyday' view. The two are often linked; and looking at them we can see why there is conflict about the value of imagining and the problems it presents in contemporary life: we can also see how methods used in schools derive from differing definitions of imagination.

Traditional definitions of imagination

We may as well begin with the square sun. For this was one of the early examples used to explain what is meant by imagining—or rather, what was meant centuries ago, and what is still meant by some people. We have seen the sun; we have seen things which are square; we can bring back to mind our impression of the sun and change it (using our impression of square things) so that we 'see' a square sun. In this way we have created, from elements provided by our past experience, something which is new and has not been experienced in reality, and which we know has not been experienced in reality.

This seems a simple enough process and one not likely to cause great excitement. It is probably not the kind of activity which most people think of if they are told to use their imagination; and not one likely to be dangerous. But if we consider how it can be elaborated and how complex these creations can become we can see how even defined in this way imagining can be important. Keeping simply to things that have been seen, we can create strange monsters—lions with human heads, a woman with the tail of a fish. If we can carve these in stone, paint them, make sculptures of them, we arrive—assuming we have enough skill in using stone, paint or wood—at artistic creations, though not perhaps the kind of artistic creation much favoured at present. If further, instead of joining together two of our past impressions we recall them at appropriate times, we can perceive that apparently different things have something in common —'my love is like a red, red rose' 'this precious stone, set in a silver sea'—and so we have poetic imagery. Similes, metaphors produced by this kind of recall of past impressions, new associations of these past impressions with each other or with present impressions, can make us perceive objects or situations in a new way. Admittedly we must make a good choice of things to be joined together or associated—some associations are more satisfying than others and some of the new constructions may be more pleasing and interesting than others; a square sun, for example, is possibly not a particularly attractive creation, especially if you have the kind of mind concerned about scientific probabilities. But the process remains the same, whether the result is worth having or not.

If the activity is extended to include not only visual or other sense impressions but ideas as well, scientific discoveries can result. The folklore of science has it that past impressions of steam moving an object like a kettle lid, combined with other past impressions, form the new construction of a machine moved by steam; or a circular formation—that of snakes head to tail in a circle, or monkeys similarly clinging together—led to the concept of a molecular ring. This can be important, though as a scientific process it is obviously incomplete.

One can see how the discussion of this kind of imagining was involved with discussion of memory, for in much remembering we do exactly the same kind of thing; initially, as in imagining, we call up impressions of what we saw or heard or touched in the past. Yet there is, normally, a difference between imagining and remembering; we know—or think we know—that we did see or hear or touch the things we remember; we may be able to say exactly when and where these events really happened. If we are imagining, we know that we did not really see or hear or touch the things we have in mind; they do not belong to any real time in our past experience. As one of the old discussions put it, we can call up images (i.e. past sense impressions) in memory and in imagination; but though we can (assuming they lived long enough) have a memory image of our grandparents we can have only an imagination image of our great-great-great-grandparents. Yet there are occasions when we do not distinguish between the two types of image; if we think of a car, for instance, we may 'see' a car without noticing whether it is some particular car which we have really seen or whether it is an impression built up from the many cars seen in the past without exactly corresponding to any of them. (This kind of remembering—i.e. when the memory is not attached to any particular experience or time—has been described as imagining (Thomistic imagination); but most people would not normally think of it as that.)

We can also note that this kind of recalling of past impressions happens in ordinary thinking, when we are not necessarily trying to remember or to imagine, though at these times the recall may be a much more involuntary process. It is difficult to think without some calling up of such impressions. Thus, St Augustine, trying to arrive at an understanding of the nature of God tried vainly to keep his mind free from all past sense impressions—*Clamabat violenter cor meum adversus omnia phantasmata mea*—but they immediately returned when banished and obscured his vision so that he could not think of God as having no physically perceived form (*Confessiones* vii, 1).

While interesting in its way, all this analysis of imagination seems rather uninspiring. It is hard to see why, if this is all there is to it, there should be such frequent references to imagination in popular songs, stories and everyday life. Why should the delights of imagination be celebrated if, for example, imagining the loved one's presence merely means looking at a kind of mental photograph? And why should there be any harm—'too much imagination'—in combining past sense impressions to make new constructions? Certainly we can see one reason for stressing imagination if it leads to the production of artistic masterpieces or scientific discoveries; but these are, on the whole, not activities which enter readily into everyday conversation.

The point is that these descriptions so far have omitted an essential element in imagining. Our ability to revive past impressions does not apply only to impressions of seeing, touching, hearing, etc. We can also revive more general associations and emotions. Better still, we feel emotions not only in response to past impressions, we not only recall past emotions but we also feel emotion in response to the new structures made from past impressions. This is the essential feature of imagining. It is not simply a matter of thinking of things abstractly, arranging past impressions to make new patterns or things which are decorative, beautiful, useful or helpful scientifically; it is a matter of using these past experiences to produce emotions and to maintain emotions, even although we know, normally, that what is causing these is not part of our real experience and is not 'really' happening. Emotions occur in response to actual happenings; they occur also in response to imagined happenings; and the latter emotions are real, happening in the present, even though they are called up by unreal situations. In fact, we give a kind of reality to imagined creations by feeling these emotions; in a way we live an imagined situation because it affects us emotionally.

It is this characteristic which explains imagination's popularity. Imagining someone's presence can produce something of the same pleasure as the real presence would give; it can be even better, in some respects, for the absent person can be imagined as saying what we want to hear; or we can have the pleasure of ourselves 'saying' the things we might want to say but, for one reason or another, have not said in reality. In this way we enjoy all the pleasure of day-dreaming, the most popular and most common use of imagining. This imagining is the kind of activity which keeps children glued to the television screen; which keeps others reading for hours when they should be asleep; which leads to floods of tears for the sad fate of heroines or heroes of books or films, or occupies attention so that monotonous work is done without being noticed and time passes unperceived.

This is the common use of imagination; but the remarkable thing is that in a great many scholarly and philosophical discussions of imagination attention has been focused exclusively on the impersonal side, on artistic products or scientific inventions only; the beauty or usefulness of new constructions, the skill with which past experiences have been combined, the differences from memory, the originality or number of new constructions are considered; but the point that the construction was an experience accompanied by emotion and possibly had emotion as its main object is somehow left out. Its presence is so obvious that it is omitted from these scholarly discussions. (It is true that in some psychological discussions the emotional factor receives exclusive attention; these in their turn often omit the conscious skill of construction which is also imagination.)

Yet some discussions of imagination have implied the importance of emotion. Francis Bacon (*Advancement of Learning*) gave imagination a place as a part of our rational behaviour when we are trying to decide whether to take action or not: 'For Sense sendeth over to Imagination before Reason have judged; and Reason sendeth over to

Imagination before the Decree can be acted; for Imagination ever precedeth Voluntary Motion.' Presumably the decree depends on how we feel. Some considerable time later, William James (1891) made something of the same point, if in less picturesque language: 'An anticipatory image, then, of the sensorial consequences of a movement, plus (on certain occasions) the fiat that these consequences shall become actual, is the only psychic state which introspection lets us discern as the forerunner of our voluntary acts.' Here too we could assume that trial runs in imagination include an emotional reaction to possible consequences.

Even more explicit recognition has at times been given to the emotional aspect. In the seventeenth century, for example, Descartes (*Principes de la Philosophie*) included both emotional and physiological reactions in his description of how imagination works when, for example, good news is received; the mind judges first if the news is good or bad; if it is good, a kind of joy is felt: 'But as soon as that spiritual joy comes from the understanding to the imagination, the imagination causes the animal spirits to flow from the brain towards the muscles which are about the heart and there they stimulate the movement of the nerves by which there is provoked another movement in the brain which gives the mind the feeling or passion of joy.' It is a sporting attempt at precise definition even if it sounds rather roundabout. (Today 'animal spirits' would possibly be replaced by something like bio-chemical reactions or electrical impulses.) Still, this is an interesting attempt to explain the emotional contribution of imagination; and a fascinating concept like animal spirits does lead to interesting further speculation. For Descartes it fitted in with a view of imagination as being at times a merely random activity: at such times, he said: 'The [animal] spirits being diversely stirred up, meeting the traces of various previous impressions made in the brain follow them, going by chance through certain pores rather than through others. Such are the illusions of our dreams and also the reveries which we often have while awake when our thought wanders nonchalantly without attending to anything of its own' (*Les Passions de l'Ame*). Possibly it is such a view of imagination as a non-purposeful activity, due to a kind of random slopping-about in the mind, which led to concentration on its more mechanical aspects and to undervaluation—until Freud and others challenged the idea of random production.

Another philosopher, Hume ('A Dissertation on the Passions'), certainly recognised clearly the power of imagination to produce and stimulate emotion; he suggested however that the emotions produced lasted longer than the imaginative construction; he also made the point (in 'An Enquiry Concerning Human Understanding') that no feeling of belief is given to the imagined situation. Later still, Ribot's exhaustive analysis of imagination displayed some of the common enthusiasm for concentrating on other issues, as he asserted the existence of so many types of imagination—diffluent, plastic, numerical, musical, practical or mechanical, scientific, commercial, mystic: but at least in the four factors of 'creative imagination' Ribot did include with intellectual, unconscious and synthesising factors the emotional factor. He also stressed the origin of imagination in an emotional need; but his concentration on creative imagination possibly distracted his attention from this vital aspect.

Thus some philosophical recognition has been given to the emotional element; but serious follow-up of this recognition has been neglected by philosophers. Even in analyses of imagination from the literary point of view, there has been at times a neglect of the emotional component—possibly in a search for intellectual respectability. Inventiveness, skill in combining sense data, evoking memory data; the scope and aptness of associations made between such data; mystic understanding—all these have been prized and emphasised. Wordsworth, for example, distinguished (in the Preface to the *Poems* of 1815) invention and imagination—very reasonably; but held the value of imagination to be in giving new insight into what is described. Coleridge's definition (in *Literary Remains*) affirmed that 'the imagination is the distinguishing characteristic of man as a progressive being'; this, though giving imagination a high value, emphasises rather its philosophical than its emotional role.

In one extreme use, the emotional element in imagination has received full weight; this is in the practice of magic. Here it is by imagination that actions of a symbolic kind acquire their power; and it is, apparently, because of the emotions of the victim that some magic has the intended effect. Malinowski (1948) suggested that those who merely read about primitive magic may fail to realise the importance of emotion in it: 'For the sorcerer has, as an essential part of the ritual performance, not merely to point the bone dart at his victim, but with an intense expression of fury and hatred he has to thrust it in the air, turn and twist it as if to bore it in the wound, then pull it back with a sudden jerk. Thus not only is the act of violence or stabbing reproduced, but the passion of violence has to be excited.' For those whose imagination is not strong enough, the ceremonies presumably provide additional reinforcement: as, again, Francis Bacon put it: 'Ceremonies, Characters and Charms . . . serve only to strengthen the imagination of him that useth it.' Similarly the magic rites associated with, e.g. initiation into adult life in primitive societies in some parts of the world, presumably serve to stimulate the imagination of those unable to realise independently the crisis in their development, and contribute to the emotional reactions necessary for a successful initiation.

Contemporary views

We have looked at some past definitions: how is 'imagination' thought of today? What problems are suggested by contemporary definitions?

If we look at the views held by ordinary members of the public today we usually find that the past theories are present in one form or another; common views are often variants of the old scholarly theories, modified by everyday use. Admittedly, with the popularisation of psychological theories, it is more and more common to find non-specialists producing specialist theories as their favourite newspaper or magazine has transmitted them. But if we ask various groups of people what they think 'imagination' is, we are likely to get definitions which fall into the following classification: (1) the ability to 'visualise' things or events or call up other sense impressions; (2) the ability to invent new things; (3) the ability to produce works of art; (4) the ability to foresee future events and plan for them; (5) the means by which one can escape from reality, enjoy emotional relief; (6) the power to deal with things or situations not actually present. A seventh, much less common definition is 'the experience of having an undirected sequence of images'.

This classification, which is based on written and spoken replies to the question by different groups of people, includes practically every type of definition used in past scholarly discussions: one exception is that ordinary members of the public are not likely to give the purely linguistic definitions (e.g. imagining as equivalent to supposing) which philosophical discussions often include. It is also improbable that they will say imagining is the ability to synthesise all experience: and most improbable of all that anyone will claim not to know the meaning of the word or assert that imagination does not exist.

Problems arising

If these are contemporary beliefs about the nature of imagination, which of them underlie or justify statements that children's imagination should be encouraged or that certain books, etc., stimulate imagination dangerously?

The ability to invent new things or to produce works of art may be what is intended when imagination is said to be worth developing.

Possibly the ability to foresee and plan for future events is intended also, though one has the impression that this is not usually what is meant in discussions of education—some educators might emphasise imaginative planning for future behaviour, but the ordinary person tends to think of planning as a firmly rational, non-emotional kind of behaviour. It seems improbable certainly that the average person would consider the ability to have sequences of images either as something to be fostered or as something to be restrained.

It is when we come to the definition of imagination as a source of emotional relief that we reach a theory of imagination which leads to strong differences of opinion. These differences are worth closer study.

Imagination and laziness

There is a relatively mild objection to this imagining, the spartan view which objects to wallowing in easily acquired comfort; imagination, it is said, encourages passivity, so those who favour strenuous living don't approve of it. Children who sit and watch television or film are being spoon-fed; they are not thinking for themselves; they are avoiding action. (Emotional enjoyment by watching live theatre presumably occurs too infrequently to arouse the same criticisms.)

Is this criticism justified? It is of course true that in the literal sense the children—or adults—may be passive; someone else has determined the course of the imaginary situation for them, and they are staying still in one place to watch—though children, in fact, are often physically active while viewing, moving sympathetically with the imaginary characters, or wriggling in excitement. But this does not prove passive minds. If the story is to be understood, they have to bring something of their own past experience to mind so that they can interpret what is shown; what they see is not real; the dimensions of the people watched on television are unrealistic (they are astoundingly distorted in some ways); there must be a constant activity of mind to perceive these as 'real' people. Spectators also need to give continuing attention to interpreting the situation shown—and the cutting technique of modern television or films demands at times a sophisticated and quick attention which is by no means passive. Listening to questions or discussions by children as they watch we also notice the constant formulation and checking of hypotheses— even if only on the 'Is he a baddie?' level. It is also true, as research surveys have shown, that from television and film viewing children do assimilate ideas, information about behaviour, customs, styles; this may be inaccurate and unconscious learning; but it does not

2

support the accusation that viewing is merely passive emotional wallowing. Some judgment and learning is going on as well.

Admittedly the spartan objection may not always centre on the fictional nature of the emotional delights; it may attack the feelings of ease accompanying this kind of activity, no matter whether the subject viewed is real or imaginary. Such critics consider that the child's imagination would be more 'active' if meanings of words had to be thought out with minimal clues—certainly without the help of pictures and sound. The implied theory seems to be that imagination can be educated only by a difficult process of struggling to put together partial information. This seems related to the construction-from-past-impressions theory of imagination: but it overlooks the need for basic materials from relevant past impressions. It is difficult to believe that anyone would argue that a child would be better imagining what the surface of the moon looks like than seeing television recordings of a landing on the moon; yet advocates of the activity method make exactly this kind of proposal with regard to other situations.

Effects of emotions produced in imagining

But the major difference of opinion about imagination considered as a means of emotional response is still more serious. On the one side the enjoyment of imagined experiences is thought to provide a safety valve; emotions stirred by imaginative experience are somehow worked off, so that dangerous emotions are not carried over into real action. On the other side are those who think that imaginative experience stirs up emotions but does not dispose of them satisfactorily; on the contrary, it leads to effects in real behaviour which are highly undesirable. The former view we will look at more closely later; it is worth noting now that the latter seems to imply a kind of belief in the immense power of imagination which goes beyond anything usually indicated in definitions offered.

This belief seems to be that whatever our experience in real life, whatever education is given by parents or school, imagined experience is so vivid and attractive that it will cancel other influences and determine our behaviour; and the behaviour determined in this way will be anti-social. Hence the allegations—made especially strongly in the fifties, when there was a forceful campaign against children's (or adults') comics—that juvenile and adult delinquency result from such imaginative activities as reading comics may provoke. Today we have campaigns against violence shown on television; we have campaigns against certain books. These must come from an immense, if pessimistic, respect for the overwhelming power of imagination.

(We should note that such a belief is long-established, for this kind of campaign is by no means new. Novels were looked on during the nineteenth century as a potent source of corruption; the spread of literacy and the development of cheaply printed books were, by some critics, said to be leading to the degradation of society in general and the working class in particular.) If imagining does affect behaviour and personality in this way it is indeed a dangerous activity which should be carefully controlled or possibly eliminated.

What are the consequences of such a belief? It is held that if we imagine ourselves (following the characters in various plays and books) committing crimes, enjoying wealth, drink, drugs or other delights we will want to carry out these actions in reality as well. So if books or plays show people behaving in an anti-social way and we experience the same emotions as they do, through imagination, we in turn will behave in an anti-social way. The logical conclusion is to impose a censorship on the kind of activity we indulge in through imagination—or at least on the kind of imaginative activity which plays, books, etc., encourage us to indulge in. That is, if people should not behave in a certain way in real life, don't let them even imagine that kind of behaviour.

The evidence of the effect of imagining on behaviour is by no means conclusive; we shall examine it in greater detail at a later point. But what is important to realise here is the remarkable power attributed to imagination. Imagined experiences must offer immense attractions; the emotions they cause must be compellingly strong; the situations must be intensely attractive, or at least part of them must be so. Let us consider these two suppositions—the vividness of imagined experience, and the priority of parts of the imaginary situations.

The power of imagined experiences

Are imagined experiences life-like? We must wonder if differences in people's attitudes to the effects of imagining are not due less to observation of effects on children and others than to individual differences in experience of imagining. Some people do experience imaginary situations more strongly than others; some apparently feel strongly as they watch or read—it is as if they were living in the situation. If this is so, they may reasonably assume that feelings as strong as these must have later effects; they must feel that these reactions were part of their real personality, and consequently that their behaviour is affected. (This, presumably, is illustrated by the feeling of guilt or contamination which some people feel after reading —even if not by their own choice—literature describing behaviour which their judgment condemns.) Other people have little or no time for imaginative enjoyment, they cannot see the point of it; they presumably react very feebly if at all to the kind of stimulation it offers; and so they feel that they themselves have not been involved in the imaginary situation; and since they have not lived it, emotionally, they are unaffected by it. It would follow, if all this is so, that the people who warn most strongly against the dangers of imagination are the people who have the most powerful imaginations. (Though there is a possible dichotomy here; warnings may also come from people who are simply shocked by the actual words or external actions of a play and not by the emotional experience which it embodies. In such cases they judge the stimulation dangerous not because of emotional involvement but on this superficial level; if they were emotionally involved they might discover that the meaning was not immoral.) So warnings about the dangers of imagination can come both from those who have very little imagination and from those who have a great deal. There is little objective evidence on this point but as we shall see later there is some biographical information which does suggest that some of those who have been most concerned about the dangers of imagining have been people of most lively imagination.

Selective attention to imaginary situations

The second aspect—the life-like and compelling qualities of imaginary situations or parts of them—is even more complex. The objective study of books, plays, etc., which are said to be dangerous does not always, or even often, show plots where anti-social behaviour is finally rewarded. But there may be a disproportionate amount of attention and time given to the intermediate trials of the virtuous and triumph of the wicked? Even in school set books, where we should expect that a certain amount of selective care has been exercised, plots of various classics offer quite a lot of sex interest and violence which might cause protest in modern dress and idiom on a television programme; certainly it is doubtful if we really want pupils to behave in the way shown most of the time by most of the characters in the books read. But ultimately, *as a rule* one might almost say, the conclusion is on the side of right behaviour; and, it is presumably hoped, the reader has perceived how unrewarding the passions of jealousy, avarice, ambition, and the rest, really are. (It is possibly a too naïve trust in the happy ending which leads to some curious choices in official syllabuses. When some protest was raised against the inclusion of *To Sir With Love* (Braithwaite, 1959) in a N. Ireland schools' syllabus, the book was replaced by *Tiger in the Smoke*

(Allingham, 1952). Granted that adolescents might not be greatly interested in a book written very much from the adult teacher's point of view, it is difficult to see what more moral principles the substitute represented—except that a crime mystery was solved; and of course the book is enjoyable and admirable in its genre.)

It is in fact astonishing to note in how many books, plays, programmes virtue does ultimately triumph. The villain seldom gets away with it in the end even though there is—even in the humble Western—the middle time when it looks as though the baddies might come out on top. The criminal is triumphant in Part 1 of *Z Cars*; but in Part 2 (usually) all is discovered and the wicked defeated. We do have an astonishingly strong tradition (imposed by a more or less conscious censorship by authors?) of this kind—which is possibly a most uneducative preparation for real life situations. (As an exercise it might be interesting—if one could bear it—to count how many stories are presented on television each week, and in how many of these the baddie is allowed to win. Excluding, of course, the middle range in which there is no clear conflict of this kind.) Yet although we may be consciously aware of some such conventions— e.g. in American films of a given era that suicide must be shown as associated with at least temporary insanity—we may not consciously notice this one of the happy ending; hence the traumatic shock when, as very seldom happens, virtue is shown as defeated. (As in *Public Eye*, when the detective hero finally, irrevocably, beyond the last-minute twist of plot, was seen entering prison to serve a legally justified sentence—though not, of course, really guilty. Skies fall on such occasions.) And the hardened reader of low- to middle-brow stories automatically becomes less involved with a character who actually commits a crime—such a one cannot possibly win. (Unless the author is cheating and deceiving the reader.) Even characters regarded as less reputable tend to have their own claim to moral standards which justify their final victory; James Bond, for example, in *Casino Royale* (Fleming, 1955) expresses bitter, self-righteous indignation at the idea of a spy on the other side having claimed to love him; in bed with one of his conquests, he reflects most moralisingly that 'he knew, and he knew the girl beside him knew, that they had done no wrong to each other' (Fleming, 1964). Only a few anti-hero productions fail to conform to this general pattern; which possibly explains their limited range of admirers.

Thus we might conclude that if belief in the character-affecting power of imagination is justified many of the attacks on works of imagination are unjust; in the end the pattern of behaviour which is shown to be rewarded is the kind which (presumably) we want children and adults to follow. The only possible reason for criticising many of the imaginary adventures would be that we—or children—select only the parts that appeal and conveniently overlook the rest; so that although the villains are defeated at the end of the story, what we remember, and what we have experienced most vividly, are the episodes in which the wrong kind of behaviour was being temporarily rewarded. Hence—the argument would continue—we should never allow bad behaviour to be successful or effective in imaginary situations. But this does seem to assume that bad behaviour is more appealing than good; otherwise why should it be more enjoyable and memorable in such imagining? Admittedly, some authors do show regrettably more skill in depicting the bad than the good; bad behaviour perhaps tends to be shown as more fun—'the snake has all the lines'. Having enjoyed this part, we withdraw our support and refuse to experience, with the defeated villains, the due punishment of their misdeeds; indeed at this point we can remind ourselves that it isn't really happening, and so benefit from one of the chief qualities of imagination—experience whose consequences can be avoided. This indeed is possibly the cause of the failure of many well-intentioned authors who have hoped to improve us by their stories—Milton's *Paradise Lost* can serve as example; Lucifer is so likeable—one cannot really see him defeated. But perhaps it need not always be so.

Possibly the opponents of imaginary experience have been too pessimistic and are too pessimistic in assuming that behaviour is affected for the worse by all these imagined situations. Possibly imagination has affected our attitudes, but not adversely. People generally do expect things to work out in the end; we do—mostly—think it wrong if in real life virtue suffers (we may recognise that it happens, but we feel the times are out of joint). This may show favourable conditioning by works of imagination. True, it cannot be said that people behave well on all occasions; but possibly this is because of the gap between virtuous behaviour and its reward; or possibly the real life situation is not perceived as clearly (in metaphorical black and white) as the situation on the television screen or the stage, so the good and bad are harder to identify. We are perhaps less selective than we think.

Censorship

In spite of the preceding considerations, there are still those whose belief in the power of imagination is such that they want some censorship of books, plays, anything which stimulates this dangerous power. Is there a case for censorship? Should parents and educators consider that imagined experiences can influence character by inducing enjoyment in imaginary actions of an anti-social kind? Milton undoubtedly put the main argument against state censorship in *Areopagitica*: the best defences of a society are not censorship laws which inevitably become ridiculous but the standards of good sense among members of the society; this good sense will lead to rejection of what is undesirable without any external controls.

But the situation does not look quite the same when we are working with children and look at the kind of things they may be reading or watching avidly. Then even the liberal educator may begin to wonder how such standards of good taste, as well as standards of good behaviour, are formed; and whether possibly children must be protected until they have the chance to form them. This kind of consideration may be reinforced when we discover, for example, that children offered a choice between a poem which is usually thought good and a poem usually thought bad do on some occasions choose the latter; or when we see that they clearly rejoice in the aggressive actions but show little interest in the moral point ultimately made. All too often we see that, given the chance to read 'good' books, many children (even the most intelligent) turn to others fairly described as trashy. (A parallel in adult life is possibly the cult of whodunnits or science fiction, even among the allegedly well-educated. Sartre (1964), in one of his most endearing remarks, says that even in adult life he retains a preference for the *Série Noire* rather than Wittgenstein.)

There is of course the argument against censorship that the child has to know the bad in order to realise the merits of the good. This sounds weak; it suggests that the good is not good in itself, but only by contrast. Certainly, even if the child has to know the bad, it is a pity to spend as much time, or more time, on it than on the good. As an advocate of censorship may reasonably remark: why worry about reading bad books when there are so many good ones you'll never have time to read? A better argument is that censorship will rouse the child to opposition; what is censored will be sought after and more eagerly studied. This is valid if the child knows that censorship is operating and if opportunities to evade it exist. But much censorship can be carried out with little or no awareness on the part of those so protected. The argument that censorship of society would fail in the world of today often does not take account of the circumstances of different countries; where travel into and out of a country is easy, undoubtedly effective censorship is wellnigh impossible; but it is much more possible where there is state controlled publishing only and restriction of travel—even if it is then not infallible. Similarly the parent can guard against the reading of undesirable books or viewing of undesirable television programmes only if children are continually under home supervision and do not visit friends or receive visits from—or even talk to—them.

It is this very freedom of communication today which may make the adult who formerly could have exercised an unobtrusive censorship, secure in the knowledge that the child was not likely to meet much in the way of dangerous imaginative stimuli in the environment, begin to wonder if more deliberate control should be exercised. Direct prohibition seems unwise and undesirable; but the more subtle kind of parental or educational censorship—presenting an alternative activity when the child could read or watch something unsuitable—is one which can be exercised less obtrusively and may be rather more palatable—if the alternative offered really is attractive. This kind of censorship is one which liberal adults and teachers can probably use with less feeling of guilt. But when confronted with the problem they should be clear in their views as to what they think imaginative stimuli can really do.

For adults undoubtedly censorship is objectionable because it implies that someone else is a better judge of what is good for us than we are ourselves; at this level it is certainly to be opposed. In dealing with children, however, we may well feel—so many parents do—that we really are better judges of what is good for children than the children are themselves; we do know more. But we have to be sure that in such judgment we are using real knowledge, real thought and not simple prejudices; not leaping to facile conclusions (based on an unanalysed theory of imagination and its effects).

Theories of imagination underlying school methods

The belief in imagination as a source of emotional enjoyment and emotional relief led us to these complex problems of censorship and the real effect, if any, of imaginary situations on the development of character. Is it this kind of belief which has determined the teaching methods found in schools today, or do schools' efforts to 'foster imagination' seem to imply yet another definition of imagination?

We can in fact distinguish a variety of definitions underlying the methods adopted; and the definitions may vary from subject to subject, or even within different teachers' interpretation of a subject. The gradual increase in attention to the study of art in schools (still too often interpreted as drawing and painting) probably has been intended to give more scope for imagination—but which kind of imagination, apart from a diffuse activity? The old-fashioned 'still life' (jar, fruit, against draped background) could be based not so much on a desire for photographic imitation as on the need to sharpen sense discrimination by studying sense impressions so as to reproduce them well on paper; thus storing clear impressions for use in future imaginative constructions. The 'free composition' of a scene would seem rather to emphasise the ability to recreate from past impressions, and possibly to express personal emotion. Construction of designs, pattern-making, again would seem to emphasise the ability to construct from past experiences, from sensory images. Abstract painting would stimulate in the spectator, if not also in the artist, the need for the kind of imagination which can construct on a minimum of sensory cues: pop art returns again to the vivid awareness of sense impressions. In all, of course, imagination would be necessarily associated with skill in using materials to express the imagined construction. But clearly the range of implied definitions is wide.

Other subjects also make claims to develop imagination—the new science and maths are devoted to that kind of scientific imagination which needs, it is said, freedom to experiment and first-hand knowledge of things, combined with intuitive thinking. History may claim rather to develop human understanding through, possibly, imaginative experience of the past, emotional experiences. But probably the major claims are made for the teaching of English, and especially of English literature; so methods there are of especial interest.

Methods of teaching English and theories they imply

(1) One rather outmoded method has been to encourage forming sensory images clearly, e.g. trying to visualise precisely when reading or listening to poetry. This is a method which clearly relates to the earliest views of imagination; it is revived from time to time—e.g. Burt suggested quite recently (1967) that the teacher should supplement intelligence tests of children with other types, such as tests of mental imagery. And a more modern method emphasises sensitivity to, and greater awareness of, sense impressions and their subsequent communication by writing or by speaking about them. Thus, for instance, a class may try the experiment of listening in silence, to discover what sounds from outside or inside the school can then be heard; or go out of doors on a spring morning to observe the sensations of sight, sound, smell characteristic of the coming of spring; or discuss their preferences for sounds of different kinds—the noise of the wind in autumn, leaves crackling underfoot, rain on the windows, bird song. Lessons of such a kind can have a variety of aims—appreciation of beauty, greater skill in the use of words, deeper awareness of experience. But the emphasis on sense perceptions seems to assume that imaginative construction uses such

impressions, so children's minds must be stored with material for future constructions.

(2) Traditionally, imagination has been fostered by the setting of themes for written compositions. Very often these have been of a melodramatic kind—burglaries, fires, floods, discoveries of smugglers' caves—which could scarcely be derived from the child's own real experience. The underlying theory would seem to be of the spartan variety, that imagination is developed by demanding exercises; the child had to combine past data to form something new, it had to escape from the limits of its own experience in such a construction; and preferably the result should be well expressed, original and readable. In practice, of course, children drew largely on the most easily available secondary material—the books they had read, the films they had seen—i.e. on someone else's imagination. Some children admittedly managed to infuse real feelings into these, and even combine borrowed material with their own real experience; they managed to live in the imagined experience (and showed how, in reading other people's fictions, they had had enough imagination to live in these and so acquire a kind of experience from them for future use). But for many children this kind of exercise has demonstrably been unhelpful; they have drearily reproduced what they could from uninspiring and conventional sources; so that nowadays more favoured subjects allow the children to draw on their own real experience and make straightforward communications of it. As the *Plowden Report* (Department of Education and Science, 1967) put it: 'It is becoming less usual for personal writing to take the form of an invented "story". Save for exceptional children who have a story telling gift, and should be given the opportunity to use it, this type of writing tends to be second rate and derivative from poorish material ... poorer story writers often have more influence, in the short run, on children's style because their conventions are mechanical and easily borrowed.' Nevertheless, it is interesting to see that continuing to write fiction is accepted as beneficial for some children —presumably it is left to the child to decide whether this kind of topic is to be attempted or not. But it is not quite clear what the benefit of this exercise of imagination is to be—possibly the creation of enjoyment in others? Here at any rate there does not seem to be any concern about the possibly bad effects of such fiction on the development of character. On the whole, the main emphasis in this kind of exercise in the past has been less on cultivating imagination as a source of emotional stimulation than on encouraging the ability to invent new situations and the ability to describe these coherently and effectively. The imagination cultivated by this method has been very much tied to skill in the use of words.

(3) An entirely different theory of imagination seems to underlie another popular technique—dramatisation and play construction; or rather two different theories. The more traditional kind of dramatisation of a set book seems to assume that weak imaginations cannot work on the cues offered by words alone; so assistance is provided by seeing people moving, speaking, struggling, etc. Dramatising serves as a kind of prop for imagination: possibly it is assumed that after getting enough assistance of this kind the individual imagination will in future work well enough, will be able to translate words sufficiently well to imagine without these external aids. (There are of course also some plays in which action is so important that even good imagination cannot give the full flavour without seeing the movement of the characters acted.) But in classroom dramatisation there is perhaps a lack of consideration for the people with good imagination who need no such crude props—are indeed much better without them, for their imagination can create the play more effectively than amateur school actors in classroom conditions—a squeaky-voiced, pale, plaintive schoolgirl as Lady Macbeth may have a most inhibiting effect on classmates' emotional involvement in the play.

In the less conventional type of dramatisation pupils construct their own play, either gradually, with much discussion and re-writing of scripts, or spontaneously, without rehearsal. The underlying theory here seems to be that imagined action serves to give an outlet for emotions; and possibly that creating one's own play stimulates imagination more than the recreation of someone else's imaginary situations can do. It is remarkable, however, that whereas the imaginative composition written by the individual on melodramatic themes is being abandoned by general consent, the construction by groups of children of similarly unrealistic, melodramatic plots is considered beneficial. Granted, there is social benefit in the co-operation necessary for this kind of activity; it is true also that weaker imaginations may again be helped by acting rather than writing, and by choosing material which is presumably within their understanding. But the acceptance of what is often fairly derivative material (based on uninspiring models) as a play constructed by a group, and the rejection of similar material when written as prose by an individual suggests some confusion of values.

There is, of course, the outward expression of emotions in these imaginary situations of drama: similarly mime, expressive movement and dance are considered to give helpful opportunities for the expression of emotions which otherwise might be suppressed or lead to trouble. In these activities, however, we can see that occasionally pupils' imagination is helped in various ways; initial suggestions for interpretation of the music accompanying mime or dance may be given, or short lengths of film used to suggest a dramatic situation. It seems to be accepted that occasionally imagination does need models to follow: though teachers are sad when pupils follow without changing the model. It is noteworthy that it generally seems to be assumed that whatever the emotions expressed, the result will be beneficial provided that they are expressed strongly and effectively. (Though it is true that the choice of accompanying music, or the guidance given in interpretation may determine the choice of emotions for the imaginary situation: and the school situation itself may automatically censor and guide some pupils' reactions.) The educators' point of view here does seem to be that all imagining is good and to be encouraged.

Similarly where creative writing of a more spontaneous individual kind is encouraged in school, when pupils write to express moods, emotions, views on self-chosen themes, censorship is improbable—indeed the expression of views on themes earlier banned seems at times to be taken as a sign that progress is being made; though here also some kind of model for imitation may be given by the teacher's expressions of interest and approval, by the choice of work read in class, by the choice of music listened to. Imagination here is recognised as being essentially emotional; the expression of imagining is accepted as beneficial.

(4) These methods emphasise active creation by the pupils. Another method commonly claimed to cultivate imagination calls for more passive behaviour; it is the reading of imaginative literature. This is by now a hallowed feature of the curriculum; it is claimed to increase the experience of the individual, to make possible a participation in varieties of experience which is not possible in one person's real existence. The underlying theory here seems to be that imagination is fostered by exercise; imagining while reading presumably improves future performance in imagining; it gives data for future constructions. It is also capable of improvement—the teacher's questions on the meaning of what is read presumably check the accuracy of the imaginative response and draw attention to details which might have been omitted; even the frequent discussion of the meaning of words can be interpreted as a way of improving imagination by helping the reader to understand more fully what the words are communicating. (Whether classroom analyses of the meanings of words and phrases do call up the relevant associations, evoke sensory impressions, make the sense more vivid is of course another matter.) And although some teachers may come to the conclusion that some members of the class are incapable of imagining, this conclusion does not seem to have been generalised into a theory of the nature of imagination.

It is also claimed occasionally that a study of well-chosen imaginative literature exercises a beneficial influence on pupils' personalities, presumably by giving them greater insight into human behaviour and more ability in recognising and emulating the good. Here it is agreed that if the desired effect is to be achieved pupils must be emotionally involved in the imaginary situations; they must feel with the characters described. But in this attempt to use imagination to influence emotional development there is less analysis than one might expect of the precise direction of the emotional involvement. Very often the fact that the pupil is interested and emotionally responsive to any literary character is taken as a sign of grace—if the enthusiasm goes to a 'bad' character, or if the emotion is mainly evoked by the chapter (even in Jane Austen) where the heroine gets her man, teachers usually seem satisfied at this display of imagination by the pupil. It is true that some schools may eliminate in advance some of the less desirable identifications by the selection of texts to be studied; but even this selectiveness leaves room for some questionable responses. What, for example, are the expected benefits of emotional involvement in *Pride and Prejudice*? Contempt for snobs and worldliness—comfortably allied to the expectation that the virtuous end up with a comfortable sufficiency of material well-being? Or what emotional effect on the personality of the adolescent or young adult is expected from a series of novels expressing the frustration of unfulfilled passion, pessimism, nausea?

Problems remaining

In general, schools' attitudes towards imagination seem to be based on a number of theories, to be at the least permissive and to be often enthusiastically in favour of any kind of manifestation of this ability. Undoubtedly some part of the schools' work in subjects said to foster imagination is more critical and analytic; but these qualities seem to relate more to the form of expression than to the effects of imagining, the content of the imaginary situation and the type of emotional response which accompanies the experience. Yet although teachers of different subjects, or teachers of any one subject may have different beliefs about imagination—and each be able to claim support by some traditional theory of the ability—there is all too seldom methodical discussion of what their theories are and whether the methods used are having the desired effect.

Given this variety of belief and definitions we have the problem of deciding what is the most reasonable definition and what educational consequences or changes in method should result from a clearer view of what imagination is. It is possible that the schools, and society generally, are showing too much permissiveness; the stimulation of emotion by imaginary situations may be a regrettable waste of human time. Fiction is possibly something which should not be widely read, let alone studied. Coleridge, for instance, while in favour of encouraging and stimulating children's imagination, considered 'modern' novel-reading as something to be avoided; in his view it harmed not only imagination but judgment and morals—novels being jumbles of fact and fiction which 'afford excitement without producing reaction'. Education, he thought, should produce rather reasoning and observation, and emotional excitement should lead to action according to principles. Coleridge therefore would have preferred to fiction 'the objects and facts of natural history' even though he considered that works of 'true imagination' 'carry the mind out of self and show the possible of the good and great in human character'. It is striking that many teachers who regard Coleridge as well worthy of study by their pupils, and regard his views on imagination with proper respect, none the less continue freely to make pupils study novels—and produce imaginative works—which suffer from the defects Coleridge condemned. Have the schools generally erred in this part of their curriculum? Does society err in its moderate permissiveness in regard to books, plays, television?

Or is imagination such an important power, giving so much enjoyment and exercising so much effect—both for good and ill—on personality that we should be giving it a much greater place in education? Is it at least a valuable safety-valve? Does it form an important part of experience for only a relatively small part of the population? Is it so differently distributed among individuals that schools should modify their approach according to the qualities of the child concerned?

Educators in fact seem to be faced with three main questions: (1) Does imagination affect behaviour, and if so, how? (2) Can imagination be developed by education or is it largely a matter of individual differences? (3) Should imaginative activity of some kinds be encouraged by education, and if so, by what methods?

The evidence required to answer these questions conclusively is by no means complete. But it is illuminating to look at some of it, and to consider more fully what various people have contributed to this subject. Imagination is such a common part of everyday life—for some people—that we can easily think of it as universal and unalterable: we can especially take it for granted that everyone's imagination is like our own. Yet as we have seen, definitions of it vary; implicit beliefs in its nature and effects vary; and scholarly discussions and theories all too often omit what seems to be the most important factor in everyday imagining. We have therefore to consider what educators in the past have said about imagination and its control or encouragement; and to consider such information as is available in objective studies and in introspective reports. In this way we can try to answer the questions important in educating imagination or at least arrive at a more reasonable view of this activity.

Chapter 2

Opposition to imagination

If we look at the arguments put forward against cultivating imagination it is rather surprising to find that they have made so little impact; for three of the most interesting denunciations have come from Plato, Rousseau and Montessori, and these writers have had immense influence in other aspects of education. It almost seems as if there had been an agreement to hush up their comments on imagination or to ignore them politely, as if these comments represented an aberration by otherwise respectable thinkers. Admittedly Plato's views on censorship have attracted a certain amount of adverse publicity—but all too often they are attacked from the political or social point of view rather than from that of understanding of the learning process. It is therefore worthwhile to look at these views and see whether they have any validity today or whether they should indeed be charitably forgotten—as Milton (*Areopagitica*) suggested Plato's proposals for the ideal state and censorship laws should be.

Rousseau's objections to imagination

In some ways, although he is not chronologically the one to begin with, Rousseau seems to be the most accessible. Certainly he is an educator whose views have been largely accepted in modern practice; not that people reading *Emile* today necessarily recognise him as a kindred spirit but much of what Rousseau said about letting children discover knowledge by first-hand experience, avoiding cramming them with information which they can repeat parrot-wise but do not understand, is fundamental to modern methods of discovering science and mathematics; more and more attempts are being made to write and use language which children can understand, and to get them away from rote learning of what is said in books to acquiring real knowledge; all this is very much in the spirit of Rousseau's proposals. The cultivation of an enquiring mind, sound common sense, independence of judgment, are all ideals accepted by modern education; so is the avoidance of empty formulas of politeness or superficial religious precepts. But it seems to many modern readers that when Rousseau (*Emile*) said: 'I hate books!' and attempted to banish them from his ideal pupil's education during childhood he was going much too far and depriving his pupil of one of the most valuable sources of knowledge, and also of one of the greatest delights—the enjoyment of fiction.

Why did he propose this omission? It was not a complete exclusion of books from education; only up to twelve or thereabouts were books excluded; between twelve and fifteen one book, *Robinson Crusoe*, could be studied because it shows the pupil the problems of the human being in keeping himself alive and in dealing with his natural environment; it must produce a great respect for the skills and knowledge essential for survival. (By a fascinating process of literary descent, this ideal led to the very unreal, information-crammed book of *Swiss Family Robinson* with its omniscient authority.) Books become more normally used only in later adolescence when history and fiction may give the learner some knowledge of human behaviour; but even at this point Rousseau emphasises the need to study people in real life, mix with them in their own surroundings, and learn in this way about their feelings and reactions.

Rousseau's deliberate policy was to keep the child's imagination dormant, if possible; to stimulate it as little as possible. Why? There seem to be four main reasons. In the first place, the human being is much happier if it is possible to live in the present and be contented with things as they are. Imagining happier and better states is likely to stir up discontent with the real, present situation; and if the real situation has to be accepted, then imagination is simply a source of frustration. 'It is imagination which extends for us the range of possibilities, whether in good or in ill, and which consequently stimulates and nourishes desires by the hope of satisfying them ... The real world has its limits, the imaginary world is infinite; being unable to enlarge the one, let us narrow down the other, for it is from their difference alone that are born all the ills which make us truly unhappy' (*Emile*, book 2).

There is some good sense in this; parents often have cause to regret the ambitions and wishes formed in children by stories of various kinds which lead to the maddening question: 'Why can't I have ... ?' (Commercials on television, which may be said to be imaginative stories in their way, do strengthen this tendency.) But on a serious level it is doubtful whether great frustration will develop in children if their actual situation is reasonably satisfying—no matter how forcibly the child may express momentary feelings of longing for what imaginative stories picture; if the child has plenty

3

of scope for real activity, good company, materials to work with, the discontent of imagining other possibilities is likely to be minor. Naturally also much depends on whether the imaginative situation includes fantastic adventures, wealth, glamour, or occurs in more normal and more possible circumstances. But for adults, for whom the thrill of discovery of the environment has worn off, there may be more truth in Rousseau's statement.

Secondly, so far as imaginative stories are used to teach children moral principles—here Rousseau was thinking of works like La Fontaine's fables—there is a great danger that the moral will not be understood. The child may make a literal interpretation and fail to see the real point. Or the child may identify with the wrong character —if the fox successfully flatters the crow and manages to deprive the crow of the cheese which the fox wants, the child may decide that being like the fox is the right line of action. In other cases the story may simply be beyond the child's comprehension but be interpreted in terms of the child's experience; Rousseau mentions a story in which Alexander the Great showed heroic trust in another human being by drinking what might have been a poisoned drink; the moral drawn by the child was that it is heroic to drink nasty-tasting medicine without making a fuss (a useful moral in its way).

Rousseau may be right here also to some extent. We do find examples of children identifying with the 'wrong' character and even adult sympathies do not go always to the apparent hero. Similarly it is not unknown for both children and adults to misinterpret the meaning of a story; one has only to listen to the account given of a film one has seen, or a book one has read to realise that the same material can convey very different meanings to different people. But of course fiction is not always used deliberately to teach morals; and while some such stories may be misinterpreted many are clearly well understood. Today's immensely improved provision of books for children might remove some of the strength of Rousseau's argument; large numbers of children's books are well adapted to their understanding and experience—so much so, sometimes, as to count as documentaries rather than fiction. But admittedly some room for misinterpretation remains.

More serious is the third of Rousseau's reasons for caution; the child will not merely misunderstand the plot but will form inaccurate ideas of the emotions and behaviour described in stories. This happens when the child has not had relevant experience and where the reactions described are beyond a child's level of development. The child forms some concept of what is intended—some kind of meaning is given to the words—and so the child has the impression of understanding and can even elaborate this happily. (On the verbal level, for example, we can still find today that the hymn lines

There is a green hill far away
Without a city wall

call up for some children a very pleasing picture of a hill far out in the country, with no kind of building in sight.) On a more important level, the child can form false expectations about life; understanding about human behaviour is not increased but instead the foundations for later failure to understand other people are laid. Some of these false impressions may be corrected by experience; but the correction may be a sadly disillusioning process, and some false beliefs will persist. The child's curiosity about adult life is fed by information which cannot be assimilated; roles attributed to adults are wrongly perceived but they are the roles which the child will try to play accordingly later on. Rousseau obviously felt that he himself had suffered in this way as a result of the novels he devoured when a child: 'These confused emotions which I experienced one after the other . . . gave me bizarre and romantic ideas of human life of which experience and reflection have never been able properly to cure me' (*Confessions*, book 1).

Much the same argument had been advanced by a rather earlier writer on education, Fénelon: '. . . girls who are badly educated and indolent have an imagination which is always straying. Lacking solid nourishment their curiosity turns eagerly towards vain and dangerous objects . . . They develop a passion for novels, for plays, for fanciful tales of adventure with a romantic love interest. They give way to empty ideas and grow accustomed to the high-flown language of the heroes of fiction. By so doing they even spoil themselves for ordinary life, for all these fine, but airy, sentiments, these noble passions, these adventures which the fiction-writer invents in order to please, have no relation to the motives which hold sway in real life and which decide actual events' (Barnard, 1966).

Associated with this argument is Rousseau's fourth objection, very similar to that made by present-day critics of television, books, plays: precocious sex interests may be encouraged. Certainly Rousseau did not think of literature as being the only source of this dangerous (as he saw it) stimulation—he was very much aware of the pernicious influence that bad company could have; but for adolescents the additional possible stimulation by reading was to be discouraged. (Rousseau's view was that the very powerful sex interest should be left dormant as long as possible, until the young man had reached a level of maturity at which he could avoid being led into undesirable expressions of it. Rousseau did recognise that in some societies ignorance about sexual behaviour could not be prolonged; he was indeed one of the earlier proposers of a positive approach to sex education—even if some of his specific proposals would not seem ideal to modern educators. But he accepted a policy of enlightenment rather because it was forced on the educator by circumstances; he would have preferred continued ignorance—innocence, as he saw it—extending into early adulthood.)

To that extent can we accept this objection? Our policy in sex education is (in theory if not in practice) more positive than Rousseau's. On the whole we accept sex interests as a more healthy and less dangerous aspect of adolescent development than Rousseau did—though our standards of acceptable sex behaviour in adolescents are perhaps less clear than our theory of normal development. It could be argued that today the conditions of urban life—or news reports—stimulate sex interests to such an extent that the additional contribution by literature and other imaginative stimulators is not important enough to make much difference. On the other hand if literature, drama and the rest give not merely information or relatively impersonal accounts but arouse the accompanying emotion in a way which factual reports cannot do, then they are possibly unhelpful in a society which is less than totally convinced that adolescent sex behaviour is to be encouraged—and possibly unhelpful to adolescents living in circumstances where sexual behaviour is not encouraged or is in conflict with other interests. But whether social custom or imaginative stimulation is at fault is a matter of doubt: we could at least deplore the inconsistency of both stimulating and suppressing interests in sexual enjoyment, and try to make education more consistent. But this problem of arousing emotions is insufficiently recognised even where sex education is given; discussions of standards of sex behaviour may be unrealistic and ineffectual if decisions are reached in a situation where emotions have not been roused; a subsequent real life situation where emotion is strong may be so different—because of the emotion—that earlier decisions seem irrelevant. Yet it is difficult to imagine a lesson in school in which—to ensure realistic decision-making—pupils' sexual feelings would be deliberately aroused. Description of the strong emotion which may dominate in real life situations can perhaps simply stimulate the wish to experience it. So that the sex educator is in a trying dilemma; to try to form standards of behaviour while leaving out one of the essential factors (emotion) influencing the behaviour; or to stimulate the appropriate feeling—as far as possible—by using imaginary situations vividly presented. Obviously, in dealing with some adolescents the educator is talking to people who know from experience the emotional factors involved—but this means that the experience has preceded discussion of the standards appropriate to it; and on the whole we prefer that sex education should come early, before experience. Possibly there is more point in Rousseau's argument than at first seems probable. We can also feel some doubt as to whether the carefully unemotional presentation of the facts about sexual reproduction (as in broadcasts for primary school children) is a kind of distortion of knowledge—though real life experiences probably redress the balance by showing that feelings are involved.

In all we may accept Rousseau's four arguments against the influence of fiction to some extent; we can agree with him that expectations are formed—if adults are shown living in luxury, living in exciting circumstances, enjoying romantic sexual love, then presumably the individual imagining these events comes to expect similar experiences; and if they do not come, life seems to have cheated. If emotions of jealousy, anger, pride are displayed, a belief is formed that these are appropriate to certain situations; similarly the expectation of altruistic, devoted friendship can be formed. So the habit of waiting for similar experience is implanted, and this can lead to continuing disappointment. The longing expressed by many adolescents to live life to the full, to experience everything—even sorrow and suffering—may be a proof of false expectations formed by fiction. Suffering can be made to seem so attractive in fiction and heartbreak so dramatic—and so sure of a sympathetic and interested audience. Flaubert's Emma Bovary, for example, had read romantic fiction voraciously and so was led to search for the romance which her real husband and lovers could not adequately provide; yet it is doubtful if Flaubert made his moral point—the book was discussed from many other angles, especially as a book likely to lead to immoral behaviour, but it was by no means seen as a warning against novel-reading. Indeed it probably strengthened some readers' delight in novels—which possibly again proves Rousseau's point that stories are often misinterpreted.

But this brings us to an apparent weakness in Rousseau's argument; it must depend on what kind of story is read whether it forms mistaken expectations of human behaviour or not. So far as children are concerned, if the reading is mainly about other children, mistaken ideas about adult behaviour can be kept to a minimum.

Nevertheless, much still depends on the individual's ability to interpret even apparently straightforward stories. Even when we are confident that we have understood them at once, we can find, re-reading some novels after a lapse of years, that they seem to take on a different meaning; the novel is constant, but experience has changed what the reader learns from it. Something which the author was trying to show may have been impatiently overlooked by a younger reader in search of something else; the romantically inclined adolescent is unlikely to note in *Anna Karenina* the impossibility of continuing happiness built on romantic love when other passions— interest in a career, love for a child, even social custom—are fighting against it; the young reader, revelling in the tragic conclusion, feels that some of the intervening chapters are somehow disappointing, something to be read rapidly and forgotten. Admittedly Tolstoy himself had some sympathy with the young reader; Vygotski (1930) reports that when a reader complained that the ending was cruel to Anna Karenina, Tolstoy said that he, like Pushkin, found his characters did what he didn't want them to do but what they had to do in real life. So books which are understood and loved at one stage in experience can be understood differently—though possibly still loved—at a later stage; and this does confirm Rousseau's doubt as to how much we do in fact learn about life from books.

Rousseau's own experience of imagining

But even if understanding is not complete, there can be delight in what is partly understood. Did Rousseau fail to realise the pleasure that fiction can give to the child? There is a great deal of evidence to show that his attempt to reduce the amount of time spent in imagination did not by any means come from failure to realise the joys of imagining. According to his account of his own childhood and later life Rousseau was one of those for whom reading is a passion, an addiction. This enthusiasm was shared by his father: he describes, in his *Confessions*, how they both found it impossible to put away a novel before it was finished, so that: 'Sometimes, my father hearing the swallows in the morning, would say shamefacedly: "Let's get to bed; I am more of a child than you are!" ' Not that this enthusiasm was entirely for light literature; Rousseau speaks of reading serious works by the age of about eight and indeed being so carried away by his identification with the heroes of classical times that: 'I would become the person whose life I was reading'—to such an extent that once when he was re-telling a story he went forward and placed his hand on a burning hot stove in imitation of the hero's action. Such reading might have been expected to encourage the development of heroic qualities and attitudes. Yet, we have seen, his later view was that this early reading harmed him. (It is of course possible that his assessment of his own personality is incorrect; he may have overlooked some beneficial effects of the addiction and exaggerated the bad effects.)

In adolescence this passion for reading continued; he describes how he read anything the local lending library could offer, spending whatever money he had on this, paying with articles of clothing when money ran out; until eventually he was in the unhappy situation of having exhausted the library's stock. (Those with a similar addiction will appreciate how distressing the loss of supplies can be.) At this point in his life he found a solution (which similar personalities seem to have found at a rather earlier age): 'In this strange situation my uneasy imagination made a decision which saved me from myself and calmed my awakening sensuality; this decision was to nourish itself on the situations which had interested me in my reading, to recall them, to vary them, to combine them, to appropriate them to myself to such an extent that I became one of the characters whom I was imagining, that I saw myself always in the situations most agreeable to my taste, in a word, to such an extent that the fictitious condition into which I succeeded in putting myself made me forget my real condition with which I was so dissatisfied. This love of imaginary objects and this facility in occupying myself with them accomplished the task of disgusting me with all that surrounded me and determined that taste for solitude which has always remained with me since that time.' The decision, he considers, was vitally important: 'More than once in what follows will be seen the strange effects of this attitude, apparently so misanthropic and gloomy, which came in reality from a heart which was too affectionate, too loving, too tender and which, being unable to find existing beings like itself is forced to nourish itself with fictions.'

Reading novels led him to prefer living in imaginary situations, and to feel that the real human beings who were around him could not reach the standards of the imagined human beings. It did have another effect, which to some people might seem to compensate for some of the disadvantages; he produced a novel in which he tried to capture the ideal countryside in which he could live happily, and to present the people in whose company he enjoyed living: 'After many vain efforts to drive away from me all these fictions, I was at last completely seduced by them, and I occupied myself with trying to put some order and continuity into them in order to make a kind of novel out of them.' He had, he tells us, some scruples about writing a novel, for his Calvinistic background—in addition to his personal feelings—had led him to distrust 'these effeminate books breathing of love and weakness' but he came to the conclusion that his work of imagination would show the triumph of virtue (his heroine Julie would overcome her feeling for her former lover and remain faithful to her husband); and it might even throw light on some philosophical principles which were in dispute at that time. So he overcame what should perhaps have been more serious scruples about misleading others, and even delighted himself by using specially elegant paper for his writing, and powder of azure and silver to dry the ink.

Even if producing a novel seems to show an attempt to communicate with real people—and the novel, *La Nouvelle Héloïse*, was immensely popular—Rousseau further emphasises how imagining disturbed his relationships with other people; when he was so much interested in his imagined situation, visits from friends were by no means welcome; 'When, ready to depart for this enchanted world, I saw arriving wretched mortals who came to keep me back on the earth I could neither moderate nor hide my annoyance.' Which does rather accord with the development, later in his life, of a belief that people were united in a conspiracy against him. (The person from Porlock who interrupted Coleridge's departure into the enchanted world of Kubla Khan has not received as much public sympathy as Rousseau's friends may seem to us to deserve.)

Rousseau certainly denounced the effects of imagination from a position of inside knowledge; it was for him a source of immense pleasure; but also, he thought—and one can see some justification for the view—a cause of his failure in dealing with people. (Yet he did recognise, in talking of the education of Emile as an adolescent that 'it is only imagination which makes us feel the ills of others' and that at this stage in life sympathy and compassion can be fostered by entering imaginatively into other people's experience; though this reaction must still be based on real observation of how others live.)

It is also possible that Rousseau's reading had an effect which he did not notice; that because he identified in imagination with so many heroic and virtuous characters he felt that he himself was of the same quality. Having shared—quite sincerely—their sentiments in imagination, he may have overlooked the fact that he had not acted in reality in accordance with these praiseworthy principles. Hence, possibly, his essentially romantic picture of himself at various times as a good person not appreciated by society—a view expanded to the theory that society in his time was not a suitable environment for the 'naturally good' human being. It is possible that the process of constant identification with heroes, with persons whose merits are recognised in the end (or even continuously by the writer), led to failure to realise exactly what qualities he himself had really displayed —or really possessed—to deserve society's approval and rewards.

It may be argued that Rousseau, though he gives some fascinating insight into an imaginative personality, is not a good exponent of the case against imagination because he was an eccentric personality. Reading fiction may have had undesirable effects in his case; it does not follow that every child would be affected in the same way.

Rousseau may have been wrong to assume that this kind of imaginative experience would occur for many other children; he may have been unable, for various reasons, to adapt to ordinary life but many others may be more able to adjust to it.

On the whole, such an argument is less likely to be applied to Plato who did not leave confessions for the enlightenment of a critical world. Yet Plato also recommended, in *The Republic*, a most rigorous control of imaginative works. Were his reasons the same as those given by Rousseau? (We should of course bear in mind that Rousseau had studied *The Republic* with enthusiasm.)

Plato's opposition to fiction

What were Plato's objections to the use, in an ideal education, of imaginative folk-tales, literature, drama? There was firstly the straightforward objection that some of the stories told to young children give a misleading picture of the gods and heroes. Stories should not picture gods committing crimes; they should not display heroes showing unheroic emotions. The first part—allowing for differences in religious views—seems reasonable. The portrayal of heroes is a matter for more uncertainty. Plato's view is that if the heroes are seen to behave in an unheroic way this sets an example to the child of allowing oneself to behave in an unworthy way. Our first reaction may be that this is unreasonable; modern fashions prefer heroes who are really 'human', who display normal weaknesses; our view of courage can include initial fear which is overcome. But if we look at the kind of heroes set before young children at present we might almost think that Plato's prescription has been followed. Admittedly we have got away from the more sanctimonious, priggish kind of hero of nineteenth-century works; but it is not common to find the heroes of children's or even adolescents' fiction showing truly unheroic qualities. Eccentricities they may have; and some likeable weaknesses; but not serious defects. (Depending, of course, on the author's judgment of what a defect is—heroes of some boys' fiction may show attitudes of deplorable racial prejudices but the author is still making them as heroic as he knows how. Possibly an exception can be made for heroines of girls' stories—and some women's magazine stories—who do at times behave unheroically, to say the least; indeed their only claim to be heroines is the romantic belief in their place as centre of attention and the conviction which continues—long after the reader has lost it—that their fate is important. But then these are scarcely heroes in the Platonic sense; they are heroes only in the sense of being the central character.) We might almost say that in some ways one of Plato's recommendations about fiction has been followed for children's stories—allowing for difference in social judgment as to what constitutes good heroic behaviour. Adult fiction is more doubtful.

We must of course keep in mind that Plato was not concerned simply about children listening to stories of undesirable behaviour, but with the effect on children of acting such behaviour, since this was part of the learning of the stories. Plato argued that throwing oneself into the character of an unpleasant sort of person or actually imitating the wrong kind of emotion and actions must leave some impression on the actor's personality. He was less concerned to cut bad behaviour out of the stories entirely than to present them so that children did not have to 'live' cowardice, unmanly displays of grief, and behaviour of that kind. Children could learn objectively about bad actions but they should impersonate and identify themselves with only the good characters behaving well. One does wonder how much drama is possible if the opposition is presented only by narrative; even the more innocuous kinds of radio serial do have to bring in occasional vivid presentation of 'badness'—though it could be said that some such serials (and some television serials also) do generally manage to avoid extremely bad behaviour and work rather on the rich field of normal stupidity and misunderstanding. Certainly Plato's argument is especially worth considering at present when so much stress has been laid on dramatic activity in the classroom and children are often rather encouraged to throw themselves into the forceful representation of thoroughly antisocial characters. (As we shall see later, there is not yet conclusive experimental evidence on the effects of such acting.) In a later section of *The Republic* (X, 606) Plato pointed out that normally we try to restrain certain emotions and certain kinds of behaviour because they seem undignified and unworthy; but in plays these emotions and behaviours may be presented and encouraged: 'And with regard to sexual desires and anger and all feelings of desire and pain and pleasure in the soul, which we say follow all our actions, you observe that poetic imitation produces all these effects in us. They should be withered, and it waters them and makes them grow. It makes them rule over us, when they ought to be subjects if we are to become better and happier, instead of worse and more miserable.' For adults equally, fiction can be damaging.

The opposing view would be that emotions of aggression and other undesirable kinds are unavoidable and that fictional presentation of them is therefore a relief rather than a reinforcement. But presumably their arousal does depend to some extent on the kind of people we are living among; in *The Republic* Plato planned to provide an ideal environment which would be more harmonious than ours and consequently—perhaps—afford less stimulus to undesirable emotions; there might be more probability of these emotions remaining dormant if not re-awakened by imaginary situations. There is also the question of the amount of social approval which is implicit in dramatic performance; it could well be that seeing various emotions expressed not only affects the emotional state of the spectator but also forms the belief that the expression of such emotions is socially acceptable. Admittedly, this belief may depend on the outcome of the drama; nevertheless the fact that this emotional behaviour has been witnessed possibly increases the readiness of the individual to act in the same way, without fear of social sanctions. Plato's view is that emotions are encouraged and strengthened if they are experienced through an imaginary situation.

But Plato's most important objection to works of fiction, in any form, is that they offer an unsatisfactory kind of knowledge. This is important; very often we are told that we (or children) learn about life and human behaviour by studying literature; we are told that by such means we acquire insight. But according to Plato such study is misleading; the people in literature are mere imitations of reality; they are less complete than people observed in real life; just as an object represented in a work of painting or sculpture is less real than the object itself so people in poems and stories are further removed from reality. In Plato's theory individual objects do not completely represent the essential qualities which are for him the true realities. Individuals may have chance peculiarities which distract attention and prevent us from realising the true characteristics of their kind. So by studying imperfect imitations of imperfect individuals we move even further from true knowledge than by studying the objects and people themselves.

Further, as Plato points out, the author may be trying to create in the play or poem a kind of person whom he does not really know, because he himself is not that kind of person. He may write about a good man or a great statesman or general; but he himself is not a good man or a great statesman or general; how therefore can he tell us what such a man will think or feel? All he can do is tell us how he himself thinks or feels (which may be quite different); or he can describe such people from the outside—in which case we have not gained much. To write with satisfactory knowledge, according to this argument, the writer would have to write only about himself or about the kind of person he is. Otherwise he is merely guessing (no matter what observations he may base his guessing on) and he may be giving very misleading information about how certain kinds of human beings think, feel, respond in certain situations. As another writer expressed it more recently: 'Novels tell you about people;

how they think, why they do things, what they say. Good ones constantly astonish us by apparently telling us something the author can't know—how *does* Mary McCarthy know that's what I'm thinking, or Angus Wilson get right inside the mind of a middle-aged woman? But a novelist without the gift tells us *wrong*: he analyses human relationships falsely, tells us people do things for reasons they never would. A bad novel, unless it happens to amuse us, is worse than useless in a way that even a bad report of a football match is not.' But Katharine Whitehorn (1969) is prepared to make honourable exceptions among novelists; Plato thought that—unless the poet or dramatist sticks to his own type—the information will always be wrong.

This is a most important criticism since it attacks one of the major reasons for including literature in the school curriculum; it also attacks one of the main justifications offered for a highly popular way of spending leisure.

Do we learn about life and other human beings from fiction? Or do we receive misleading information from it? There has been a great deal in the development of literature, drama and other sources of imaginary experience since Plato's time which would seem to support his main contention. It is worth while to consider this in some detail for if fiction really is a source of false information, should it have a place in education at all?

Support for Plato's contention may be found even in the developments that take place from time to time in novel-writing. We know that the conventional novel leaves out a great deal—all sorts of physical sensations, events, background perceptions; if some boring time occurs, the novelist can evade it by beginning a new chapter 'weeks later' or by some such device. Which certainly does not give a true picture of life, attractive as the idea of cutting out or skipping the boring bits may be. As a reaction to this incompleteness we find techniques trying to give more exact impressions of how people live: 'stream of consciousness' narration in an attempt to convey the unorganised sequence of thoughts, feelings and actions of real individual experience; or a much reduced time span for the whole of the story so that more detail can be introduced and actions last as long in the imaginary situation as they do in reality; a breakaway from the conventional narrator who can see all that is happening to a presentation of thoughts, words, impressions which the reader has to sort out and attach, if possible, to actions and people. (In visual terms, the disjointed images of *cinéma vérité*.) Whether these techniques give better insight into human behaviour is debatable; but possibly the impression is more true to life in some respects. There have been other developments of realism in the novel—a move from the exceptional characters of romantic tales or gothic horrors to more ordinary people and environments. Language has become more colloquial; situations formerly politely omitted are now included to make the fictional life more real. (One can engage in a rather entertaining game of spotting the first mention—or the first recurrence after a period of taboo—of various everyday situations in novels. Child-birth scenes—detailed descriptions of—made their appearance some time ago; A. P. Herbert's *Water Gipsies* scored with a description of a heroine's discovery that she was not, after all, pregnant; and Mary McCarthy probably merits high marks for her mention in *The Group* of the problems of having a contraceptive fitted.) Consideration of the occurrences which do not make their appearance in so many fictional works illustrates the extent to which fiction does not present an accurate picture of experience. Some of the omissions may not be significant; but they still distort the picture. And physical details may be of major importance at some times; recent hypotheses that Napoleon was physically ill at the time of Waterloo offer an example of the way in which official accounts, like fictional ones, could through omission give an inaccurate report of how events really are determined. Thus developments in novel-writing suggest some truth in Plato's view; since authors have clearly been preoccupied in making fiction more life-like they too must recognise that it can be misleading. (One recognises, of course, that not all authors accept the view that fiction should increase the reader's knowledge of human existence. Others may argue that the reader can fill in the missing elements from personal experience—but this is to assume that the reader already knows about the situation, so is not increasing in knowledge of life.)

Secondly, there is an even greater amount of evidence to suggest that individual authors cannot satisfactorily create a wide range of characters. We find a popular belief that everyone could write one book—possibly this would be the one valid contribution to know-ledge that each individual can make, the account of the individual's own personality and experience. (Sometimes in an otherwise poor book some description of a way of life or scenery or a character stands out and remains in the reader's memory; this is, perhaps, the one real experience which the writer had to convey, and it is an enlargement of knowledge, even if the rest of the book is contrived and without value. Hence the rather surprising but justifiable attachment which we sometimes feel for a book read in childhood or regarded as generally inferior.) We certainly find that authors repeat what are evidently the same characters in various forms—and indeed some authors are popular because they can be relied on to do this (readers who like that kind of character or situation want to be able to return to it—i.e. do not want their knowledge enlarged). Various whodunnit writers can be enjoyed on a basis of spotting the culprit not by the elaborate process of deduction from clues ingeniously offered by the writer but simply by knowing that with this author it's always the personable young man or the rather likeable quiet woman. (Coleridge pointed out that it is the mark of a rare genius to be able to present a wide range of subjects; which also seems to give some support to the Platonic argument, rare geniuses being in fact rare.)

There are also some kinds of character which authors are notoriously bad at depicting; the sugary or wooden sweetness of many 'good' characters—Dickens' Little Nell, for example—or the gullibility and weakness of the supposedly good characters in some of Balzac's stories. These would seem to suggest that in fact writers do find it difficult to present characters very far from their own—or possibly of a type they have never actually observed in reality. A similar problem for many writers is to create a character who is a genius; they tend to do it most successfully by describing other people's reactions to this character; when they try to present the genius directly speaking or acting, the result can be remarkably unconvincing. Proust, for obvious reasons, is perhaps the most successful of authors in depicting the personality of geniuses. (Sherlock Holmes is largely presented through the contrasting stupidity of Dr Watson; when he is allowed to speak directly he does rather distress the reader at times.)

Thirdly, some paradoxical support for Plato's view that knowledge is distorted in fiction comes from the technique of deliberate distortion—possibly used to secure the alienation effect. In some historical novels or dramas characters speak in a modern idiom and express present-day views and attitudes. One can see the advantages of this technique: Anouilh, for example, uses it very effectively in *L'Alouette* and Shaw similarly used it effectively in *Saint Joan*. But what kind of knowledge then results? If it is clear that we have not learned about the real historical personalities, well and good; it may in any case be vain to think that we could really know how they thought and felt. But if the impression is left that we have received insight into their minds rather than into the mind of the dramatist interpreting historical data we are misled. (It is possibly true that all human beings are much the same and therefore authors are justified in presenting contemporary views in historical dress; but there are differences caused by social environment, physical conditions of life, education or lack of it, and it seems unwise to ignore these— experience is certainly not enlarged if we simply concentrate on the common elements of experience.) Admittedly we may receive some protection if more than one author deals with the same character; we may then realise that both versions are fictional.

A variant of this problem occurs in contemporary plays which offer the author's interpretation of recent events and apparently present historical personages who died only recently—e.g. Churchill. In some such cases the dramatist is at pains to state that this *is* fiction and not a historical event, but the attachment of real names and the interweaving of real events with imagined discussions must affect the reader or spectator's impression of knowing the personalities involved and therefore knowing how real events are determined. It is true that here, as in more ancient history, knowledge is given incidentally of facts, events, customs, costume; but while this may indeed be a gain of some knowledge to the spectator it does not invalidate our concern for the possibly false knowledge of motives and character. And fiction is insidious; it is astonishing, for example, that many intelligent people (and many more less intelligent people) can slip into the error of talking about fictional characters as if they really did exist or talking about a situation in a book of fiction as a proof of certain principles of human behaviour; thus in discussing *Lord of the Flies* some people argue that this *proves* what child nature—or human nature—is really like if left to develop freely and naturally. (Oddly enough, few people argue that *Peter Pan* proves the natural charm of small boys.) If fiction about non-existent beings can make such a convincing impression, what chance has the historical personage that people who have seen a dramatic presentation of his life will take the trouble and thought to discover how much of it was fiction and how much corresponded to real events? So it may be clear to the writer of historical drama what kind of knowledge the play is intended to give; but the writer expects too much of the spectator if such a thoughtful sifting of knowledge is necessary. (And there is the other possibly superficial complication, in historical drama, that from the time of viewing the spectator is convinced that the historical personage looked just like the star who played the part.)

Fourthly, if we consider the knowledge that fiction gives, there is the delightfully satisfying completeness of the pattern offered by so many dramas and novels. The story comes to a conclusion; we know what became of the characters and we know how their problems were solved—indeed we also know that their problems *were* solved. This tidy provision can be seen at its most naïve in the old-fashioned novel where the author sorts out all the strands in the last chapter, telling us authoritatively who married whom and how many children they had and where they lived and when they died. As Camus points out in *L'Homme Révolté*, this is the great charm of imaginative works;

they give unity to life, they allow consistency of emotion and control over the duration of emotions; whereas in reality emotions change, die away; a pattern is not so clearly perceptible; even supreme heartbreak may prove curable. Camus remarks that in the *Princesse de Clèves* the heroine dies enthrallingly and—to the reader—satisfyingly of a broken heart; but the writer of the novel who, it seems probable, had experienced something of the same suffering as her heroine lived on to a relatively good old age. The novel is a world where 'suffering can, at will, go on till death, where passions are never distracted from their object, where people are completely enslaved by their dominant idea and are always present in each other's minds. Man indeed constructs there for himself the clear shape and comforting boundary lines which he seeks for in vain in human existence. The novel produces destinies made to measure.' In this way, Camus asserts, we have a world which competes with the real one and in which we can, temporarily, conquer death. This is a great glory of art, that it imposes form on life, emphasises and perpetuates the highlights; but it is not a way of increasing knowledge. If we look in life for the same ingenious patterns, the same supreme moments and undying passions, the absolutely faithful memory of things past, we have again been deceived by false information.

We do admittedly find imaginative works which come close to showing more realistically the unfinished qualities of real-life situations; Proust is rather good at creating this kind of impression, at showing the change of feelings, the way in which an action in the past can suddenly be seen in a new light some time later; but he also affirms the shaping and preserving power of art. Some more modern writers, in presenting formless situations and actions which do not lead to any 'solution'—which rather convince us of the lack of insight and the planlessness of human behaviour—may come closer to giving a realistic view; but then they do not give the satisfaction which the shaping imaginative construction does give. This conflict between being true to life but satisfying a human need for form and pattern in existence does pose a difficult problem for the writer; but the educator's problem is the kind of knowledge of life the finished masterpiece offers.

And in this survey of the kind of knowledge offered we might note lastly that fiction normally focuses on one or more main characters; and so the impression may be created that life consists of a main character, and his or her friends and immediate circle, and other less interesting and less important people. Admittedly some writers excel in making formerly insignificant characters suddenly appear as important in their own right. Even television serials or series, in their attempts to maintain interest, may have the merit of gradually showing formerly minor characters as central in their own circle of events. But the general tendency is to encourage us to identify with someone in particular and feel that events are to be viewed as they concern that person. (Robbe-Grillet's *La Jalousie* with its recurrent description of inanimate objects is a rare example of success in getting away from the human being or human beings as centre; except that there is still, presumably, a human eye observing.) Identification with a main character is of course in accordance with our normal tendency to consider events and people as they concern a central character, ourself. But it is a way of reinforcing self-centredness. Sometimes it is claimed that imaginative works make us less self-centred, because we concern ourselves with the fate of others; but if the success or happiness of the fictional character symbolises our own success or happiness, and if that character's survival represents our own, we have not really moved out of our own central concern. Possibly the experience of identifying with a minor character —Horatio instead of Hamlet—would give the necessary change of emphasis; but it doesn't seem to happen very often. It is in fact difficult to see how one can get away from the main feature of individual life, the interest in one's own continued existence; as Modesty Blaise put it neatly in the film of that name: 'I can't be killed. I am the heroine of this story.' Which is very much the attitude of the human being going through life, and the attitude reinforced by fiction. Yet knowing that one's own concerns are of merely peripheral interest to practically everyone else is a useful piece of knowledge.

Thus we can see very considerable support for the Platonic objection to fiction as conveying false knowledge. But yet we can argue that in spite of these weaknesses some value is obtained. How valid are the defences of knowledge given through fiction? One defence is that we are not misled because we are aware that the imagined situations are not real. We know that things don't happen in real life as they do in plays or books: but this surely means that we do not learn from fiction? And are we in any case constantly and logically aware that the imaginary situation is not real? Certainly the acceptance of puppet shows would seem to indicate that we recognise unreality while we still enjoy imaginary situations; we know the puppets are not real just as we know that actors are merely acting and their actions will have no real consequences. But does this mean a dangerous separation of emotions and actions and their consequences? As a representative of the BBC remarked on one occasion: 'Cowboys never bleed' (Weldon, 1967). The child therefore can happily watch the cowboy and Indian battle, knowing that there will be no real unpleasant consequences to face—no burying of the dead

4

(except simply and gracefully), no nursing of the horribly wounded in distressing detail, no really untidy disfigurement. The frequent participation in a 'Bang! You're dead!' situation can possibly develop a lack of attention to normal consequences. If this is so, then possibly the kind of film which is normally considered unfit for children—the film in which physical suffering and death are shown in realistic detail—could be a better source of information about life and develop more reasonable behaviour. Escape from the consequences of action is probably one of the greatest advantages of imagination, but we cannot enjoy this and simultaneously claim that imaginary situations are giving us knowledge of life. The argument that we are safeguarded by our awareness of the unreality of the situation is weak—especially where children are concerned. They might learn more from gory realism.

Possibly a more valid defence of fiction is that even although one author can depict accurately only a few characters like himself, or herself, the reader is not restricted to only one author. By reading a variety of authors we can learn something about a variety of human beings, each author contributing a few examples in his or her own image. The reader can possibly form composite pictures from the images thus collected, verifying what one author says by comparing it with what others say. Or individuals can check their own observations of personality and human behaviour by comparing them with what various authors have observed. People do recognise themselves or others of their acquaintance in some novels or plays and this in itself is a great source of enjoyment (though recognising oneself can sometimes be disillusioning—especially if something one thought rather original on one's own part is said or done by the imaginary characters; but possibly the discovery that one is not unique is extremely valuable). Thus it is a defence of fiction that it offers this opportunity of comparing notes—even if the process is rather one-sided. Disagreement with the author on some occasions, feeling that a certain character could not possibly have acted in the way described, is not necessarily a disadvantage; it can lead to a review of one's own ideas, and it can give some protection against being misled by some authors. There is admittedly still the danger that if an author introduces an unfamiliar kind of character we may accept the author as correct because what is said about the other characters fits in with our own impressions; and yet the author could be totally mistaken in this instance—as, for example, in trying to describe a psychopathic murderer's feelings.

As to the argument that fictional knowledge is incomplete and biased by individual peculiarities—the whole process of communication between human beings suffers from this weakness. To understand words we have to put into them something of our own experience; if we hear of anger, we must assume that the person feeling it has the kind of feelings we have when we feel what we have learned to call anger. Some objective observation of behaviour—loud speech, gestures, redness of face—may convince us that our assumption is correct or—in other cases—convince us that the word is not being used in the same sense as we would use it. (The same kind of problem occurs in naming colours; we learn to call certain perceptions 'green'; this works, for most people, in a satisfactory way on most occasions; but we do have occasions on which we argue whether something should be called green or not and we discover that people are understanding the word more or less differently; or we undergo scientific tests and find that as compared to some other people we judge a wider or narrower band of the light spectrum to be green—when matching patches of light with other patches of light we find we match differently. But for practical purposes on most occasions the differences are small enough to make communication possible and let most of us act effectively—except for those who are colour-blind where green is concerned.) In the same way, we don't communicate fully—we take for granted that people we are talking to can supplement what we say from their own experience; when we are telling them about an event, we can't tell it all. We often discover that we have not said what we meant to—or what we said has not been understood as we expected it to be, either because of our personal qualities or those of our listeners—or both. But we can only report as well as possible what we experience, and assume that we have understood other people's imperfect reports. The whole process of communication demands imagination, the ability to use one's own personal experience in the past to create the situation which someone else is referring to. Some items of knowledge can be passed on objectively and without reference to personal memories; but they are remarkably limited in scope. We communicate because we make the assumption—which works within limits—that although there are individual differences and no two people perceive things in exactly the same way, there are sufficient similarities to make our imagined constructions of what others mean reasonable approximations to what is really meant. Words are symbols; they have to be interpreted. If we insist on complete, detailed, unbiased knowledge we should have to abandon communication by their means; and it is difficult to see an alternative method.

Nevertheless, there are degrees of inaccuracy in communication; and it still is important in education to recognise the extent of the inaccuracies which can be introduced by the demands of imaginary situations, the love of emotional stimulation and the personal characteristics of some authors. Even if Plato's argument about the misleading quality of knowledge given through fiction is not to be entirely accepted, it remains important for educators to consider whether too much inaccuracy is being introduced by the fiction studied, whether inaccuracies can be corrected or lessened by comparisons and analyses.

Montessori's criticism

A more positive and practical approach to the effects of imaginative literature on children was offered by our third opponent of fiction in education, Maria Montessori. She distinguished (1917) between types of imaginative activity: the creative and the illusory imagination. Creative imagination, on her definition, is the kind which is based on truth and leads to new inventions and new scientific discovery—but also to artistic work. It seems in fact to be the kind of imagination which depends on the reconstruction of the data given by past experience of the material world. In the early part of her career, Montessori was especially interested in the way in which children receive sense impressions and use them as the basis of subsequent ideas. (This led to the development of her didactic apparatus which initially emphasised very strongly the development of the child's sense perceptions.) This emphasis on sense impressions has a fascinating line of descent from the philosophical belief that ideas come first from sense impressions; thus if sense impressions can be made very clear and distinct there is a greater possibility of having clear and distinct ideas. (Itard and others used this theory as basis for attempts to educate children of subnormal ability.) Therefore, in Montessori's opinion, the way to educate the creative imagination is to provide plenty of raw material in the shape of sense impressions gained from actual experience. The child must be allowed to work with real objects and discover the qualities of the physical environment in this way; then it will be possible to produce new constructions which will be of real value. Montessori even suggested that different forms of artistic creation—in music or painting, for example—could be traced to the kind of sense impressions which the individual was most interested in—the musician being most interested in auditory sense impressions, the painter in visual impressions, and so on; (but attempts made by others to check this hypothesis seem to have given disappointing results).

But while advocating the kind of education which would make this creative imagination possible, Montessori opposed strongly the kinds of attitudes towards children which foster the 'illusory' imagination. This is the imagination which is not based on real experiences and indeed which is in opposition to them. For example, adults at her time—and now—might consider that the child playing with toys is showing imagination. But in Montessori's view it is only a child who is deprived of real experience, who has no chance to work with real things, who finds satisfaction in this kind of play. It is merely a compensation for poverty; the child wants something which the environment is not providing: 'An adult resigns himself to his lot, a child creates an illusion.' If, for example, the child has a real horse to ride on, there will be no imaginative play at riding on a stick which is said to be a horse.

The use of toys is not only a poor substitute for what the child really wants but is also—in Montessori's opinion—a way of keeping the child from making progress in mastering the real world. A child playing with a toy tea-set is not getting the opportunity to discover the properties of real dishes, is not developing the physical skill necessary to handle them successfully, to know their weight and capacity. Real objects would be more satisfying to the child and would help it more. (Modern playthings probably do show a tendency in this direction—in fact some do really work—some toy typewriters, for example.) Montessori's view is well supported by the enthusiasm which children can show for using household gadgets and the brief attention they give to toy models of these which do not work. The passion of small boys for playing with model cars may be thought of as disproving Montessori's view; but we can scarcely test the alternative of giving them the real thing and seeing what this does to their interest in models (riding in someone else's car is not quite the same thing). Girls' play with dolls has seemed compatible with Montessori's theory since it can be interpreted as compensatory; recent boys' play with dolls like Action Man is perhaps more difficult to interpret, though conceivably it is compensation for not being able to wear the various uniforms the dolls can wear—or live the life which the uniforms denote.

For the same kinds of reasons Montessori criticised those who think that the child's imagination is stimulated by legendary stories, like that of Santa Claus. In this case, she pointed out, it is the adult who is exercising imagination; the child is simply believing; and the adult is taking rather a mean advantage by enjoying the child's credulity while giving the child false information about the real world. If we want the child to speak properly we do not waste its time in talking baby talk; so why should the child's time be wasted with ideas which are not true? From the indignation with which many people greet this suggestion that the Santa Claus story should not be told to children one can judge that Montessori was right in alleging that it is the adult who gets pleasure and satisfaction out of telling it

—though one wonders also if, in an obscure way, some adults have come to think it part of religious doctrine.

The view Montessori gives of the child is of someone with an essentially serious attitude towards life—someone who wants to discover as much as possible about the world without wasting time on false trails. The child should develop imaginative powers, but not those of constructing fantastic situations. Montessori felt that schools of the time very often demanded the wrong kind of creative work from the children. Teachers asked them to write on topics which were supposed to test the child's originality but which were much too remote from the child's experience; the child had not the raw materials of real experience from which to build imaginative constructions on such topics: 'The child must create his interior life before he can express anything . . . he must exercise his intelligence freely before he can be ready to find the logical connection between things. We ought to offer the child that which is necessary for his internal life, and leave him free to produce . . . If imaginative creation comes late, it will be because the intelligence is not sufficiently mature to create until late; and we should no more force it with a fiction than we would put a false moustache on a child because otherwise he will not have one till he is twenty.'

It is perhaps reassuring to note that many schools now follow some of Montessori's advice when they encourage children to write about what they know from experience, but the Plowden Committee quotation given earlier shows how long the tradition of setting children to write on fantastic topics has lingered.

Montessori is thus less vehement in the denunciation of fiction than were our other two opponents of imagination in education; she was, of course, writing about development in childhood rather than about the place of fiction in life generally. She did emphasise, as the others did not, the positive development of a kind of imagination based on real experience. This means that, oddly enough, the conclusions arrived at by all three have some measure of agreement. Rousseau emphasised the heuristic approach in education; he did want his ideal pupil to learn by experience. Plato, though much less concerned with observation and study of the physical world, was also concerned that the mind of the learner should carefully analyse impressions and the perception of relationships. So that the three at least concur in trying to reduce—or eliminate entirely—the part played by fiction in the education of the human being, and in emphasising instead the attainment of objective knowledge. They are not necessarily opposed to all kinds of imagining; but they are opposed to the use of imagination to create fictional situations for the sake of emotional satisfaction; they certainly want to avoid the development of the habit of living in unreal situations and accepting as knowledge the impressions that fiction can convey. But since they have some doubt as to whether the dangers of exposure to fiction can be guarded against, they do tend to limit the use of fiction very strictly.

It may be of some comfort to enthusiasts for the illusory imagination and the delights it offers if we note that other educators have been much less extreme in their reaction to its dangers. Fénelon who, as we saw, pointed out the dangers of imagination, at the same time considered it useful in education, especially in religious training. Children's enjoyment of fairy-tales could, he thought, be channelled into enthusiasm for fables with a moral, and especially into realisation of the interest of Bible stories: 'Enliven your stories by couching them in vivid and familiar language. Make your characters talk. Children whose imagination is lively will feel they see and hear them. For example, tell the story of Joseph. Make his brothers speak brutally and Jacob like a loving and afflicted father . . . If you have several children accustom them gradually to act the characters in the stories which they have learnt . . . All these stories, if properly handled, will pleasantly fill the imagination of young and intelligent children with the history of religion from the creation of the world down to our own times and will give them an exalted idea of it which will never fade . . .' (Barnard, 1966). Fénelon was clearly unworried by the dangers of a false view of customs and speech in Biblical times being presented in such play, and unconcerned about individual characteristics of the actors distorting the child's knowledge of the historical personages; but he did point out the need to give eventually a rational basis for belief and to lead on to spiritual things. Parents, however, must still avoid the error of taking children to entertainments of the wrong kind: 'They accustom the volatile imagination of children to the violent agitations produced by emotional play or music, and after that they cannot settle down to study. They give them the taste for unbridled emotions and make them consider innocent pleasures as insipid. After this they still expect education to succeed, and they regard it as dull and harsh if it does not admit of this mixture of good and evil.' So imaginative situations are to be used only with caution; and one cannot help feeling that possibly Fénelon was a little too ambitious in intending to have imagination active only in religious plays and not used for emotional enjoyment at other times. It is also of interest to notice that he assumes some children to have a lively imagination—and others presumably to lack it; it is the former whom he obviously hopes to have as pupils.

Again, the delights of fiction were given a generous place in education in Friedrich Froebel's proposals (*The Education of Man*).

Children, he noted, enjoy stories; and stories can contribute positively to their development. For one thing, they complement what
the child can learn from his environment (for Froebel also was
concerned that children should learn from the environment and
discover its qualities). The present does not give enough material for
the child's intellectual energy; and as the child grows older it often
develops curiosity about the past and a wish to hear about people who
lived in earlier times; although this eventually leads to studying
history, imaginative stories are the first approach to satisfying this
curiosity (presumably they need not be highly illusory; they may be
more or less factual). Indeed, even if the educator does not provide
the imaginative material, the children may still insist: 'This craving
especially in its first appearance, is very intense; so much so that,
when others fail to gratify it, the boys seek to gratify it themselves,
particularly on days of leisure, and in times when the regular employ-
ments of the day are ended.' (This view in some ways seems to agree
with Montessori's, since it is at times when practical activity is not
possible that imaginative activity is enjoyed.)

Another purpose is to be served by imaginative stories, and it is
one which we might feel was overlooked when Montessori dismissed
play with toys as unhelpful: children need to have their own experience put into words and their feelings made articulate. The child's
understanding of what is happening round about is made clearer
if stories are told about these things. 'Even the present in which the
boy lives still contains much that at this period of development he
cannot interpret, and yet would like to interpret . . . He wishes that
others might furnish him with this interpretation, and impart a
language to the silent objects; that they might put into clear words
the living connection of all things which his mind vaguely appre-
hends. Yet these others frequently are quite unable to gratify the
boy's wish, and thus there is developed in him the intense desire for
fables and fairy-tales which impart language and reason to speechless
things, the one within, and the other beyond the limits of human
relations and human earthly phenomena of life.' Here admittedly we
become involved with Froebel's philosophy of the interconnected-
ness of all things, and the presence of the divine in all created objects.
Froebel believed the child to have some perception of this—so the
child was not simply searching for factual, scientific information
about the real world but also faintly perceiving this divine element
in everything. Nevertheless, it is true that the child's enjoyment of
stories expressing experience of things round about, explaining them
as it were, has often been noticed.

But these recommendations do not completely oppose the spirit
of the recommendations made by the previous educationists. At

least one of the kinds of story that Froebel approves of is realistic; it does deal with the child's own experience, and so is less likely to be misleading. The purpose of improving the use of language, of enriching the child's vocabulary and understanding by talking about experience is one which all the educators would accept. We can also note that this kind of realistic 'story' is very popular in young children's books today. Indeed the word 'story' is possibly misleading here; the situation described is unreal in so far as it is not related to a specific event but it does not really offer a new or novel reconstruction of past data; it rather recalls what is already known.

Nevertheless, some of Froebel's advocacy of stories in education does relate to the other kind of fiction. He points out that children enjoy stories of heroes—heroes of the past or of imagination—and this enjoyment, he suggests, arises because the child can identify with the heroes and enjoy their triumphs; they give a foretaste of what the child hopes to become. 'The story concerns other men, other circumstances, other times and places, nay, wholly different forms; yet the hearer seeks his own image, he beholds it, and no one knows that he sees it.' This, to Froebel, is a legitimate way of building up the child's self-concept; he does not seem perturbed at the possibly misleading pictures of behaviour that the child may form, nor at the kind of emotions—power-seeking, superiority, self-conceit, self-centredness—that the child may be indulging in. There is in this instance a direct opposition of views between Froebel and the critics of imagination. Presumably it is Froebel's point of view which is accepted in the use of literature in schools; the identification with heroes is expected to benefit the learner's personality by building up ambition, hopes, the self-concept. Dangers of false expectations of the future, of false concepts of a non-heroic real world, and of overvaluing the self in this process of identification, are apparently considered negligible.

Can conclusions be arrived at on this difference of opinion? Generally people seem rather to have reached conclusions implicitly, so far as current educational practice is concerned. To some extent, as we have noted, the positive proposals of all the educators considered here are being put into practice; but the negative recommendations are still surprisingly neglected. We still are content to see children absorbing less realistic stories, tales of heroes and others. Yet there seems to be some substance in some of the arguments urged by Plato and Rousseau. Misleading information can result from fiction's enjoyment, individuals' emotions and concepts—if not behaviour—can be adversely affected. Admittedly there is little scientific evidence on these points; but in the absence of conclusive evidence educators today have apparently given the benefit of the doubt to fiction. The prescriptions of Plato and Rousseau are here neglected while other parts of their theories flourish or at least receive more attention and interest. Attacks are made on flamboyant fiction, certainly—anti-sex and anti-violence —but not on the more subtle and more pervasive effects which any kind of fictional stories can have. In the following chapters the consideration of some of the evidence and some of the theories about imaginative activity can perhaps show how reasonable or unreasonable is the tolerant attitude in education today.

Chapter 3

Images and imagining

Possibly images seem remote from the emotional and moral problems just considered; but it has been thought that the essential element in imagining is the ability to have images, i.e. to reproduce past sense impressions when the actual objects or situations are not really present, and to recombine these impressions. The word 'image' has of course various other meanings—in literature, with reference to metaphor, in religion, with reference to representations of objects or people by statue or picture—but these usages introduce elements which are not our main concern here.

The earliest definitions of imagining concentrated on this ability to have images. Even today some people still seem to think that images of one kind or another are the most important part of imagining; and this leads easily to the view that if we can cultivate the ability to call up images of past impressions we shall be more imaginative and even able to think more efficiently. (It doesn't necessarily follow that it really is possible to increase this ability.) The curious point is that there has been quite a lot of research which has shown having images—in the sense of clear recall of past sense impressions—to be comparatively unimportant; but since the research has not been widely studied, and since the imaging idea is attractive, every now and then we find it revived. Solemn pronouncements are made about the need to encourage children to visualise or about the powers of imagery necessary for artistic creation and artistic appreciation: and the appearance of tests of imagery in new creativity batteries may well give renewed impetus to this kind of proposal.

Undoubtedly the experience of imaging can be one of the most interesting in everyday life, and its study does reveal some of the most fascinating differences between people. Studying it can also make people much more aware of the powers they have and of how their mind works. So it is a worthwhile study even although it may prove irrelevant to the development of methods of education and the best kind of education.

It is not clear what happens when we experience an image or a succession of images. It seems that some physiological reactions take place; they may be the same as those which take place in real present perception; it is tempting to assume that the image represents the same kind of perceiving but at a lower degree of intensity; yet there is the major difference that there is not a present stimulus. It has been found that some changes in EEG recordings do seem to correspond to imaging; changes in breathing frequency have been found for people claiming to have auditory (speaking) images; changes in psycho-galvanic reactions have been found to correspond to dream experiences accompanied by images; and changes in muscle potential have been found when physical activities were being 'imaged'—though such changes were not necessarily only in the muscles directly involved in the activity—some were in muscles merely associated with it. This study of physiological reactions in some ways is the most satisfying line of investigation of images for it means that some objective and comparable measurements are possible, whereas other methods of testing the presence of imagery do depend very much on taking people's word for what is going on. Even if people are trying to be scrupulously honest, they may not be able to describe accurately and effectively what they are experiencing; they may also use words in different ways. On the other hand one has to admit that the attachment of gadgets necessary to make physiological measurements can have a distracting effect; and even then, unless some method can be found to make people have images as required, we must still depend on individual reports, from the inside point of view, as to whether imagery is being experienced when the physiological reaction is observed.

Tests of imagery

More amusing, if less easy to control scientifically, are the ways of discovering what kinds of imagery different people claim to have and how vivid these images are or are said to be. Various tests of this kind have been developed. The simplest is perhaps the one used by Galton (1883) who asked people to assess whether the picture they could call up of their breakfast table was (1) brightly lit, (2) had clearly defined objects, (3) was coloured. He found remarkable variations here, ranging from the kind of person who claimed to see the table as brightly and clearly as it was seen in reality to the kind of person who could not 'see' it at all but merely recollected that it was there. (There were also people who claimed not to know what he meant by 'images' and 'seeing' the table.) One can do this kind of testing for the various kinds of sensory experience—e.g.

ask people to 'hear' a telephone bell ringing, to 'smell' a rose, to 'feel' velvet (when these objects are not actually present)—and use a kind of descriptive scale ranging from 'as if it were real' to 'very faint and indistinct' to 'no image at all'. In this way one can also discover the differences among people in experiencing different kinds of images—there are some who have particularly distinct images of things heard, others who can 'smell' in imagery with no difficulty and so on. But one can't assume that reports of these experiences are completely accurate.

Yet various fascinating aspects of imagery have been discovered by this relatively uncontrolled kind of enquiry; for example, that some people 'see' letters of the alphabet or the days of the week as having a characteristic colour; Tuesday dark green, Thursday blue and so on: or as Rimbaud's sonnet about French vowels asserted, 'A black, E white, I red, O blue, U green'. Various theories have been advanced to account for this (e.g. that these are unrecognised memories of childhood books in which the names were printed in these colours) but the interesting point is rather that people have the habit of thinking of the words or letters in this way and do it so normally that it seldom occurs to them—unless a discussion arises—that other people don't do this and don't have the same feeling about the letters or days in question. Similarly there is the existence of 'number forms' which Galton (1880) also discovered; that is, some people 'see' numbers placed in some kind of constant position in a vaguely defined space; e.g. 5 half-way along a line with 10 at the end of it; a spiral leading up to 15 and so on. He even got people to draw these—though, as often happens, they were not satisfied that the drawings accurately represented what they saw.

Other tests have been devised to discover which kind of imagery people use most often; for example, they may be asked to write, in a limited amount of time, a list of (1) things one can see, (2) things one can hear, (3) things one can taste, etc. The relative length of the lists is supposed to show which kind of imagery is strongest—obviously one has to rely on people's co-operation here (it would be easy to cheat if one knew the purpose of the test), but as most people are rather interested in studying themselves, they are, on the whole, likely to give a reliable response. In this respect, the technique used in the creativity battery described by C. J. Mullins (1964), making people compare the strength of different types of images may make it easier for replies to be given; e.g. it may be easier to reply to a question asking whether the image of 'a red rose' is stronger than 'the feel of running your finger over a towel'. Such a test does of course decide the possibilities open to the person doing the test, whereas the open-ended approach earlier mentioned leaves it more to individual habits to determine which kinds of images come to mind. It is interesting all the same to note that the use of the creativity battery containing this imagery test has suggested that 'the tendency to choose the tactual or kin-aesthetic images is supposed to be indicative of ego strength, which, in turn, should be an important component of the creative person-ality, in its continuing struggle with more conservative opinion' (Mullins, 1964) but there is not yet conclusive evidence on this point.

Alternatively, tests of learning have been devised in which the material to be learned is presented through sight or through hearing; it is then assumed that the better success in learning shows which is the stronger kind of imagery for the individual. (This obviously is a rather risky assumption, for the individual may very well translate any-thing that has to be learned into the preferred kind of imagery—e.g. construct a verbal description of what is seen, or form a picture of the information that is heard. There is even some evidence to suggest that normal learning proceeds by coding in words, no matter how the material is presented; though schizophrenic thinking may differ significantly from normal here.) An ingenious attempt to prevent learning by the 'wrong' method in experiments is to try to prevent inner speech by making people hold their tongues between their teeth as they learn: since this sometimes seems effective it may confirm the view that imagery is very close to the normal perception or action. Another device is to use something like the Binet Square in which sixteen letters or digits are printed in square formation and have to be memorised; in such cases the numbers can be printed in Roman or Arabic form, randomly; it is then hoped that the good visualiser will reproduce the numbers in the appropriate Roman or Arabic form while the non-visualiser will get the value of the numbers right but reproduce them in the wrong form. (Again, there seems to be nothing to prevent a sophisticated learner from memorising 'Roman six, Arabic two' or 'vi then two'.)

Frequency of imagery types

At one time it looked as if this kind of testing made it possible to classify people as 'visiles' 'audiles' 'tactiles' and so on (though the words for describing people whose main images were of smell and taste do not seem to have survived); it also seemed that visual imagery was the most widespread and vivid. Various researches have in fact given the percentages of different types of dominant imagery reported; thus P. McKellar (1965) lists: 'Visual 83·4%

Auditory 26·0% Tactile 3·2% Olfactory 3·2% Motor 3·0% Gustatory 1·8% Pain 1·8% Temperature 1·8%.' Other lists give a slightly different impression; e.g. D. Brower (1947) gave visual imagery as again the strongest; followed by auditory, motor, thermal; then tactual and pain; then olfactory; with gustatory weakest. Others have given a higher rank to auditory or to motor imagery; but gustatory, olfactory, thermal, pain do seem to rank low in almost all reports. However, as McKellar points out: 'Some individuals reported more than one kind of imagery as predominant.' The method of study may also help to decide which type or types of imagery will be experienced. Certainly, as A. A. Mackinnon, S. Wilson, P. McKellar (1969) comment: 'It becomes increasingly apparent that visualizer/non-visualizer dichotomies are precarious.' It is difficult to be sure that one is experiencing a 'pure' image in any case—i.e. an image which is only visual or only auditory, without accompaniments of other kinds of sensory impressions. There are amazing variations in the kind of image possible; there is indeed the probability that images will be 'mixed'—that is, we recapture not simply the visual aspect of an object but at the same time have an accompanying impression of how it smells or how it would feel to the touch, and so on. Using the metaphor of music, we could say that asking people for their experience of one form of imagery alone is like asking which instrument they hear playing when in fact an orchestra is performing; one or other instrument may dominate at that point and be named; but it is heard in the context of and probably with accompaniment from, other instruments. Many images are a combination of impressions rather than a clear and unique impression in one sense mode only.

Problems of defining images

The use of words describing imagery complicates the problem further; for example 'auditory image' may be used for hearing the sound of the word describing an object; or for hearing the object (or stimulus) itself; or some people may be hearing a sound as if they themselves were producing it (possibly with a feeling of moving speech muscles), others may be hearing it made by someone else. In the same way people may have visual images of a scene as if they themselves were part of it—they know where they are standing in it or they see themselves standing to the side of it; others may see it in a completely detached way as if they were looking at an illustration in a book.

This latter kind of imagery leads to consideration of another kind which may be much more common than is realised—the imagery which consists of knowing one's position relative to things which are being imaged, of moving one's position in space. Angyal (1930) illustrated this rather neatly in the experiment of asking people to draw a plan showing how to get from one place in their town to another. Some people drew the plan according to the positions in which they actually found themselves at the time of drawing— i.e. the streets were represented as they ran from the actual position of the individual. Other people seemed to be using some kind of orientation which did not correspond to their actual position but which also did not correspond to the conventional scheme of putting north at the top of the sketch, south at the foot, and so on. (Some people did of course use this convention in their sketch.) It became evident, on further study, that the people with the odd orientation were drawing the plan as it would appear if they were in a familiar position—e.g. standing in front of the place where they lived. This seemed to indicate that they had some image of position. This could be called spatial imagery but in some ways it also seems to be associated with the body image (the schema which we automatically build up of our present position, posture, etc.). Another experimenter, Erickson (1929), similarly found that people listening to a description of a scene had—without direction or instruction—'placed' themselves mentally in various positions related to the objects mentioned; e.g. one was 'observing' the scene from a position on the left of the table. It is reasonable to suppose that since we have sense perceptions of our bodily positions we can also have imagery of this kind, which is not altogether kin-aesthetic. What is interesting, however, is that in what could be described as visual imagery some people have this kind of accompanying awareness of their own position relative to what is seen, an awareness which makes the experience rather different from a 'flat' visual image which could be perceived without any kind of personal involvement.

Galton himself found it necessary to use a special term to describe the kind of mixed imagery which he himself experienced; he referred (1879) to his 'histrionic' reactions and described them in this way; in response to stimulus words he would 'act a part in imagination . . . I feel a nascent sense of some muscular action while I simultaneously witness a puppet of my brain—a part of myself—perform that action, and I assume a mental attitude appropriate to the occasion'. For example: 'The word "abasement" presented itself to me in one of my experiments, by my mentally placing myself in a pantomimic attitude of humiliation, with half-closed eyes, bowed head and uplifted palms, while at the same time I was aware of a mental puppet in that position.' Admittedly one can raise all sorts of queries as to what is meant by 'assuming a mental attitude' but the description does seem to convey the kind of mixed reaction that many people have when asked how they respond, and this reaction is not adequately described as having a visual image (or an auditory or kinaesthetic image).

Incomplete images

Similarly, many people have noticed that their images also differ from real sense impressions by being more or less incomplete; some images may be considerably less complete than others. Descartes (*Méditations*) was one of the earliest to remark on this when he pointed out that he could have an image of a triangle which was clear and distinct but in thinking of a thousand-sided figure he could have only a confused sort of representation—some sort of image, it seemed, but one which was vague enough to have done equally well as an image for a hundred- or million-sided figure. Titchener (1909) makes the experience of having such partial images particularly clear when he describes his reaction to reading books; he mentions that he has the habit of thinking of writers in visual terms, attributing to the writer a kind of characteristic visual pattern (which sounds rather like other people's number forms or coloured vowels): 'I must warn the others, to whom this sort of imagery is unknown, not to think of a geometrical figure printed black on white, or of anything a hundredth part as definite. I should be sorely puzzled to say what colours appear in my schemata, and I certainly could not draw on paper my pattern of a particular writer or a particular book. I get a suggestion of dull red, and I get a suggestion of angles rather than curves; I get, pretty clearly, the picture of movement along lines, and of neatness or confusion where the moving lines come together. But that is all . . .' (It would be interesting to discover whether modern computer analyses of writers' styles would show any relationship with such imagery—i.e. if a subliminal perception of a writer's preferred sentence structures leads the reader to form images like those Titchener describes, and so the qualities expressed in the image (e.g. neatness, clarity) do correspond to qualities of the structure patterns in the style).

Titchener further describes his partial images thus: 'Whenever I read or hear that somebody has done something modestly, or gravely . . . I see a visual hint of the modesty or gravity . . . The stately heroine gives me a flash of a tall figure, the only clear part of which is a hand holding up a steely grey skirt . . . The stately form that steps through the French window to the lawn may be

5

clothed in all the colours of the rainbow; but its stateliness is the hand on the grey skirt.' And again, showing something like Galton's reaction: 'Not only do I see gravity and modesty and pride and courtesy and stateliness, but I feel or act them in the mind's muscles.'

All this, of course, may be to some people totally meaningless; so that they are likely to query furiously as to what is meant by 'the mind's muscles' and how any intelligent reader could so blatantly disregard what a writer says about the colour of a character's clothes. Yet Titchener, like Galton, has provided what is to other people a very apt description of common experiences. (Unfortunately there is not enough evidence to show conclusively how many people fall into these two categories, though Mackinnon, Wilson, McKellar (1969) state that 'available data suggest that perhaps only 10% of the population can be regarded as non-imagers'.)

Pre-sleep (and post-sleep) images

There is perhaps one form of pure imagery, the kind which is rather remarkably named hypnagogic imagery (and its even more interestingly named companion hypnopompic imagery). This is the kind of imagery which happens spontaneously when we are in the process of falling asleep (hypnagogic) or waking up (hypnopompic). In the former state visual imagery seems the most popular, though auditory imagery is also fairly frequent; so people about to fall asleep suddenly 'see' (with closed eyes) what are often odd and fantastic shapes and objects; often these are vividly coloured; people, faces, geometrical or other designs, landscapes—all kinds of things may be 'seen'. In some cases these images appear totally different from memory images for they are not related to anything in the individual's real experience—distorted faces, monsters, weird landscapes; in other cases, more normal objects and scenes appear. Sometimes indeed they may seem like after-images of things seen during the day, except that they are not exact reproductions of them—for instance after many hours of driving, one may see, when falling asleep at night, a road unwinding as if before a car. Another such instance was noted by students who had been working on a holiday job of picking strawberries: they began to wait expectantly, in the dormitory at night, for newcomers to the job to exclaim that they were 'seeing strawberries' as they settled down to sleep; but again, as the strawberries were described as being more beautiful and perfect (sometimes even conventionalised in form, with perfectly regular leaves) than the real strawberries handled during the day, these images did seem to be something other than simple memory images or after-images.

Hypnopompic imagery, while emerging from sleep, seems to be rather less common; certainly it has been less studied. Perhaps children would find it less frightening, for it has been suggested that hypnagogic images add to fear of the dark in some children and they are reluctant to go to bed if they have imagery of monsters or other inexplicable and frightening things.

Hypnagogic imagery in other sense modes does present problems if we are to distinguish between images and hallucinations or errors of perception. It is evident that things 'seen' in such falling-asleep circumstances are not real, since they obviously are not present in the actual surroundings; but if there is an image of something heard— e.g. a phone bell or someone's voice calling—it may be difficult for the individual to decide that this is an image and not an actual perception; similarly (and agonisingly) a smell of burning may be hard to classify (though other smells, e.g. of exotic flowers, would obviously be images since the real stimulus was absent).

Visual images of this kind are said to be due to characteristics of the eye—e.g. to residual light affecting the retina—in some authors' explanation; other characteristics would presumably apply to other sense organs, each may have its own peculiar way of 'running down' before sleep and thus produce the odd perceptions called images. Studies of sleep behaviour, providing further detailed information about physiological processes during different stages of sleep, may soon help to explain image formation in the pre-sleep or after-sleep period.

If these images do result from such physiological processes, we should expect everyone to have them; but they may be so common as to be overlooked. Certainly one finds that after discussions of this kind of imagery many people find that they have been having hypnagogic images without noticing them—or rather, when they hear them discussed, they begin to notice that they happen; other people are so familiar with the experience that they have learned to welcome the appearance of hypnagogic images as a sign that they are finally falling asleep. For those who have no personal acquaintance with this imagery a milder prescription than the hallucinogenic drugs currently fashionable would seem to be suggested by John Locke's observation (in the *Essay on the Conduct of the Understanding*) that a lady began to experience hypnagogic images when she took a cup of tea before bedtime. (Again, it would be useful to know whether those who try drugs in their search for vivid images are the kind of people who have already experienced vivid hypnagogic images or who do not normally have them.)

Individual differences in imaging

All these reports and investigations emphasise the great variety of experiences covered by the term 'images' and the great range of individual differences in this kind of experience. A further important individual difference, for those who do have images, is in the ability to control their imagery. Some people claim to have superlative control, to be able to produce images as they choose, change them into any shape or position; others find it difficult to call them to mind at will or, having once produced them, to alter them. A test of this kind of ability was devised by R. Gordon (1949) who proposed that one should try to 'see' a car standing in front of a garden gate; then try to change its colour; then make it move to different surroundings; then involve it in a crash; then make it move again normally; then see it 'old and dismantled in a car cemetery'. Anyone who can make the imaged car go through these transformations on demand can certainly be said to have controlled imagery; those who cannot—who find that the car remains obstinately the same, or vanishes, or who find that they cannot image the car on request—are said to have autonomous imagery. There are intermediate stages between full control and autonomy; some people can make some changes, but only at a certain speed or for a limited number of situations.

This could be an important difference between people. It has been proposed at times that children's fears (and those of adults, possibly) can be overcome if, for example, the child who is afraid of dogs is told to picture a dog in its mind, then to change the colour and size of the dog, to make it disappear, become larger or smaller, do tricks, and so on. Thus by controlling the images the child might become more confident of power to control the real animal. But very obviously this kind of device will work only if imagery can be controlled effectively by the child—the consequences for one with autonomous imagery might be highly unpleasant; a large, ferocious dog might be imaged advancing on the child and so reinforce the child's fear. Unless, possibly, the surrounding real circumstances could be made pleasant enough to let the child realise that the image did not really hurt and, gradually, to feel more relaxed about the real life situation. This proposed cure by imaging indeed is similar to the technique of desensitisation which, as we shall see later, is sometimes used in psychotherapy to help people to overcome phobias of various kinds: though in such work there is not always a clear distinction between forming images and imagining (e.g. Lazarus, Abramovitz, 1962).

A more common example of failure to allow for individual difference is possibly found when directions on how to reach a certain place are asked for and given; too often a direction-giver may begin: 'You know the white church on the corner . . .' only to be told that the enquirer has no knowledge of it, cannot remember seeing it, cannot think where it is. The informant who has clear visual imagery of any familiar scene—or even of a route which has once been followed—often cannot accept the fact that another individual who has as much experience of the scene is not able to call on a similar imagery. It is possible that educators make a similar mistake by taking for granted that words call up for all children the same amount or kind of imagery; that a poem must therefore produce the same kinds of response if the children really give it their attention.

The usefulness of images

But at various times educators have considered that all children should be encouraged to have clearer and more frequent images, since this seemed likely to be associated with clearer and more efficient thinking. Galton himself had such an idea when he first began to investigate imagery, and wrote (1883) that: 'I believe that a serious study of the best method of developing and utilising this faculty, without prejudice to the practice of abstract thought in symbols, is one of the many pressing desiderata in the yet unformed science of education.' Yet, knowing a great deal about individual differences in imaging, he also commented: 'Another general experience is that the power of seeing vivid images in the mind's eye has little connection with high or low ability, or any other obvious characteristic, so that at present I am often puzzled to gauge from my general knowledge of a friend whether he will prove on inquiry to have the faculty or not. I have instances in which the highest ability is accompanied by a large measure of this gift, and others in which the faculty appears to be almost wholly absent. It is not possessed by all artists, nor by all mathematicians, nor by all mechanics, nor by all men of science.' So Galton at least came round to the conclusion that forming images was not an essential ability; and one can sympathise with Bain's (1880) comment that if people become less able to form images as they grow older, this may well be because the power of forming images is of no great use.

Not that there is firm proof that people do in fact lose the power to form images as they grow older, though the development of the ability to use language may well affect the value of images in thought. It is true that one kind of imagery—eidetic imagery—has been more often observed in children and may in fact be more frequent in childhood. By such imagery the child can—apparently—have so clear a visual memory image of some object or scene as to be able to see it in as much detail as if it were actually present. Children having this imagery are reported to be able to 'read' from a picture they are recalling even words in a foreign language which they do not know. One report of such imagery (Haber, 1969) says that most children in a group of twenty having this ability did find there were limits in the extent to which they could 'move' the eidetic image—though one girl claimed complete control of it, even to being able to turn it upside down. These children reported that the images faded bit by bit, keeping their vividness to the end; but, oddly enough, if a part of a picture was named, or the child concentrated on it, it vanished. No connection between intelligence or personality factors and this ability was found; and the twenty children were apparently the only ones in a group of more than 500 who had this kind of imagery.

It is of course part of student folk-lore that some students have the happy gift of being able to use imagery of this kind to 'read' textbooks or notes in exam situations; it is interesting to consider that it might happen; and how useful it would be to the professional spy.

Dominance of visual imagery?

This belief in a marvellous power which is lost with the passing of childhood seems related to another belief about imagery—that children have especially strong and frequent visual imagery and that this affects their thinking greatly. Is visual imagery really dominant? As we have seen, it is reported with high frequency by many adults; and visual impressions are certainly a tremendously important source of knowledge. But there are other sources of knowledge; we clearly have images in other sense modes as well—are they underestimated while the importance of visual impressions is exaggerated? There are some reasons which could lead to such exaggeration.

One may be the use of words. If we think about it, we find that we have a lot more words at our disposal to describe what we see—or what we see as a visual image—than to describe what we hear, taste, touch or feel. We can convey to other people some idea of what we are seeing as a visual image by making a drawing of it. But there does not seem to be any other way of conveying other kinds of image (except that possibly we may imitate sounds—difficult as this may be if we are having an image of a ship's siren or of an orchestra). But if we have a very vivid image of, for example, sliding rapidly down a snowy slope, we cannot convey this very adequately even by words; our vocabulary sets limits; we have certainly some adverbs—smoothly, rapidly, bumpily—but these do not seem to give much scope in conveying our feelings—not as much as the very many words of colour, shape, size which we could use to give the visual impressions. Or consider attempts to convey the bouquet of wines—the absurd and justly mocked pieces of descriptive writing, the 'presumptuous little wine' and so forth, which just possibly arise from this deficiency in words which can convey precise taste sensations. (Of course the fact that we have more words for visual experiences may possibly indicate that they really are more important than the others.)

In the same way, when children are being questioned about their experiences, it is probably easier to ask them about 'seeing' things than about 'tasting' them or 'feeling' them; and it is easier for the child to talk as if simply seeing something when in fact other kinds of imagery are being experienced. How, for example, can the child convey an image of swinging, muscular movements, the feeling of pressure, the rush of air? It is simpler for the child to say 'a swing' and leave it unclear whether the situation is seen or felt—especially if the question was: 'What are you thinking about?' or 'What did you dream about?' While tests can be devised to find out whether a child has eidetic imagery of a visual kind it is very difficult to think of a similar test for eidetic imagery of movement or of tasting.

Certainly the statement that children think in visual images because this is the most primitive form of sensation is unreasonable. Other sensations are present at equally early—or earlier—stages in the child's life and these sensations of warmth, touch, movement, pressure are as important, if not more important in the most primitive stages of existence. Indeed the ability to see things appears to develop relatively late in the baby's experience of the world.

So far as thinking is concerned, visual images are in any case clearly not an ideal method. If we consider the handicap that deaf children suffer in intellectual development unless they are made capable of using words and forming abstract concepts through the medium of words, it becomes clear how unsatisfactory visual images can be. Teachers of physically handicapped children have pointed out that deaf children are in some ways more handicapped than blind children, precisely because of the greater usefulness of words in thinking. And the problems of educating autistic children are a further indication of the essential contribution of words rather than visual images in thinking.

Nevertheless people have found this theory that thinking could be improved by developing better visual imagery singularly attractive.

It is plausible to suggest that children would learn better if they could call up instant pictures of material—of maps, scenes shown in history or geography books, described in poetry and other writing. So from time to time the method of encouraging image formation crops up again.

Investigations of the use of imagery

What have experimental studies shown about the effects of such a method? They have focused on the usefulness of images in (1) intellectual performance, (2) memory, (3) learning skills and (4) appreciation of poetry and other literature. How have these various activities benefited by the use of imagery?

Intellectual performance

At one stage in the development of psychology it was questioned whether thinking proceeds by a kind of auditory imagery—by internal speech, so that when we think, we hear an inner voice (possibly accompanied by an awareness of muscular contractions of speech organs). But these early studies came to the conclusion that thinking does not normally proceed in coherent sentences, and that ideas can in some way be present in consciousness without any words or images of words. The effectiveness of imagery in solving geometrical problems, in tonal or other musical discrimination and in academic achievement has also been studied. The conclusion generally reached is that although imagery may be present in dealing with some problems and in completing some tests it does not seem to be an essential feature of finding solutions; thus, for example, though most musicians in one study (Seashore, 1919) rated themselves high on auditory imagery, some did not seem 'able to grasp either the fact of the existence or the significance of imagery of any sort'. Nor has imagery proved essential in dealing with academic problems; even problems with geometrical figures have been found capable of solution without imagery—in other cases the imagery used was decidedly incomplete. Imagery may come into activities involving spatial ability—i.e. being able to deal with forms and shapes, fit them together (as in a dressmaking pattern) without actually manipulating them: but even such problems can apparently be solved without imagery. As early as 1928, a symposium in the *British Journal of Psychology* by Aveling, Bartlett, Pear indicated this general agreement about the slight value of imagery—or at least agreement on the possibility of highly effective thinking without clear and distinct imagery. Similarly Bruner (1966) cites Kuhlman's research as showing the inadequacy of imagery in the developing of concept formation by children.

Memory

Bartlett (1932) carried out experiments which produced fascinating evidence of what happens when people reproduce stories and pictures which they think they remember; these studies showed various effects of imagery, but also demonstrated clearly that the presence of imagery was no guarantee of effective remembering. It was in fact notable that people were confident that they had remembered a picture correctly when in fact it had been modified and changed in memory so that the final reproduction differed considerably from the original. Also intriguing was the discovery that visual images seemed to give a feeling of confidence in one's memory, while auditory images did not necessarily do so. (This seems to be borne out by common experience; it is especially hard to convince people that their memory is at fault if they can 'see' someone doing something or wearing some particular dress or costume; yet experiment after experiment has shown that such clear visual memories can be totally mistaken. And again, the lack of confidence which may accompany images in other sense modes— auditory images, for example—bears no relation to the accuracy of these memories; they may be perfectly reliable even if not confidently asserted.)

It has been suggested however that some experiments showing that visually presented material is not well remembered have been misleading; the conclusive test of memory has not called for visual reproductions, but, possibly, tested ability to reproduce the material in words. Thus Magne and Parknäs (1963) found that visually presented material did prove to be well remembered in some types of test. But against this there is also much evidence that help is often needed to interpret visual information; for example, seeing a film of a technical process will not necessarily help people to understand the process or to remember it; both understanding and remembering benefit by explanations being given in words also. And of course, the purpose of the learning is important; if later use of the material requires the ability to explain it in words, then testing memory by verbal tests is justified.

So although it has so often been argued that encouraging children to form clear images might increase their learning power, there does not seem to be conclusive evidence that it really would increase their learning power. (And little is known about their power to learn to form images more clearly.) Admittedly some individuals feel that it helps them if they try to learn by using visual or other imagery. They may prefer to arrange information to be learned so that certain kinds of image are encouraged; some like to tabulate it, to draw diagrams, use visual representations; others like to repeat it aloud. These devices are sensible enough; they introduce some kind of order, they process the information and this seems to make learning more efficient even if the images resulting from the process are incomplete. But this is different from establishing general rules about how other people will learn best. Indeed, since people have such individual preferences, the simpler rule for teachers is probably to present information in such a way that it appeals to a variety of senses (if possible); it is then the learner's responsibility to select the mode that suits best and process the information accordingly. (Here one must sympathise with those whose preferred method of processing is not currently in fashion; those, for example, who really prefer words at a time when contemporary fashion insists on flow diagrams.)

Learning skills

This is where a good many learners do use imagery, whether it helps them or not—in the process of learning physical skills. The novice golf player watches experts on television and inwardly (or even outwardly) plays that masterly iron shot; the young footballer feels the contact of boot on leather as the ball sizzles towards the goal—even if he is prosaically walking along the street. It would be pleasing to discover that such mental rehearsals do improve the acquisition of skills; and various investigations have set out to discover if in fact they help. In one example (Start, 1960) a group was asked to form distinct images of making a basketball shot; to feel, in detail and in the proper sequence, the various movements that would have to be made. Groups were thus given a session of 'imaginary practice' for controlled periods of time, and their final success compared with that of groups who had had real practice instead. On the whole, in this instance, the method does not seem to have been clearly successful; though in a similar study (Verdelle Clark, 1960) one experimenter did claim success with some groups using 'imaginary' practice of the 'Pacific Coast one-hand foul shot'—indeed stating that 'mental practice was almost as effective as physical practice for the varsity and junior varsity groups, and not as effective for the novice groups'. (It is uncertain, admittedly, whether we should call this 'mental practice' imaging or imagining; as it seems to be very much restricted to sensory impressions, imaging seems a fair description.) In other experiments people have been invited to go through sorting procedures (much less interesting than basketball) and gains in speed have been reported; but in this kind of activity practice by imaging could be affecting other elements —especially in the way of developing concepts and categorisation of the material; so the effect of imaging on the sheer motor skill would possibly be insignificant.

It's attractive to think that we can become better at a sport by sitting quietly imaging that we are performing. It would of course be an alternative interpretation of William James' oft-quoted comment about learning to skate in summer and learning to swim in winter—it would not, as he suggested, be a matter of plateaux in learning, but a demonstration of the power of imagery. Unhappily spectators of various sports do not seem to improve much in performance despite the sympathetic imagery which they probably experience. Possibly they just don't control their imagery systematically enough. It is true also that the factor of motivation complicates this question. Anyone interested enough to indulge in systematic 'imaginary practice' may be more likely than others to go in for real practice also and so make progress in the skill. Again, there does not seem to be much evidence on how much practice of this kind the real expert does—thinking about the sport even when not actually training. In Verdelle Clark's study (1960) it was reported that 'introspective analyses suggested a strong relationship between the subject's ability to visualize the motor skill and the amount of improvement experienced' but in this case one would need to know which had priority—'visualizing' clearly or being rather promising at the skill (and therefore able to image it clearly). And even suggestibility could affect this kind of response. At least individual differences in ability to control imagery seem to have been found here too; one player practising a shot in imagery reported: 'mentally attempting to bounce the ball preparatory to shooting only to image that it would not bounce and stuck to the floor.'

Appreciation of poetry or literature

Probably it is here that the best results would be expected from being able to form images clearly and well; but it is extremely difficult to carry out experiments on people's images while they are enjoying poetry or a book or a play. The trouble is also that being asked especially about images can make people much more conscious of images, and so they produce more than they normally would. On the other hand, if we simply ask people whether they liked a certain poem, and if so, why they liked it, they may give a variety of reasons without mentioning images—not because they did not have any images as they heard or read the poem but because they have not previously discussed this kind of activity and are not aware enough of it to think it worth mentioning. Possibly the ideal subjects are people who have at some stage studied imagery but have passed the stage of giving it exaggerated attention—but such people tend to be a rather specialised group. On the whole, contemporary studies of appreciation of literature tend to ask general questions, leaving it to people to give their own reasons for liking or disliking a work; or to avoid asking for reasons but to carry out an analysis of stated preferences and so try to identify underlying factors in appreciation. In some ways the older studies which made a point of investigating imagery give more interesting results, even if these are not statistically reliable and even if the conditions of the investigations left room for a great many personal influences.

We can see this kind of situation in an early investigation by G. H. Betts (1909) in which forty-two students (and others) were asked to state their favourite poems or pieces of literature and then asked whether the piece they had chosen produced imagery in their minds; all but four did report at least two types of image (though we should note that this was not unanimous); yet they did not think that it was of the greatest importance in making them like the poem or other writing. (Oddly enough, the poem *The Cottar's Saturday Night* was said to evoke no imagery.) But one must admit that the way in which the question was put—'If the images suggested above do appear when you think of the piece, is it the images you love to think about and dwell upon, or is it the *thoughts*, the *meaning*, the *feeling*, the *sentiments*, the *language* or the *rhythm*, or some other qualities?'—does rather discourage anyone who might have wanted to emphasise the major and unique importance of the images.

From the teacher's point of view, the work carried out by E. Allison Peers (1913) with rather small groups of schoolboys is possibly more illuminating. The groups were not totally unbiased since they had previously had tests of imagery and knew something about it. They were presented with a verse of a poem which was thought to be fairly difficult for them (*A Sea Shell* by D. G. Rossetti) and asked how well they had understood it; then they were asked to write out any images they had experienced. Mainly visual images were reported (and it was noticed that the boys with the strongest visual imagery nearly always added details of their own to what was given by the poet). About 10 per cent seemed to have no imagery. Further work was done by re-reading the poem, explaining the images and again asking for reactions; not altogether surprisingly, this produced more images on the part of the boys. Later, poems of different types were read to them, the experimenter having chosen poems which in his opinion (a) conveyed the main idea through images, (b) could produce images but did not require them for understanding, (c) did not seem to call up images. The boys were asked to explain the ideas of the poems and say what images they had had during the reading. The relationship between marks gained for understanding and the amount of imagery reported was studied. As would have been expected, high marks seemed to go with full imagery in dealing with the first kind of poem; for the second type, medium or no imagery went with better marks for understanding; and in the third, good understanding and no imagery seemed to go together.

Asking the boys for their impressions, the investigator found that some who had the strongest images claimed that in order to understand poems of the first two types, they had to disregard the images and reason out the meaning; two found that they could not interpret the poem if the images were too strong. This perhaps illustrates the common-sense view that the usefulness of imagery depends on the kind of poem or prose that is in question; but the investigation is still interesting.

Valentine (1923) found further reinforcement of a common-sense view when he studied, with a group of students, the place of imagery in the enjoyment of poems. Initially he asked the group of fifty to say whether they liked a poem or not (assessing it on a seven point scale) and to say why; they were then asked to notice the imagery it produced and to notice whether there was any change in their liking or disliking when the poem was re-read; during a third reading they were asked to try to get appropriate images, and to say what effect this had. Fifteen found that practising imagery in this way was partly helpful and partly unhelpful; seventeen found it had no effect. From the objective results and from the students' reports Valentine concluded that most of those tested had experienced imagery, especially when natural objects were described, and this added to their enjoyment; but some people can enjoy even poems describing natural objects or scenery without the help of imagery. Even the same individual can have imagery on one occasion when a poem is read and not on another, and yet enjoy the poem on both occasions. (Here, of course, it can be argued that memory must affect reactions; possibly we enjoy a poem on later occasions partly because we remember that it is a poem we have enjoyed.) Valentine further noted that there can be conflicts between kinds of imagery, and between images and rhythm, sound or meaning. Sometimes too clear images may spoil the enjoyment; so may a deliberate attempt to produce images. Some imagery may be irrelevant—though this did not seem to matter to Valentine's subjects if it fitted in with the feelings which the poem normally produced. Thus Valentine came to the perhaps rather remarkable conclusion that schools should encourage the cultivation of visual and auditory imagery, but not with respect to any one poem. He did at the same time point out that harm could be done by emphasising imagery, by trying to make images too distinct or by thinking that they were absolutely necessary for appreciation. So much depends on the kind of writing that is to be enjoyed, and on the kind of individual having the enjoyment—and even on the occasion of reading or re-reading.

Similar results seem to have emerged from other studies on the same lines; for example Wheeler's (1923) investigation of the effects of reading a poem, re-reading with attention to the images that occurred, then re-reading as usual; this, for most people, seemed to lead to greater enjoyment; but some people found that noting images reduced enjoyment. Further study with a conscious attempt to develop relevant imagery led to reduced enjoyment for the majority. This investigator suggested that enjoyment is increased if poems are read aloud in an appropriate way—which might well affect the images likely to occur.

Irrelevant imagery

The question of relevant or irrelevant imagery is interesting. Analysis of our own reactions—in a discussion about other people's reactions —sometimes shows that we have formed pictures which are not really justified by the words we have read; and yet we may rather cherish them. One teacher (Tudor Owen, 1920) who was anxious to encourage image formation tried the method of asking a class to draw their impressions of a scene as it was described by a member of the class, thus, presumably, indicating the images produced. Even apart from differences in artistic skill very great differences were found in the scenes pictured in this way; but as one pupil remarked with reasonable common sense: 'That's because our natures are different.' But perhaps a better illustration of the irrelevant image comes from Feasey's (1927) report of a study of imagery with a group of 550 children who gave reasons for preferences of one of six poems they had studied in schools. (This was at a time when, the author commented: 'The method of image formation is so frequent in schools.') A large number of children included imagery as one of the main reasons for their preference—which is not surprising, in such circumstances; but one child explained her preference for Masefield's poem, *Sea Fever*, in this way: 'I seem to smell the sea and feel the breeze as it comes over the sea onto my face. I seem to imagine a little boat with white sails sailing on a blue sea towards a land of adventure where there are cannibals and treasure in some corner of the island.' One can see how this kind of imagery might give great satisfaction to the child (and it is interesting to note that not only visual imagery is reported but the smell of the sea and the touch of the breeze) but it scarcely seems likely to lead to a good understanding of the poem in question. (Of course the child may simply have been trying to please teacher by saying what seemed to be the right thing.) It is sad to reflect that quite a few enthusiastic feelings about poems are probably built—or partly built—on responses as irrelevant as these. Admittedly it all adds to enjoyment; but it can scarcely be said to enlarge experience or improve communication; it might well annoy poets.

Imagery and aesthetic enjoyment

More objective and more scientific attempts to discover what importance imagery has in the enjoyment of poems likewise seem to indicate imagery having some effect but not being a major factor. Gunn's study in 1951 asked schoolboys and students to assess the part played by nine qualities in their appreciation of nineteen poems, one of the nine qualities being 'mental imagery'. But in only one sub-group was mental imagery highly associated with the main general factor of which liking was the main component; in all the other sub-groups imagery had a positive but low correlation with this general factor. And as Gunn pointed out, many studies of aesthetic appreciation find some such general factor (which is variously interpreted as liking, good taste, aesthetic feeling) and a bi-polar factor which is interpreted usually as classical/romantic; and possibly a further bi-polar interpreted as simple/complex. Similar factors appeared in Eysenck's study (1940).

When we think about the importance of imagery in aesthetic appreciation we tend to be most concerned with verbal arts, since in other arts we enjoy actual, present sense impressions which would seem to exclude images—at least images in the same sensory mode. But some attention has been given to the appearance of imagery in response to non-verbal works of art—indeed Baudelaire's theory of aesthetics would suggest that response to all aesthetic experience has overtones of this kind: *Il est des parfums doux comme des chairs d'enfant.* . . . Architecture is said to evoke musical structures. Visual images accompanying music are often noted; they have perhaps been embodied in Walt Disney films (*Pastoral Symphony*) and, possibly, in various ballets. Attributing a 'story' to music, or giving it titles of story-like kinds can be regarded as an attempt to suggest to the listener the visual imagery appropriate while listening, and many listeners do apparently experience relevant visual imagery during the playing of such music. But it by no means follows that music must evoke visual imagery for its appreciation, or even that it will evoke the same kinds of visual image in all listeners, especially if they have not all been given the title in advance or read the same programme notes. People listening to an unidentified piece of music and asked for images evoked by it (if any) show considerable divergences in their reponses; though they may possibly agree on the same kind of emotional tone or mood indicated by the music and the images (Downey, 1897). It is of course possible that in such cases many of the images, though divergent, are relevant. Some recent radio panel game performances (*My Music*) have asked the players to give titles for a piece of music not previously known to them—possibly composed for the occasion—and the convergence of ideas between guesser and composer has sometimes been remarkable. (It would be interesting to discover what effects the prevalent background music in film or television drama has in deciding the kind of images which similar music will evoke in future.)

And of course there are the many instances of songs, or poems set to music, in which music is presumably allied to appropriate images: though precisely here some people may consider that the music produces the 'wrong' images—e.g. Fingal's Cave is worth looking at and remembering visually, but not in conjunction with Mendelssohn's music; Debussy's *Prélude à l'Après-Midi d'un Faune* may give delight but produce, for some listeners, imagery quite different from that called up by Mallarmé's poem. Yet such conflicts still reinforce the belief that imagery contributes to enjoyment, even if different people have different images in response to the same stimulus.

Images while reading or listening

The difference already noticed in individual reactions should make clear what part we can expect imagery to play in reactions to longer literary experiences—to reading a book or to listening to a radio play. Some people enjoy a lot of accompanying visual imagery, or other imagery, others have little or none. Sartre (1948) suggests that in intensive reading there is practically no imagery; this is, at any rate, his own experience and, he says, that of others of his acquaintance: 'Writers are agreed that reading is accompanied by few images. In fact, most subjects have few of them and they are also incomplete. It should even be added that images appear apart from the reading process itself, that is, when the reader is thinking of the events of the preceding chapter, when he is dreaming over the book, etc. In short, the images appear when we cease reading or when our attention begins to wander. But when the reader is engrossed, there are no mental images. We have demonstrated this on ourselves over and over again and it has also been confirmed for us by several persons. A flow of images is characteristic of disturbed and frequently interrupted reading. . . .'

Certainly imagery does often take place when people are thinking about the characters of a book or play they have read or a play they have listened to. The BBC has noted that followers of the serial *The Archers* have quite definite ideas of what the characters look like—which can be rather trying when they meet the actors who actually play these parts. It is a common experience to feel dissatisfied (at least initially) with the stage or film version of a book because the characters do not correspond in appearance to our own view of them. Some people indeed claim to find their conception of a character in a book totally altered by the different appearance (different from the images they formed) of the actor in a play—for example in the BBC version of *The Forsyte Saga*, sympathies are said to have shifted from one character to another because of the difference between the former image of the character and the appearance of the actor or actress. It is in fact an amusing exercise to ask people to describe someone whose voice they have heard on the radio or a tape-recorder; some qualities of personality may actually be agreed upon in various descriptions; but the important point is that one discovers how some people—some much more than others—do build up distinct visual images of someone whose voice only has been heard.

These points are reinforced by an early investigation (Pear, Kerr, 1931) of people's reactions to radio plays. Here recordings of two types of play were presented to groups of university and WEA students; they listened in a darkened room and then answered a questionnaire about their imagery during the time of listening. (Again it is noteworthy that those who had no psychological training gave their own imagery higher ratings for vividness than did those with psychological training. Though this again is a reminder of the difficulty of knowing how much to rely on people's accounts of their own imagery—unless we assume that psychological training lessens the ability to have images, or that those who are interested in psychology are those with low ability in imaging.) The two plays in this study had been deliberately chosen as representing different types of experience; one was domestic, *Making the Christmas Pudding*, the other dramatic, *The Safe* (in which a woman office worker was shut in a safe by her married lover and left to suffocate). It seemed here that vivid visual imagery was experienced both

6

by people who liked the plays and by people who disliked them. Of those reporting visual imagery of a vivid kind thirty-two liked the first play while seventeen disliked it; eighteen with imagery liked, and seven disliked the second. But again it was reported that visualising the characters in the plays was not always complete—at some points their faces might not be seen; when tension increased, then it was more likely that their faces would be visualised. There was also a kind of focusing on limbs when action was taking place— which suggests precognition of the television technique of focusing on the significant parts of scenes. There was also a difference in the time at which visualising took place; more was done when it came to writing reports about the first play than had actually happened while the play was being performed, but it was while the groups were actually listening to the second play that images occurred. This investigation underlines the fact that imagery may not necessarily increase enjoyment, and that incomplete images are as effective as complete—indeed possibly more so, at some times: and that the importance of imagery depends on the type of stimulus situation.

Conclusions

From this review of images, various general conclusions have emerged. It is evident that images are widely experienced and that they can be valuable when we are appreciating poems, fiction, music, etc. It is also repeatedly evident that there are great individual differences in the capacity to have images, and that images themselves are by no means simple repetitions of earlier sense impressions —they can be of a variety of sense impressions, they can combine various sensory modes, they can also be more or less complete and distinct. Thus it has become evident that we would not necessarily gain by making our images more precise and distinct—indeed, the effort to do this might well be a considerable handicap in the enjoyment of poetry and similar experiences. Images can be too vivid and dominating for enjoyment or even for understanding of a total experience; they can be irrelevant even when enjoyable; and an attempt to have the 'right' images could be futile and disastrous.

So far as intellectual operations are concerned, it is clear that for some people imagery is part of the process of solving problems of various kinds, but not an essential part, since other people claim to solve the same problems and exercise the same skills without imagery. The amount of help given by images in the practice of athletic skills is unclear; again, there seem to be notable individual differences. In memory also images play varying roles; different individuals have preferences for learning by different sense modes, but experiments have shown that clear images do not guarantee the reliability and accuracy of the memory.

All this is not unexpected. In a way the image is a return to our first impression of objects or situations, it reassures us or refreshes our knowledge of their qualities (within the limits of accuracy just mentioned; unless we enjoy eidetic imagery). But when we learn words, we develop a system of greater speed of reference; we use symbols which can be manipulated more easily than the objects or their images. In reading words we develop such speed and skill that we do not pause on the individual word nor consider all the qualities of the object which it represents; it may be that we are little concerned with the object itself—it may be only a tool, or we may be concerned with only one of its qualities. If we accompany the process of using words by images of the objects or situations to which the words refer and if we are at pains to make these images clear and distinct, the speed of the process is probably greatly reduced; we also find ourselves supplied with information which is not needed in the operation we are carrying out. It is not always or even often necessary to renew completely all our knowledge of the subjects of our thoughts even though in some circumstances this may be useful.

But although we do not use this return to the original perception very frequently we should be able to do so when we wish to. We should be able at least to recall the full meaning of a word; and images may be part of this recall, even if they are not always essential to it. So we realise the importance of letting children have sense impressions of objects or situations in the first place, in order that words used concerning these objects and situations really do have meaning for them; it is highly undesirable that children should use words without being able to recall the qualities or situations to which they refer, without being able (if the word is of the right kind) to incorporate it, to give it perceptible form, to know what sensory impressions it produces—or rather, what are the sensory impressions produced by the thing to which it refers. One can (and should) sympathise with the irritation which children and adults show when they find themselves in a situation where they cannot refer back to this kind of foundation; when they are brought to a halt and, exploring their understanding of the words being used, discover that they cannot call up any relevant imagery or memory of real experience. (Thus a child queried: 'How would I go to foreign countries?' 'You would get a passport?' 'How?' 'At the passport office!' 'But'—furiously, though near tears—'what *is* a passport? Where is a passport office—I haven't seen one, I couldn't find it!') Unfortunately children become accustomed too soon to concealing this uneasiness, forgetting about it, or inventing some kind of substitute explanation; it would be so much better for them if they persisted in demanding further knowledge, real knowledge. ('Show me a passport!' in fact.) But although this foundation of original sense-perception should be given where possible, and will often provide relevant images, it does not follow that children must always call up a clear image of what is under discussion.

Thus, though we should have the possibility of recall of this kind, and although images can be very convenient when we have temporarily become uncertain of the meaning of a word or find it hard to recall a piece of information, there seems to be no need to rely constantly on the illustration they provide. Making a habit of imaging every situation we think of or talk about would be as tedious and pointless as being unable to read without speaking every word aloud.

Imagery does remain a fascinating and pleasing kind of occasional illustration, and one which some people may use more effectively than others. But as there does not appear to be any clear method of eliminating individual differences in this respect (simply urging people to concentrate does not seem a method to recommend) we have to accept that the differences exist. Educationally the important thing is to make sure that children have both the original sense impressions and the words by which to refer to experience and to understand other people's communication of experience. Whether we should make children conscious of having images is a doubtful matter. Certainly this is part of the general knowledge of psychology that is spreading more and more widely in society today; and it would be worth making clear at least that images can deceive us about the accuracy of our memory. There is also the tremendous appeal of discovering how one differs from other people—as Bartlett pointed out, discussions of imagery so often turn into autobiographical confessions; so knowledge about imagery can be a welcome part of general culture (and a good reinforcement of the principle that people do differ). But images themselves seem to be mainly secondary in importance; one of the things that happen as we think; not in themselves a vital kind of activity.

Chapter 4

Everyday imagining

Since the ability to form images is less essential than is often assumed we now turn to the wider activity of imagining. It is generally believed that imagination is important, that it can be used and abused, that some people have more of it than others. But in practice how do people use imagination? What makes them begin to use it? In what circumstances do they imagine? We can find some answers to these questions if we look at examples of imagining as it develops in childhood.

Theories of infant fantasies

But if we are to know where to begin we must be clear about the kind of activity we are thinking of as imagining. In imagining, as we have defined it earlier, we construct from material provided by past experience new objects or situations which we know are not real, and this construction includes emotional responses or leads to them: in 'externally-directed' imagining we respond emotionally to other people's constructions of what we know to be unreal situations. But in references to children's thinking we often find mentions of fantasy and of unconscious fantasy. The two words—fantasy and imagination—can sometimes be used as equivalents; but when 'fantasy' is used, it often carries the suggestion of an activity that is uncontrolled or that cannot be directed by the individual; fantasy may not even be consciously noticed by the individual and the individual may become involved in it to the exclusion of reality. In 'imagination'—as the word is being used here—the process is conscious and largely under conscious control; the individual is aware that the imagined situation is not real. In practice this difference may mean very little—indeed on many occasions there is little or no difference between fantasy and imagination; but the word 'imagination' is to be preferred here because of the association the word 'fantasy' often has with speculations

77

about unconscious or subconscious processes: (the form 'phantasy' may indicate this psycho-analytic association).

It would take rather long to discuss the merits and demerits of the psycho-analytic interpretation of children's behaviour; but it must be noted that some statements about fantasy in the earliest stages of childhood do seem unreasonable if we are using words in the normal way. Take the suggestion that in the earliest stages of existence the child's thinking is entirely fantasy; and that, e.g., at this stage the child has fantasies of attacking and killing or wounding the mother (because in some way she frustrates the child's wishes); so the child develops a guilt complex, since it cannot distinguish between what has been done in reality and what has been done in fantasy. This point of view is exemplified in such statements as: 'This confusion so common in childhood, between what really happens, what is actually done, and what is simply wished or feared, emanates from early infantile phantasies. Angry feelings do seem to have the power to hurt, to do real physical injury, and loving feelings to comfort and do good ... Very early in his life a child feels grief at the damage he feels he has done, at his destruction of the bad, hated mother whom more and more he recognises to be the same person as the good, loved mother. Although he may be shown repeatedly that in reality he has not harmed her and that she does come back, whole and loving, to feed and care for him, this is not always enough to convince him, for phantasy can be stronger than reality. Thus he suffers anxiety at the harm he may do, and grief and depression over the harm he feels he has done' (Davidson, Fay, 1952). On this theory, imagination—or fantasy—would serve as a serious handicap from the very beginning of life, since it would produce rather unnecessary guilt feelings.

But not everyone can accept this kind of statement. Obviously the child at the very early stage cannot know what real physical injury (in the normal sense of the words) is, nor what destruction is. (It does not really improve the argument to suggest that eating is a symbolic destruction; it may be symbolic of something—it can symbolise other relationships—but it is not a way in which the child learns to know the nature of destruction as we normally know it.) The child cannot have any indication at all that harm has been done by rage, apart from the fact that the effort of screaming with fury can hurt the child or leave it feeling exhausted; but this scarcely seems harm attached to the mother. The child has no experience of damage, so cannot know it and what its consequences are. (If one is going to read adult meanings into the child's reactions one might as well argue that the slightly older child who exclaims: 'I hate you! I wish you were dead!' really does want the adult in question to drop dead, literally. In such cases undoubtedly the child wants the adult out of the way, non-existent, totally frustrated; this is expressed by a word which the child knows to have immense significance; but since the child at this stage often does not know what death is (having had no experience of it) the child would be considerably astonished and distressed if its words had the real effect. Adult shock at such statements comes from too literal interpretation, from reading adult meanings into the words; though of course we should be in no doubt about the intensity of the child's hostility at that moment.)

As for the death-dealing infant, it does seem an odd kind of reasoning (if we can call it that) which is attributed to the baby who apparently makes a causal connection between the expression of its rage and consequent harm to the mother, but is apparently incapable of perceiving the sequence of outburst of rage and reappearance of good, loving mother. One can accept that the baby does not perceive causal sequences at all; but to affirm that the baby forms one sequence—rage-harm-guilt—while remaining incapable of noting the rage-continuing-attention-and-love sequence is surely rather extreme. If one does credit the infant with ability to note sequences and to learn by experience at this stage, one might rather expect it to become conditioned to believe that expressions of rage are the way to get wishes fulfilled; screaming with fury is followed at greater or lesser intervals by the appearance of the desired food or feeling of comfort; people keep coming, unaltered, in response to the outburst. If this is so, the temper tantrums often noted at the age of two to four can be regarded as a deconditioning process by which the child learns that the expression of rage does not always achieve the desired result. (Some adults, of course, do not seem to have gone through this deconditioning process.) It is at a rather later stage, when the young child has really experienced undesirable consequences—such as the loss of social approval—that imagined or fantasied assaults are more likely to lead to the development of guilt or anxiety (not at having killed but at having offended the mother or other adult). Of course if we attribute to the child various racial memories, or traces in the universal subconscious, then these raw materials will be available for imagining harm, and all kinds of fantasy sequences could go forward without waiting for the child's own real experience. But assumptions about the availability of such racial memories are not being made in this discussion.

Children and the real world

We do not include an alleged fantasy activity in the earliest stages of childhood as the beginning of imagining. Can we accept the other view, dealing with a slightly later stage in development, that the child's early thinking is all imaginative, and that the child cannot distinguish between what is real and what is imagined? Certainly the child cannot tell, lacking experience, whether all imagined situations can really happen; the child cannot foresee how various situations are likely to develop and may therefore make 'plans' for them and talk about future activities in a totally unrealistic way. But this is not an indication of living in an imaginary world, in the sense of ignoring reality or preferring an unreal world to it; it is simply an indication of inefficiency in dealing with circumstances about which the child has not yet enough information. (Similar behaviour can be observed in adults when they have to plan for situations for which their previous experience has given little or no relevant data; their proposals are 'airy-fairy', unworkable.) It is not, however, either for the adult or the child, a deliberate choice or construction of an unreal environment—they are trying to interpret the real one.

There are other occasions on which the child is said to be imaginative simply because of unsatisfactory communication with adults. The child uses a word it doesn't know properly: the word is therefore used in an unusual way which happens to be refreshing, or, apparently, poetic. It is out of the ordinary because the child has not yet acquired ordinary ways of saying things. So the adult gives credit for imagination and originality where the child was simply trying to express a perceived factual resemblance; admittedly the perception may be refreshing to the adult, since the child is looking at the world freshly, without the acquired frames of reference which can make the adult notice things less clearly. At other times the child makes a statement which is challenged; unwilling to lose face by admitting that the word has been used wrongly or that something has been misunderstood, the child sticks to the statement—and the adult thinks that the child does not distinguish between the real and the imagined. (This kind of situation is most likely to develop when the adult is rather stupid, slow-thinking and literal-minded.) And of course there are the situations when the child is simply making the exhilarating discovery that one can play with words—that one can say things, detaching words from the real objects they represent—'I saw an elephant in the garden this morning'—and people pay attention and make a fuss.

Admittedly there may be some situations in which the distinction is not so clear—where the child's memory of a dream is confused with real happenings or where memory of real events and dream memory are hard to distinguish. But these confusions do not occur only in childhood, even if the adult is generally better at deciding what really happened, having developed a technique for doing this kind of thing.

On some occasions children may be really uncertain about the difference between imagined and real events; they really expect supernatural happenings, they expect to see (or claim that they have seen) fairies or ghosts or other beings of that kind—possibly because they believe other people have seen them, and with a little bending of real perception, what the child saw might have been a fairy—or ghost; distortions of memory help the process along until the child really does seem to be talking without reference to the real world. Or, having received some religious teaching, children expect miracles (of the most naïve kind) to happen—to be able to walk on water, or to have objects transformed into something else. These show the greater credulity of children, their too ready acceptance that what adult authority has assured them can happen, does happen—an acceptance against which experience of adult fallibility has not yet provided a defence. But this is still not an indication that the child's thinking is of a different kind from the adult's, or that the child is making unreal constructions for the fun of it; the child is living in the same world, even if with less skill in using past experience for interpretations of events. (And adults do see flying saucers.)

If then we are to consider conscious imaginative activity as it normally shows itself during the child's development, it is not helpful to begin by assuming that the child thinks differently from adults in the sense of having a rich and strange imaginary existence. The child reasons, admittedly, on different levels from adults—at least from adults who are reasoning in a mature way; but it is unlikely that the child can imagine in a different way from adults—it has to proceed in the same way by building on past experiences. In the child's thinking there may also be fewer claims on attention by the need to work or take practical action.

Imagination in play activity

Avoiding these misinterpretations of children's behaviour, what early displays of imaginative activity can we discover? We have to wait until the child is talking before we can be sure that imagining is going on. Various actions of non-speaking children may seem to show imagining, but it is too easy to project into them our own behaviour and reactions; when, however, the child is able to use language we can know whether the child is reacting to the situation as it actually is, or using its past experience to construct something different. Possibly this makes us overvalue the verbal element in imagining; but other evidence seems to show that it is in fact of major importance, not only in making the child's imagining possible but also in developing the general ability to think. Thus we see the earliest evidence of imagining when the child plays with toys or other objects and pretends that things are not what they actually are. When, for example, the child offers or 'eats' a meal whose ingredients are sand and pebbles, contained in pails, spades or other handy things, or when a sea-shell becomes 'a Jaguar car' and another shell becomes 'a sports car' and they engage in fast and furious driving along a carpet; or when toy cars go under bridges made of building blocks and into garages constructed from cardboard boxes; then imagining can be said with some confidence to be going on. This play seems commonplace but it is really very clever. The child has not only managed to learn the words for these various things, but can disregard present sense impressions (which indicate what the thing really is) and attach to the objects words related to sense impressions of a very different kind in the past; the child has therefore achieved quite a remarkable mastery of words—it can play with them, as well as with objects; it has discovered that they are detachable from the objects to which (with some effort and skill) they have only recently become attached. And in this play the child shows that it notices qualities which different objects have in common, and can separate this feature from all the others—it singles out the arch of the bridge and the blocks; it recognises the differences of size and reproduces them— roughly—in other objects; it accepts the idea of transfer from one container to another smaller one and reproduces this in the imitation of pouring out tea or coffee.

Not that all children do this kind of thing: Gesell and Ilg (1943) commented on the difference between realist and imaginative types of children, saying of the latter: 'If they ask for materials that are not available they are generally satisfied when handed imaginary substitutes. The realist, on the other hand, is annoyed by any such play, has to have the real object, and calls each toy by its correct name.' Why there should be this difference in children is not clear; it may be a matter of temperament or it may result from environment. Since there seems to be some kind of connection between the development of language skills and this kind of play, social class differences may be influential. Smilansky (1965), studying an American group, suggested that children from lower social class background had to be taught how to engage in imaginative play. This connection between parents' relationships with children was further investigated (Smilansky, 1968) with nursery school groups in Israel, where a study was made of children who came from ethnic groups where parents did not play with the children. Showing the children how to play (e.g. by acting various situations with them) did seem to lead to more such activity; but not all the group developed this kind of play even when stimulated by adults: on the whole, the girls in the groups studied seem to have developed socio-dramatic play rather more than the boys. Thus although the influence of parents and teachers may encourage this kind of behaviour it is not certain that adult influence can produce it in all children.

We can see how likely it is that in some social environments adult interest will reinforce imaginative play. Imaginative chatter requires an audience, or is helped by it—especially when the imagined situation requires subordinate characters, to receive the teacups or admire the collapse of the bridge that the car has crashed into. So adults or other children are called in. For the child who enjoys adult attention—as almost all do—there is the additional motivation of keeping the adult talking. At this stage the child's ability to keep a conversation going is limited, if untiring; so a play sequence of an imaginative kind may be valued for its conversational holding power. There are of course also occasions on which the child's imagination is powerful enough also to provide an imagined audience, and the child plays happily alone in this way.

From the adult point of view a practical advantage of such play is that it provides a way of guiding or controlling the child more easily. Playing with objects in the bath, making up stories about them, can make the child accept without protest either the annoyance of having to get into the bath or the annoyance of having to get out of it, or both. Much of the routine of getting the child to bed, of tidying away toys, even of meal-times, can be made easier if the child's attention is diverted to playing with submarines, parking lorries, attacking fortresses and so on. The annoying real actions are carried out before the child has quite noticed what is going on; and of course the possibility of further play with toys in bed may induce acceptance of the horrible fate of going to bed—as may the prospect of the bedtime story. So the adult who can do so has probably considerable inducement to foster this kind of imaginative play in the child. It can also of course be considered educative, since it improves the child's vocabulary, sentence structure and knowledge of everyday events—even correct behaviour in social situations (e.g. shopping) can be painlessly taught and imitated in this way.

Imaginary companions

This kind of imaginative activity can lead on easily to another widely observed activity—the creation of 'imaginary companions'. Quite a large number of children do create such companions from the age of two onwards. The companion can appear in a number of ways. Sometimes the companion has an actual physical presence as a battered and decrepit toy, possibly, or some object rejoicing in a peculiar-sounding name: but often the companion is visible only to the child. And for some time this companion has to be attended to, talked about, respected. 'Wattybottle' has to have a seat at table (if the adults will humour the child so far) or a biscuit has to be provided for him (and eaten probably by proxy); he has to come shopping; he doesn't like people not to talk to him. Until the sad day when Wattybottle for some reason falls into disgrace, is popped into the refrigerator or some other uncongenial place, and is heard of no more.

Companions can be of a really remarkable variety. Some companions are of the same sex and age as the child; others may be older and much wiser—sometimes wiser in a socially accepted way, sometimes in a way which is decidedly opposed to adult rules. Or the companion may be younger and excessively naughty; or simply a companionable sort of person—possibly protective, defending the child's rights on all occasions. The companion needn't be human; animals or unidentified objects serve the same purpose. And the life span of the companion is equally varied. Some make a very brief appearance on the scene (though they may be succeeded by another companion); some continue for months at a time. (Looking back at their childhood some adults have admitted that a companion lasted much longer than anyone suspected; the child simply stopped talking about the companion when in company.)

Varied also is the seriousness with which the child takes the companion. Some children insist that the companion is constantly present and become seriously upset if adults do not respect the companion's claims; others are prepared to regard the companion as a shared joke, and to forget about it from time to time. Some regard the companion as someone to talk to when they are alone, so that the companion makes very few appearances in company— may indeed never join the social circle—whereas other companions seem to appear only in that circle where they can make their presence felt—and cause maximum inconvenience.

We can see many possible uses of the companions. Some clearly serve as scapegoat; others are a kind of defence against adult domination—the companion is an adult who understands the child's point of view and supports the child's action. In other cases the companions offer company that is sympathetic and on the child's side. Or the companion is simply an audience. It can be seen how a child with religious training can take for a companion a patron saint, or develop as companion a figure who serves as conscience, critic, judge of the child's actions. A child who has the habit of living in the company of an imaginary companion should find transition to belief in supernatural witnesses and supernatural company not in the least difficult. The internal conversation with the companion, the sense of the companion's presence seem readily adaptable to religious forms; and the habit of an internal dialogue with this conscience-companion can easily become constant. Fénelon's recommendations on prayer (Barnard, 1966) illustrate this kind of link: 'tell her (the young girl to be educated) that prayer is like simple, familiar and tender fellowship with God—in fact, it is that fellowship . . . This is no longer a formal conversation; it is free and friendly intercourse.' Bettelheim (1969) offers a rather different interpretation: 'according to psychoanalytic theory . . . it is the felt (or feared) loss of important persons on whom one is wholly dependent that leads to the process of introjection' and he suggests that as children of the kibbutz do not go through such a process, they are later not able to put themselves imaginatively in the position of others—'these youngsters have not introjected persons with whom they hold inner conversations, talks that require them to recognize the introject's viewpoint and their own at the same time.' Yet it seems doubtful whether participants in imaginary conversations do enforce attention to another point of view: for some, at least, the imagined companion or conversation-sharer is very much a yes-man.

The reasons producing the companions are as varied as the companions. In some cases, reaction against authority provides the motive; in others, the motivation is social interest—this is probable in families where the creation of the companion is sympathetically received and where other people in the family are willing to co-operate in building up the personality and behaviour of the companion. In other cases, it is persuasively argued, the companion is the result of loneliness; the child who is deprived of the companionship of other children is driven to creating this substitute.

It is notable that some parents are very little aware—or not aware at all—of the child's imaginary companion; and clearly they cannot always know the full extent of the companion's life—how much the companion is present when the child is alone.

Various attempts have been made to find out more about the personalities of children who do create this kind of company for themselves. The results are surprising if one sets off with the commonly held belief that the child creating a companion is lonely or maladjusted in all cases. Ames and Learned (1946) did find in one enquiry about forty-five children who had imaginary companions or some such 'creation' that there were in fact twenty-one 'only' children in the group and most of the others came from small families; but they noted that many of the children did have opportunities for play with other children. Terman's (1926) study of gifted children suggested that imaginary companions might occur more often when the child had no real playmate, but may well depend on how satisfactory the real playmates are; Svendsen (1934) found that possibly if the gap between the child and the next member of the family is about five years, an imaginary companion may give more satisfactory companionship than the brother or sister. But in the enquiry by Hurlock and Burstein (1932) no connection between the size of family, the number of companions available, and the creation of imaginary companions was found. Admittedly, this last investigation depended on the reports given by students looking back on their own childhood; their memories could have misled them about the company that had been available in their past—though not about family size. The family situation was important in another way in the case histories studied by Friedmann (1932) for the conclusion was reached that companions are often created when the child's security is threatened by some event like the arrival of a new baby, or the first experience of death, or a move to new surroundings; and such companions naturally disappear when the child feels secure again.

There seems to be little if any convincing evidence of maladjustment in children who create companions: Wingfield (1949) who was, admittedly, testing people who were recalling childhood creations, found that Bernreuter test scores for those who had had imaginary companions showed less neuroticism, less introversion, less self-sufficiency, more dominance in face-to-face situations, more sociability and a greater degree of self-confidence than the scores of those who had not had them. Harriman (1937), similarly asking college students for introspective reports, did not find evidence of harm resulting from having had imaginary companions, or of maladjustment. (Such groups may of course be a bad sample; where creators of imaginary companions are maladjusted seriously they may simply fail to get to college and so fail to appear in such investigations; but at least it can be said that some creators of imaginary companions have made a successful adjustment.) Bender (1954) considering a differently selected group—children under observation in a hospital psychiatric ward—commented that the creation of imaginary companions 'is a positive and healthful mechanism called forth during a time of need but immediately given up when the need no longer exists'. Further: 'the presence of imaginary companions in the psychological phenomena of a child is a good prognostic sign of ego-strength.' Ames and Learned (*op. cit.*), dealing with a more normal group, thought that the child most likely to have imaginary companions is the 'highly intelligent, highly verbal type'.

How many children in fact go through this stage? The percentages reported for different groups show some variations; Ames and Learned found about 21 per cent in a group of 210. Terman's study had 136 cases reported in a group of 554. Wingfield (asking women college students for memories of childhood) found that 67 out of 229 (i.e. about 29 per cent) recalled such behaviour. A. and C. Jersild, F. Markey (1933), found 143 out of 400 (i.e. about 36 per cent). Hurlock and Burstein found in a group of 701 high school and college students, that 31 per cent of the women and 23 per cent of the men remembered such behaviour. In Svendsen's study of 119 children, aged 3–16 (in 46 families), 13·4 per cent were found to have or to have had imaginary companions; but the smaller proportion found here may be due to the fact that sustained creation over a period of time was required before the companion was counted. This study, however, suggested that having companions may run in certain families; some families had several—e.g. four companions for two children; in others, the phenomenon was unknown. (This, in view of the effect that the attitudes of the rest of the family can have, seems highly probable.) This study had the additional advantage of asking the children and their mothers separately about the existence of the companions; it was found that the mothers were not fully informed about them and under-estimated the number of companions then in existence; it also became clear that some of the older children were hesitant about admitting and discussing the fact that they had, or had had, 'companions'.

From some of these reports it seems possible that there is a sex difference. A rather greater proportion of girls than boys is reported as having companions: e.g. in Terman's group 85 girls and 51 boys were so reported. Svendsen found a 3 to 1 proportion in favour of girls; Hurlock and Burstein 31 to 23; Jersild and Markey found that girls gave more detail in descriptions of imaginary companions (82 to 61). The last investigation also found a tendency for the companion to be associated with high intelligence, which, it was thought, might be a more important factor than that of having few brothers or sisters to play with; average I.Q. for children with companions was 115·7; for those without them, 108·3.

Imaginary personality

Associated with the creation of companions is another more unusual kind; it is the attempt by the child to create another personality and to be that personality. In such a case the child may ask to be called by another name and to be treated in a way which would be suitable to this other person; for example, a girl may want to be—for part of the time—a domestic help, having another name and relationship to the family; and she may try—temporarily again—to behave in what seems to be the appropriate way, possibly trying to divide the day between being the 'help' and being her normal self. Other children may adopt other types of role; as animal, adult, baby, as a character read about in a book. The duration of this play also varies; naturally it is even more dependent on the co-operation of adults than the imaginary companion creation; where the adopted extra personality is not one that the adults want to live with, the creation is likely to be short-lived; it is possible too that adults who can tolerate talking about a non-existent companion are less willing to encourage the child to behave in an uncharacteristic way, to practise what seems an inappropriate role. Ames and Learned suggested that children who practise this kind of creation are 'apt to have high social abilities and to get on well with other children' but the group they studied was very small. In this kind of creation at least two kinds of motive might affect the child; in some cases, an attempt to escape from a personality that is not much liked; in other cases, a lively curiosity, an attempt to find out what it is like to be someone else, to live more than one life.

Continued stories and pre-sleep imagining

The transition from these kinds of creative imagining to another widespread form also seems easy and gradual; it is the move to the 'continued story' which many children enjoy—the story which goes on, in their minds, with themselves as central character, hero or heroine, for quite considerable periods of time, being taken up when there is a suitable opportunity, repeated and modified as more material comes to hand, or as feeling changes. The child can have more than one such story, of course; and stories can go on for any desirable length of time. This kind of development can occur after the time of the transition which Vygotski (1962) has noted as significant in the development of thinking—the transition to internalised speech. For some children the development may be simply the process by which the imaginary companion is no longer addressed aloud, in the presence of the parents, but continues to carry on long conversations in the child's mind. Thus, for example, the experience of one student as reported by Harriman (1937) was that: 'Imaginary companions began when he was four and went with him through high school. Eager to commence school and to share in the experiences related by two older brothers, he invented a teacher who conducted school for him at home. When he began attendance at school he was accompanied by an imaginary friend named Bill who remained with him for four years. Bill never made a mistake in class and took highest honours in school. In the 5th grade Bill gave way to Joe, also imaginary. Joe was a stellar athlete who achieved great fame for his exploits. A year later Joe was joined by Helen, who was attractive personally, brilliant in class and outstanding in extra-curricular activities. Not until this young man had reached 18 years of age did he give up this imaginative play.' Other companions and their stories seem to have survived even longer; and the story need not necessarily be about a companion; the child can be and often is the hero or heroine, possibly with constant attendant admirers, possibly alone.

This is obviously a kind of day-dreaming, but it differs from the ordinary day-dream in some ways; it is more consciously controlled and it has much greater continuity—the main theme can, as we have seen, last for years. For many if not for all whose minds work in this way, the time before falling asleep at night is especially favourable for the enjoyment of the continued story or stories—though naturally the story can also continue at convenient times during the day. Robert Louis Stevenson (1892) has given a well-known account of this kind of use of imagination: 'This honest fellow had long been in the custom of setting himself to sleep with tales, and so had his father before him; but these were irresponsible inventions, told for the teller's pleasure, with no eye to the crass public or the thwart reviewer; tales where a thread might be dropped, or one adventure quitted for another, on fancy's least suggestion.' In Stevenson's case these pre-sleep imaginings apparently formed the basis of stories published later, with suitable editing and improvement.

An early investigation (Smith, 1904) showed this kind of imagining to be common; in a group of 980 pupils aged 7–16 and 469 students aged 17–25, and a group of 23 adults, it was found that: 'some children regularly get themselves to sleep by making up stories, the same one sometimes being continued for several nights... Closely akin to the story form of the day-dream is the imaginary conversation which is sometimes carried on with actual friends and acquaintances, sometimes with strangers casually seen or with

7

characters in books or history, or in some cases with purely imaginary characters.'

Those who have enjoyed this kind of story find it hard to believe that other people have not engaged in the same activity: as one person quoted by McKellar (1965) put it: 'I used to shut my eyes and let my mind go free and into it would come what I used to call my "night stories" . . . and all kinds of imaginings in story form . . . I thought all children had the same night stories and was amazed one day when I found they hadn't.'

An autobiographical account of this process suggests what is perhaps an unusual degree of control of the situation. Sartre (1964) writes: 'Every evening I would wait impatiently for the end of the daily farce, I would hurry to bed, gabble my prayers, slip between the sheets; I was longing to get back to my reckless daring. I grew older in the dark, I became a lone adult, without father or mother, without home or habitation, almost without name. I was walking over a burning roof, carrying an unconscious woman in my arms: below me, the crowd was shouting: it was clear that the roof was about to collapse. At that moment I uttered the fateful words: "To be continued in the next instalment." "What are you saying?" asked my mother. I replied prudently: "I am leaving myself in suspense." And the fact is that I would fall asleep in the midst of the dangers, in delightful uncertainty. The next evening, true to plan, I would return to my roof, the flames, certain death. Suddenly I caught sight of a drain-pipe which I had not noticed the night before . . .' Still showing this admirable control of the activity he further describes how he would change his mind as to whether to allow his burden to regain consciousness, or plunge her back into unconsciousness again because her conscious help would detract from his heroic solo performance; or, having come to an unsatisfactory development—official thanks for his deed of heroism—he would again return to the really enjoyable part, and begin again at the beginning, hearing a girl crying for help.

This kind of activity, with varying degrees of control of the situation, and varying durations and repetitions, seems to be widespread, though again there is no conclusive evidence to show exactly what proportion of the population engages in it. It can shade over into less clearly imaginative activities, for example, into recalling pleasant memories—which similarly can be broken off at suitable points or repeated when they produce particularly happy feelings. Or there can be a kind of imagining of possible future events which may not be as dramatic as the stories described above (they may even be realistic), but which also give the same kind of satisfaction. Foulds (1950), studying a group of 75 normal boys of average age $9\frac{1}{2}$, and 59 mentally defective boys of average age $14\frac{1}{2}$ (mental age approximately $9\frac{1}{2}$), found that 31 per cent of the normals and 41 per cent of the others thought in bed about their 'fancies' while 23 per cent normals and 14 per cent of the others thought at that time about 'tomorrow'. Learoyd's early enquiry (1895) into the continued story habit among 362 adults and 114 children (average age 12) found that about 33 per cent of the adults and 60 per cent of the children definitely had this habit. Another enquiry (Sutherland, 1962) among 234 ten-year-old children showed approximately half of the group claiming that they did imagine in this way—making up stories, or re-living stories—before falling asleep. It is true that questionnaire answers (as used here) are not always a reliable source of evidence, but the proportion does seem to accord in more than one investigation. Variations of technique also appeared in this last group; some children claimed that they had continuous stories, repeated or continued from one night to another, while some claimed to make up new stories each night.

Such pre-sleep or continued stories differ from the haphazard daydream in this conscious decision to plunge into the imaginary world; there is also a clearer recognition of separation between this activity and the other activities of life because it occurs in clearly defined circumstances, and in circumstances which make it particularly easy to shut out interruptions and to disregard stimuli coming from the real environment. In bed, with closed eyes, there is less conflict of claims on attention, the imaginary construction can be enjoyed more completely; and from the point of view of parents, this willingness to go to sleep (apparently) is often a virtue for which children receive a bonus of approval.

Again, as for imaginary companions, it seems possible that there may be a sex difference in the frequency of this behaviour. Learoyd's study found that 100 women claimed to have such stories, while 114 were doubtful or definitely did not have them; whereas only 20 men claimed to have such stories, 128 being doubtful or negative in their replies. The same trend appeared in the children's reactions: 41 girls, 29 boys claimed to have a continued story, while 21 girls, 23 boys did not have one or were doubtful. Possibly, of course, the conventions of the time (1895) discouraged admissions of this kind on the part even of young men. The more recent enquiry (Sutherland, 1962) among ten-year-old children did not show a sex difference in pre-sleep constructions; 59 of 123 girls, 55 of 111 boys claimed to practise pre-sleep imagining. Yet an investigation by Pitcher and Prelinger (1963) into the 'stories' related by 137 children of nursery school and kindergarten age showed that 'the girls tend to present people more vividly and realistically and to identify themselves with the personality and experiences of others'. This might indicate a greater readiness of girls to imagine stories for their own satisfaction rather than that of investigators. (It may be noted also that Galton (1883) found that: 'the power of visualising is higher in the female sex than in the male'—though he was studying imagery rather than imagining.)

Characteristics of 'continued stories'

It is impossible to be sure what age limit there is to this kind of activity—indeed it seems probable that there is no upper age limit and that many people continue in such imagining in some form or other well into adult life, or throughout their whole life. Anthony Trollope (1883) refers to continuous story-construction (not only as pre-sleep activity) in late adolescence and early adulthood, though in his case, as in Stevenson's, it became the foundation of novel-writing: 'I will mention here another habit that had grown upon me from still earlier years which I myself often regarded with dismay when I thought of the hours devoted to it, but which, I suppose, must have tended to make me what I have been. As a boy, even as a child, I was thrown much upon myself . . . I was therefore alone, and had to form my plays within myself. Play of some kind was necessary to me then, as it has always been. Study was not my bent, and I could not please myself by being all idle. Thus it came to pass that I was always going about with some castle in the air firmly built in my mind. Nor were these efforts in architecture spasmodic, or subject to constant change from day to day. For weeks, for months, if I remember rightly, from year to year, I would carry on the same tale, binding myself down to certain laws, to certain proportions and proprieties and unities. Nothing impossible was ever introduced—not even anything which, from outward circumstances, would seem to be violently improbable. I was of course my own hero. Such is a necessity of castle-building. But I never became a king, or a duke—much less when my height and personal appearance were fixed could I be an Antinous, or six feet high. I never was a learned man, nor even a philosopher. But I was a very clever person, and beautiful young women used to be fond of me. And I strove to be kind of heart, and open of hand, and noble in thought, despising mean things; and altogether I was a very much better fellow than I have ever succeeded in being since. This had been the occupation of my life for six or seven years before I went to the Post Office [at age nineteen]: and was by no means abandoned when I commenced my work. There can, I imagine, hardly be a more dangerous mental practice; but I have often doubted whether, had it not been my practice, I should ever have written a novel.'

The similarities in some of Rousseau's reports and Trollope's are interesting, though in his strict adherence to probabilities Trollope seems to have been more scrupulous than many other imaginers—though Sir John Adams (1914) made the point that the true imaginer does stick to some rules; events must normally be possible. But some variations in personal qualities are usually thought permissible. Interesting too is Trollope's comment on the dangers of this practice, and apparent feeling of guilt about it; though he does concede its value in his own case as a foundation for later publications.

Trollope's autobiography thus suggests continuing systematic imagining in adult life. The example of the Brontë family similarly indicates that imaginative creations (which in their case were originally a joint effort, all four children collaborating in making up stories about their country, Angria) can continue into adult years (Du Maurier, 1960). And another fascinating comment similarly supports the view that imagining of this kind continues well into adulthood, for some people at least—others may of course abandon it in adolescence or early adulthood.

This further comment is in a work by Florence Nightingale, a work privately printed, not published in her life-time, entitled *Cassandra*: it was written in 1852, revised and finally printed in 1859 after her return from the Crimea (Strachey, 1928). It is worth looking at fully, since it contains so many useful indications about this use of imagination, though the writer's main purpose was to point out the appalling restrictions placed on the activity of young women of her time: 'If the young girls of the "higher classes" who never commit a false step, whose justly earned reputations were never sullied even by the stain which the fruit of mere "knowledge of good and evil" leaves behind, were to speak and say what are their thoughts employed upon, their *thoughts*, which alone are free, what would they say? That, with the phantom companion of their fancy, they talk (not love, they are too innocent, too pure, too full of genius and imagination for that, but) they talk, in fancy, of that which interests them most; they seek a companion for their every thought; the companion they find not in reality they seek in fancy, or if not that, if not absorbed in endless conversations, they see themselves engaged with him in stirring events, circumstances which call out the interest wanting to them. Yes, fathers, mothers, you who see your daughter proudly rejecting all semblance of flirtation, primly engaged in the duties of the breakfast table, you little think how her fancy compensates itself by endless interviews and sympathies (sympathies either for ideas or events) with the fancy's companion of the hour.

'And you say, "She is not susceptible. Women have no passion." Mothers, who cardel yourselves in visions about the domestic hearth, how many of your sons and daughters are *there*, do you think, while sitting round under your complacent eye? Were you there yourself during your own (now forgotten) girlhood? What are the thoughts of these young girls while one is singing Schubert, another is reading the *Review* and a third is busy embroidering? Is not one fancying herself the nurse of some new friend in sickness; another engaging in romantic dangers with him, such as call on the character and afford more food for sympathy than the monotonous events of domestic society; another undergoing unheard-of trials under the observation of someone whom she has chosen as the companion of her dream; another having a loving and loved companion in the life she is living, which many do not want to change? And is not this all most natural, inevitable? Are they, who are too much ashamed of it to confess it even to themselves, to be blamed for that which cannot be otherwise, the causes of which stare one in the face, if one's eyes were not closed? Many struggle against this as a "snare". No Trappist ascetic watches or fasts more in the body than these do in the soul. They understand the discipline of the Thebaïd—the lifelong agonies to which those strong moral Mohicans subjected themselves. How cordially they would do the same in order to escape the worse torture of wandering "vain imaginations". We fast mentally, scourge ourselves morally, use the intellectual hair-shirt in order to subdue that perpetual day-dreaming which is so danger-ous ... Never with the slightest success ... It is the want of interest in our life which produces it; by filling up that want of interest in our life we can alone remedy it.'

This of course does not prove that such continuous story-making or systematic day-dreaming was in universal or even widespread use in the time of Florence Nightingale or at our own time. Possibly she had some objective proofs that in fact large numbers of her girl friends or women friends did think in this way; it is also possible that she was mainly projecting her own reactions on others. But it is valuable to note the reason which she attributes to this activity (the want of worth-while occupation in reality) *and* the strong disapproval with which she views this imagining.

Attitudes towards systematic imagining

One finds possibly something of the same disapproval for the wilder flights of such constructions in Charlotte Brontë's (1856) stated determination to deal not with romantic situations and characters but to try to bring to the reader knowledge of the plain, ordinary human being; she seems at times to be justifying a continuation of the day-dreaming activity which she, like others of the time, thought morally deplorable—it becomes permissible if it is realistic and morally right. But in more modern forms, the activity seems to be regarded more neutrally—though possibly its description for comic effect shows still some uneasiness about it. *The Secret Life of Walter Mitty*, with its hero 'living' with unusual facility a variety of stereotyped, fiction-fed heroic roles, is a useful example; it produces amusement (a kind of punishment for the imaginer?) but at the same time clearly relies on ready understanding of his behaviour—i.e. assumes that this kind of thinking is not unknown to the majority of readers or viewers. This assumption is noteworthy, especially if we consider Florence Nightingale's theory that it is those who are kept from worth-while real activity who enjoy such imaginary existences; it may be the case that conditions of life and work in relatively affluent societies offer uninteresting and un-demanding occupations to many people (not only to women); if so, imagining would seem at least to be a less damaging solution than refuge in alcohol or drugs. (The less affluent society is excluded since hard physical labour, anxiety and attention centred on means of survival seem unlikely to provide conditions in which imagining will go on.) But in the affluent society not everyone is as able as Florence Nightingale to escape from a cramping environment to a kind of work which demands all possible powers of attention: hence perhaps widespread use of 'continued stories'.

The opinion that a restrictive environment favours imaginative activity is given by yet another autobiography, that of Viscountess Rhondda (1933): 'There are disadvantages about being an only child. But there are also advantages . . . One gets time to think. Too much time, perhaps. For hours together I used to sit up in the branches of the great beech trees . . . and tell myself stories. That is not good for any child. At best it teaches it to withdraw into a world of unreality; at worst it can become an overpowering disease or drug-taking which makes all real contact with the visible world illusory. At night also I told stories to myself, but then my mother . . . used to put her hand on my forehead, and if it was hot she said: "You've been telling yourself stories" and invariably I had. And then she would make me promise to stop and go to sleep . . . In the early days the stories were always about huge families of children . . . By the time I was fifteen or sixteen—and the habit was too strongly formed to be broken by going to school—they usually concerned strong emotional conflicts between married couples . . . Sometimes I myself was the heroine, in which case—at that stage—the love interest vanished and was replaced by a tale in which I, dressed in a strikingly beautiful frock—usually white—having come out first in the Cambridge Tripos, rescued large portions of my family from a burning house . . . Telling myself stories went on all through my 'teens and twenties. Sometimes I would go for weeks or even months at a time without telling myself one, and then a new and enthralling story would start and for days I would go about scarcely conscious of the world around me, refusing to speak more than I could help, longing all the while to get back to my tale, and at night I would lie awake till three and even four in the morning, whilst the tale grew more and more passionate and emotional and impossible as the hours wore on. I broke myself of the habit, with a big effort, in my middle thirties.' In a later comment she adds: 'Another way of using up surplus energy. For the rest there was amazingly little to do . . . The dreaming time itself which in a normally busy person would have been squeezed into a precious five minutes or so here and there, stretched and stretched itself until at times it came to occupy half my days.'

Possibly a more gradual transition from imagining to realistic thinking was shown in the case of Herbert Spencer (1904), who as a child was also a reading addict (he concealed his addiction to reading in bed at night by the simple expedient of leaping out of bed and putting his lighted candle in a cupboard when his mother came up to see if he was sleeping): in his childhood he could become so engrossed in his 'castle-building' that he could set off to do an errand in town, forget to stop when he reached his destination and so walk right through the town to the other side; remembering his errand then, he would turn back into town, but again become so enthralled by his imaginary constructions that he would walk right back home with his errand still unaccomplished. In later life, he claimed, this kind of thinking was directed rather to the working out of theories of a scientific kind. (Admittedly T. H. Huxley's comment, when Spencer told him he had written a tragedy—that Spencer's tragedy must be the killing of a beautiful theory by a nasty ugly little fact—suggests that the transition to realistic thinking may have been incomplete.)

Another shading over of the distinction may be seen in Virginia Woolf's novel *Orlando* which seems to embody a typical series of 'continued stories'— living at different historical epochs, changing sex at will (or as suits the situations imagined), continuing as the undying hero or heroine; a kind of transformation of private imagining for communication in literature, like Stevenson's and others', but nearer to the original imagining.

There is clearly a strong tendency to make this kind of transition to published works, so that we remain uncertain how far this kind of imagining is characteristic of a large proportion of the population or restricted to future novelists, dramatists, writers of autobiographies, poets. Certainly the habit is widespread in adolescence. (And this imaginative construction is independent of work set by schools—very often it is unsuspected by the school.) It is not clear whether the increase in writing at adolescence is due to an 'enrichment of inner life' with puberty or to greater facility in the sheer mechanism of writing—or possibly to greater awareness of the possibilities of publication and desires for individual self-assertion in this way. (Vygotski (1930) suggested that younger children express imagination through drawing or acting rather than by writing; and these products seem even less likely than adolescent fiction to reach a wide audience and so to show the frequency of the activity.) Writing, however, means a change from the freedom of purely internal imagining; the constraint of sentence structure, choice of words, limit to number of words that can be written in a given time—all these, as well as the need to tidy up the story to make it socially acceptable, are likely to change the quality of the experience and possibly mean that in fact only a minority choose to accept these limitations: the majority may continue in the less restricted individual way.

Sexual interests in imagining

But a further complication in adolescent expression of imagining is the development of sex interests and their inclusion in the imagined situations. Whether the sex interest of the adolescent includes physical love-making in imagining or not, whether the imagining is accompanied by masturbation or is a prelude to it, the sex element has probably led to some concealment of the habit of imagining in adolescence—at least among those who live in an environment where sex interests are socially disapproved. Where the imagining is in fact linked to physical masturbation any guilt feeling attached to this behaviour would very probably transfer to the imagining also. Hence possibly some of the moral disapproval which various writers have expressed for the habit of living in imaginary situations. It would however be a mistake to assume that the kind of systematic day-dreaming we have been discussing is replaced by masturbatory fantasies in adolescence or that it is identical with masturbatory fantasies. The accounts quoted, and other descriptions of a similar kind, show that the main emotion is very often not sexual, and that the habit can continue after adolescent or adult interests in sex have been otherwise satisfied. The ability to imagine can of course be used equally to construct sexually exciting situations. In this respect it is interesting to note that according to the *Kinsey Report* (1953) 2 per cent of women reported ability to achieve orgasm by fantasy alone without physical stimulation, but 'exceedingly few males are capable of reaching orgasm in this fashion while they are awake'. However, 36 per cent of females reported no fantasy during masturbation and 'for a fair number fantasies had not begun until some years after the masturbation'. There seems, according to the *Report*, to be a decided sex difference in the use of fantasy in masturbation—'Fantasies . . . often provide the stimulus which initiates the male's masturbation.' It was also found that for women fantasy was limited by the degree of real overt sex experience: possibly some cultural elements contribute to an apparent sex difference in this use of imagining.

Strong sexual elements in imagining, especially if they lead to physical excitement and physical masturbation, would possibly remove one of the main advantages attributed to pre-sleep imagining, that of enabling the individual to fall asleep easily; though if pursued to physical climax such imagining might ultimately produce the relaxation necessary for falling asleep. Sexual elements thus are likely to affect considerably the individual's assessment of the value of imagining at this stage of development; in some cases they may lead to guilt about the imagining process and a decision to desist from it: in other cases merely alter the type of situation created for enjoyment.

Evaluation of imagining

But the habit of imagining is by no means always regarded as being a cause for guilt or as being morally unsatisfactory. Certainly there is social criticism if day-dreaming causes lack of attention to work or to the demands of the present situation. Teachers protest strongly when children are obviously day-dreaming in class. Still, there are many adults, adolescents, children who calmly accept imagining as part of their normal activity, though some restrict it, consciously or otherwise, to the pre-sleep period. Opinions as to its value vary widely; thus when 234 ten-year-olds (Sutherland, 1962) were asked if they thought pre-sleep imagining a good or bad thing to do, the answers were:

	Girls	Boys
Yes	55	47
No	29	34

(Some children, mostly those who did not imagine, did not answer the question.) The reasons given for the answers also varied, but the most popular reason in its favour was that 'it helps you to sleep'. Thirty girls and eighteen boys said this. (And this question put to other groups has very frequently received the same response.) This sleep-inducing effect does seem probable if imagining (1) distracts attention from stimulation by real surroundings, and (2) induces a happy emotional state. Or, as two children said: 'It puts worry out of one's head' and 'It keeps you from thinking bad happenings.' Other advantages claimed are help in school composition-writing or in understanding books. In this context it is illuminating to note the report by Gollwitzer (1954) that in a prisoner-of-war camp the telling of a bed-time story (an activity which might seem simply regression to early childhood) was highly popular; any sort of material would do, so that the story-teller racked his memory for all sorts of material. In this case, distraction from the real circumstances would seem to have been the advantage of the activity—not wish-fulfilment, since many listeners fell asleep before the end of the story (though they asked for the ending the next day). Poetry had similar value in these circumstances.

Yet a disadvantage of imagining is also said to be that it keeps people from sleeping or leads to bad dreams—thirteen children who did imagine and twenty-four who did not imagine mentioned these possible drawbacks. One boy remarked: 'You will not have a clear head in the morning'—leaving it uncertain whether this would be due to lack of sleep or excessive excitement. But in this group there did not appear any great belief in moral fault in the process of imagining. It should admittedly be recognised that the question was introduced in a way which might give the activity prestige, since it was mentioned that a writer of books had said he made up stories before falling asleep. (But this did not, at least, introduce a serious influence towards attributing literary merit to the activity.) Smith's investigation (1904) found children aged between seven and nine had no opinion on the value of day-dreaming; a few thought it all right if the dreams were true, but bad if they were not. At a later age, day-dreaming was thought bad because it was associated with failure to attend to lessons; but a few children considered it wrong because they were cross when interrupted, or dreamed about 'bad things' (unspecified) or became dissatisfied with real things or wasted their time. (It is fascinating to see how views mentioned by Rousseau and others have been given this independent expression by children at a different time and place.)

Certainly day-dreaming is recognised in adult life as a fairly frequent activity: so much so, that it seems too vast a topic for specific research (though it has been the theme of various books and articles—e.g. Wagman (1968) found a negative relationship between day-dreaming and university achievement for female students, though not for males). Many adults are familiar with day-dreaming: some day-dreams are more systematic, longer-lived, more realistic than others: and unless the habit is carried to excess (making the individual unsociable or inefficient) it is generally well accepted.

In addition to this spontaneous private imagining there is of course a great deal of overt enjoyment of imagining with assistance from various media—magazines, books, films, radio, television. Though a minority of people opt for non-fiction books and broadcasts, imagining with the aid of other people's creations, and often with the help of cues from the sight or sound of actors, is nearly universal in our society and would seem to disprove any theory of a loss of interest in imagining once adult life is reached. Indeed, looking at the immense production of books of fiction one is astounded at the amount of imagining required to create and to respond to them. One is also astounded and possibly appalled to think of the evidence they give of the number of hours which must be spent in imaginary situations by so many people. Yet society generally does not seem to suffer from guilt feelings about this employment of its time. Granted, there are occasional comments that some groups might do better to take more exercise, get out of doors, be less passive. There have been in the past Puritan attacks on the theatre, and all fiction. But today on the whole our widespread enjoyment of stimulants of imagination is viewed with complacency.

Addiction to imagining

Yet it is suggested that in some cases individual development goes astray: imagining becomes an addiction. When there is concern about addiction, it tends to be more or less acute according to the mode of stimulation. Addiction to books (comics are different) is normally considered fairly harmless, even if annoying to people who want to claim the reader's attention for something else. At times people rather approve of it; they think it promises well for a child's future; the example of some of the greatest writers suggests that it can be predictive of later achievement; and it is often associated with school success. In practice, admittedly, parents of the less educated levels of society have been known to denounce addiction to books; but for practical or social reasons rather than out of concern for the child's emotional development. They may be annoyed that the child absorbed in reading fails to attend to what it is told to do, or that it seems to be enjoying a kind of leisure not available for other members of the family, or that it seems like an insult, that the child prefers the book to the conversation of the people round about—and this last impression may be completely accurate. Other families may worry that the child is not going out enough, or not playing with other children enough. But on the whole the reading addict has escaped much of the public censure that falls on those with addictions to other stimuli of imagination: little blame attaches to those indulging in this overt imagining.

Possibly people are right in feeling different degrees of concern. It is likely that children (and adults) with very different character- istics form different kinds of addiction; the reading addict probably has high verbal ability since words by themselves are an adequate stimulus. Other children need more aid from sense perceptions; some may need a special kind of environment—the darkness of the cinema—in order to enjoy imaginary situations. Himmelweit's (1958) Nuffield Foundation investigation found that children who were 'television addicts' tended to 'come more often from working-class than from middle-class homes' and that the more intelligent the child the less likely it is to become addicted to television. Other characteristics of the TV addict were noted: 'It was not the only child, or the child whose mother goes out to work, who was a heavy viewer, but the insecure child, in particular the child who had difficulties in making friends with other children. The addict, more often than other viewers, was described by his teacher as a follower, not a leader, and as submissive, shy and retiring.' Those who viewed a lot of television also tended to go rather more frequently than others to the cinema and even combined comic-reading and television viewing: 'Book-reading does not suit addicts, and fewer of them, compared with occasional viewers, had read a book or even part of a book during the preceding four weeks.' (We must note, however, that this investigation was carried out when fewer hours of television were available daily; it is possible that the viewing pattern and the type of children who most enjoy viewing have altered slightly since.) Nevertheless the results here are rather what would have been expected from introspective accounts. The survey also noted the 'transient addict' 'who temporarily finds himself in an environment which provides him with insufficient outlets'. The conclusion was that: 'The child who, for his age, intelligence, and social class, watches television a great deal is either temporarily restricted by his environment or is faced with personal problems which he cannot solve.'

There was no sex difference in addiction; which is interesting since 'girls . . . tend to respond more to the medium than boys, to think more about the plays they see, and to be more affected in their outlook by the content of television programmes'.

But although there may be differences in the kind of medium chosen, the characteristics of the TV addict do correspond to some extent to those evident in introspective accounts from reading addicts. At least they seem to have in common some absence of satisfactory companionship with other children, and lack of other outlets in the environment. The emotional need and presumably the emotional satisfaction are similar. But there remains a basic difference, that some children (and adults) can respond to words while others need additional cues for imagining. We must note that there are secondary effects of addictions too; reading can affect the ability to use language; incidental factual information can be acquired from stories or dramas, read or seen; possibly greater knowledge of various forms of human behaviour is gained, though this, we have suggested, is doubtful.

Conclusions

What conclusions have emerged from our survey of imagining in everyday life? There are surroundings and circumstances which are particularly favourable to its development. Imagining is likely to happen when the stimulus from the real environment is not demanding; pre-sleep imagining is a clear example of a situation with minimum demand—less light, absence of speech, comparative warmth and comfort; similarly, cinema viewing; television viewing may be subject to more distractions. (Reading is perhaps the one instance where imagining often continues to go on in spite of rival claims for attention; the keen reader can simply ignore other stimuli.)

Again, imagining seems likely to occur when the events in the real environment are (1) not demanding or (2) unsatisfactory. It does not seem possible to imagine when something unusual is happening (to do so then would seem pathological). Routine tasks not requiring much conscious control make imagining easy. These conditions, we have seen, may be associated with a possible sex difference in imagining; if women are more often confined to the house and occupied mainly with routine work (in the house or elsewhere) they may—as Florence Nightingale suggested—have more opportunity and more need to imagine. But a sex difference in imagining has not been clearly established in all studies (though another possible indication of it is the number of women who have investigated topics relating to imagining; it seems greater than would be expected by considering the total number of women research workers). But we must note that men also can spend much waking time in undemanding occupations. (Sperber (1944), studying stories and day-dreaming, suggested that imagining even occurs as a rejection of the female role; that girls characteristically go through a phase of imagining situations in which they do not occupy the 'typically' feminine place; but this also would seem to depend greatly on the society in which such observations are made). We must also consider possible effects of cultural conditioning; if girls are expected to be more responsive to people than boys are, this might increase their interest in imagining situations dealing with people.

Continued absence of congenial companionship seems to be another probable cause of imagining; it also lessens the actual social demands of the real environment—the child is left to play alone. All the same, it must be noted that the evidence does not suggest that only the solitary child engages in imagining. The Brontë children engaged in co-operative imaginative constructions; other children have done the same; a social interest can be developed by imagining and can encourage imaginative construction as well as give emotional satisfaction.

Values set on imagining clearly differ. As we have seen, in some ways it is tolerated and indeed encouraged. But some imaginers have denounced it as waste of time, misleading, a diversion of energies; and while association with sexual feelings may have been influential in some cases, it is clear that other reasons for guilt feelings have been strongly held. Yet it is obviously impossible to work or act constructively in some situations—e.g. in the pre-sleep situation (though admittedly planning for future activity can be done then, and is sometimes done): similarly in waking life, in some situations of childhood or adulthood (e.g. the prisoner-of-war camp) there is no possibility of alternative real action; imagining then does not seem reasonable cause for guilt feelings. This possibly explains the calm continuation of spontaneous imagining by many people in adult life; and conceivably explains also something of society's calm acceptance of much imaginative activity—imagining is acceptable when there is no need for real action or even no possibility of it.

What must also be noted is a kind of negative evidence; we do not find, among the people who felt guilty about wasting their time in this sort of imagining, any suggestion that their real behaviour became like that of the people in the imagined situations. Thus although they might imagine violent action or passionate disputes, there does not seem to be any evidence that they carried over this imaginative behaviour into their everyday life. It is only from the outside point of view that a simple relationship between enjoying the stimulation of fictions of violence and acting violently in real life is expected to be formed. We do hear of delinquents saying they found a method in television or books—but a method only; the enthusiastic imaginers certainly do not seem to have reproached themselves with determining their real actions by their imaginary experiences—they accuse themselves rather of sins of omission. It may be, of course, that they are a selected group—people of good moral background, whose material for imaginative construction did not include much violence or crime; (though it possibly did include actions which they would have regarded as wrong or socially not permissible—actions which they did not carry out in reality).

We find too that in many cases imagining occurs when the individual is well adjusted to the environment: as, for instance, the writer who adapts imagining to social ends (if writing novels can be so described); or the individual who leads a normal life but returns happily to some kind of pre-sleep or other imagining in moments of leisure.

But we still do not know the proportion of people who spontaneously construct for themselves and enjoy imaginary situations, and we do not know what proportion of their time is spent in this and more casual day-dreaming; even the large proportion of people who enjoy imagining with external aids is not clearly defined— possibly almost everyone can imagine in this way to some extent (but exceptions would be very well worth study: how many 'realist' children remain realist throughout life?).

Finally, an essential observation for educators is that the kind of development we have been looking at seems to continue to a large extent independently of what goes on in school. Children who are addicts to reading and who enjoy pre-sleep imagining may not have been led to this by any stimulus from school teaching (though they may use as their materials books reached through the school). Their activities may be unknown to their teachers and may not bear much relationship to the activities described in school as 'encouraging imagination'. (The investigation of ten-year-olds showed correlations between dramatisation in school and composition-writing to be significant for girls but not significant for boys.) And indeed being asked to write in a school classroom about a theme chosen by the teacher is rather a trifling event compared to one's continuing existence as a great hero of ancient times or as a modern Amazon —though the imaginer of really flexible powers may well be willing to oblige, though irked by the constraints of writing in the school situation. Certainly the stimulus and the raw material offered by books—and some school lessons—may be considerable, a rich source of future imagining; but it is doubtful whether a child discovers the delights of the 'continued story' by writing 'poetry' in the classroom. (One Russian child who composed poetry was reported (Tchernikova, 1950) to be able to compose only when walking about; other creators have similar quirks.) Whether the methods of play construction in current use in schools, or similar stimuli—finishing off a story dramatically presented by film or television—have more lasting consequences is something worth investigation; they may simply add useful raw materials for private enjoyment.

The important point is that imagining flourishes as a common experience in human development; and this activity seems in many instances unaffected by education of a formal kind—apart from the basic skill of reading given by formal education. It is a deliberate activity; it is chosen and enjoyed by the individual and is largely under the individual's control. What is still of concern to us, is whether this imagining does affect behaviour in a way more subtle than is popularly assumed; whether the guilt feelings of some imaginers are at all justified; and whether education could usefully influence or guide this spontaneous activity.

Chapter 5

Uses and effects of imagining

We have seen that imagining begins from an early age and gives considerable satisfaction to many people. We have now to consider the ways in which it may affect or control behaviour; if indeed it does affect behaviour. If imagining leaves us just as we were before, then educators' criticisms, the censorship of imaginative literature and popular campaigns against television violence, comics, etc., are a remarkable waste of energy and time.

As we have seen, it is difficult to know exactly how much imagining, controlled or less controlled, most people go in for; so it is difficult to decide whether their behaviour would have been different without this imagined experience, or whether their thinking about themselves or about other people would have been different. Because the scope of the problem is so large, most investigations confine themselves to studying a limited form of imagining; individuals are asked to imagine some specific situation or series of situations; their real behaviour is then observed in situations likely to be affected by this imagining. But such evidence relates to what may happen when imagining is controlled or directed by someone else; the effect of the individual's own chosen and self-directed imagining may be rather different. There are also important differences between imagination which is unsupported by actual, present sense perceptions—which is, possibly, a response to words only—and imagining which is elicited by presenting a film or some other kind of imitation of reality. However, if we can discover something of the effects of imagining even in special circumstances, in a limited way, it may give us some idea of what is likely to occur in more general circumstances.

We are concerned mainly with the effects of imaginative activity in changing personality and behaviour; but it is worth recalling initially that sometimes people are asked to imagine simply so that an estimate can be made of their existing personality or so that understanding of their attitudes and problems can be arrived at. This is the kind of imagining called for in diagnostic test situations—e.g.

those which ask people to make up a story about a picture or some similar stimulus; and this we must look at more fully later. There is also the kind of imagining referred to in Chapter 3, the forming of images; people are exhorted to form images or imagine themselves carrying out some action so that they can improve their skill in some game or sport: this is certainly a kind of effect on behaviour, but a limited kind; and since little or no emotion seems to be involved in the process (however much may come into real behaviour when playing the game) this is not imagining in the sense that mainly concerns us at present, so this kind will be neglected for the moment.

What, then, are the effects which imagining—in the sense of responding emotionally to an unreal situation constructed by oneself (or other people) as if it were real—is likely to have on the behaviour and personality of the individual?

A number of results of such imagining have been suggested as probable: they are (1) finding the solution to problems, (2) getting rid of emotions which cannot be expressed in direct, real action, and (3) forming attitudes and standards of behaviour, perhaps leading to imitation and in some cases producing delinquency. It is remarkable that with so little experimental evidence so many different claims have been made for imagining, and that such diverse effects can exist—allegedly—side by side. Do these claims seem justified?

Imagination and problem-solving

One of the most optimistic beliefs about imagining is that it helps many people, and especially children, to arrive at solutions to problems which are bothering them. By a series of imagined situations, it is suggested, the individual tries out various solutions and eventually discovers and settles on the right one. Griffiths (1945) made a study of children's dreams, paintings, stories and imagery, and found that in some cases children made a series of paintings related to their problem, and seemed to show progress through the series to a satisfactory solution; or their stories showed a trying-out of different solutions until finally one which was socially acceptable was arrived at. For example, a small boy who was worried about the problem of possessions made up stories which initially included theft as a way of getting things; then a story showed that theft was punished; then a possession—fruit—was bought; then the idea of growing fruit for oneself was imagined; but the problem of possessing the ground necessary for this activity arose (which makes the boy sound rather like a reincarnation of Rousseau's Emile, who met a similar difficulty): so there was regression to theft; then fruit was simply found. Unfortunately this particular series had to be ended before a final solution was reached; but it does illustrate well the trying-out process. In the same kind of way a child worried by the problem of damage or loss made up stories in which, to begin with, loss was simply endured; then other people helped her; then she repaired a damaged object; then she went to look for the thing that had been lost. Griffiths concluded that fantasy 'provides the normal means for the solution of problems of development'. Though she also noted that a child who has a serious emotional problem is likely to be inhibited in activities like painting and playing, so that the experimental process may not be possible.

Interesting as such illustrations are, it seems doubtful if they prove the merits of imagination as a way of finding solutions to problems. There are limits to what the investigator can discover about this trying-out of solutions; the investigation may occur at the wrong point in the process, before a final solution is reached; or it may stop before it is certain whether the present solution is the one which the child is really going to accept. There is also the possibility that the constant presence of the investigator and the need to respond to the investigator may make the child concentrate on the theme first chosen and so the child will show more consistency in tackling the problem—and indeed a greater pre-occupation with it—than would normally be the case. (This of course depends on whether the observer is a noticeable part of the child's normal play conditions.) Even so, it is clear that the situation is by no means always cleared up by imagining solutions; some of the solutions are not satisfactory; some regression appears; or the child may simply choose an escape solution—as did one of the children studied by Griffiths, who talked of birds flying away to a foreign country. It is also possible, as Griffiths remarked, that 'the child is only vaguely aware of the end towards which he is striving'.

We must further know what other attempts are being made to find solutions before we can give credit to imagination. If, for example, the child is also talking to adults about the problem, then the 'solution' may come from what the adult suggests—even if the solution is then reinforced by imagining it. It depends also on the child's real behaviour whether we can accept the view that a solution has been found—if the behaviour remains unaltered, then imagining a solution has not had much value.

Another investigation (Alschuler, Hattwick, 1947) dealt with children's paintings and found indications that imagining is not in fact a simple way of finding solutions to problems. From a study of 150 nursery school children the investigators suggested that children may certainly express problems in their paintings but: 'The painting experience for these children apparently never eventuated in clarification or real release. For them, painting could perhaps be compared to the adult experience of communicating troubles to a sympathetic listener.' They commented also that the child's problems were most usefully dealt with by a more explicit method, by talking to adults; indeed, getting to the stage of putting the problem into words seemed in itself to mean that adjustment could be made in some cases. Of one child suffering from jealousy of a new baby, they observed: 'It is of interest to note that once she could accept the baby's coming enough to talk about it, bit by bit she lost her need to paint.' In such circumstances, dramatic play may replace painting as a method of communicating the problem, though not necessarily lead to a solution.

A great deal of any usefulness of imagining as a means of finding the solution to problems must depend on the nature of the problem—and of course on whether it has a solution which the individual can put into practice. In many cases more than imagination would be needed to decide whether the ideal solution had been found. One of the beauties of imagining is precisely that in the imagined situation people can be made to behave as we would like them to; (many imaginers make it a point of honour to conform to rules of probability; but even these leave considerable scope). Consequently one of the easiest imaginary solutions is to think of a situation minus the person who is causing trouble; thus, for instance, a jealous child imagines the family without the baby. There is nothing in this imagined situation to prove or demonstrate that this is not an adequate solution. Admittedly the circumstances of everyday life will not fit in with it; but this may be all the more reason for pursuing the enjoyment of imagining. Alternatively the baby could be imagined as dying, or getting lost; and there is no self-correcting mechanism to show that this is a poor solution. The 'good' solution of behaving kindly towards the baby, of becoming protective and becoming its special friend may easily not occur in imagination, unless there is some experience in real life which has shown that this is a rewarded response; in which case, this data from real life may be incorporated into the imagined situation and this solution reinforced. Again we see that much depends on the store of relevant data from real experience that the child can draw on, and on how capable the child is of collating imagined situations with real situations—or possibly on how capable the child is of perceiving the connection between behaviour and reward.

Nevertheless imaginative behaviour which is observed by others can indirectly contribute to solving problems. If the problem is a general one—e.g. the problem of feeling inferior and undervalued—and if this problem has been brought into prominence by some special event in the child's daily life, then praise, admiration, appreciation of the child's imaginative behaviour in painting, acting or telling a story does solve the problem, at least for the time being. It is not necessarily the imagining that has provided the solution (no matter how much the problem may have been worked over in the imaginary construction) but the real response of the audience or observer. And this kind of reassurance can help the child (or adult) to face the real life situation more competently. (It may also strengthen the enjoyment of imaginative activity and make the child more likely to practise it in future, even if this is not ultimately the best way of dealing with the problem situation.) There are of course other activities which may produce similar reassurance—at adult level, playing a round of golf may have the same kind of relaxing effect; children too may find that success in games provides the temporary solution to their problem; though in all such balancing activities there is the necessary condition that the standard of performance is good enough to evoke praise or a feeling of achievement—they can, unfortunately, sometimes reinforce the feeling of inadequacy.

When the problem situation is dealt with by imagining events borrowed from fiction there is possibly even greater danger of solutions which are wrong in reality being satisfactory in imagination; the wrong solution has, after all, apparently been rewarded in the 'real' situation of the book or television drama; it may well have been highly satisfying emotionally. If, for example, the solution imagined is some kind of intervention by a fairy godmother (or other god or goddess from the machine) or if the problem is 'solved' by helpful coincidence or powerful assistance from someone else, the individual may expect that this kind of solution will occur in reality, and happily go on imagining its arrival. The individual then drifts on, failing to take the necessary real action or solve the problem because one day Prince Charming or the fairy godmother will arrive. It seems likely that children who have become accustomed to fictional solutions of this type would tend to imagine similar solutions to their own problems. Some very slight indication that this attitude to problem-solving may be produced is given in an early investigation (Shuttleworth, May, 1933) which was concerned with children who went three or four times a week to the cinema compared with others who attended only once or twice a month. In a questionnaire offering multiple choices of solutions to some trying situations, the two groups had to deal with this example: 'Dick and Betty had led rather disreputable lives. Their ship took fire in mid-ocean. They realized that the end was near and promised to reform if they were saved. What is the most likely to happen? (1) The ship burned up and all on

board were lost. (2) A sudden cloudburst of rain put out the fire.'
The 'movie' group significantly more often than the other chose the
second answer (though one must note that quite a large proportion
of them did choose the first one). It is of course possible that they
would not have expected a similar happy conclusion in their own lives.

Accepting imaginary solutions to a problem also depends on the
kind of problem and our attitude to it. One investigation (Mahler,
1932) tried to assess people's willingness to accept unrealistic
imagined solutions by first interrupting them at some problem-
solving tasks they had been set—thus producing the problem of
wanting to complete the work—and then offering alternatives which
were more or less realistic—(1) carrying out similar tasks, (2) talking
about how the original problem would have been finished, (3) thinking about finishing it, (4) using 'magic' to find the solution. The
acceptability of these alternatives was judged by noting whether
people later took the opportunity to complete the original task or
whether, having been apparently satisfied by the alternative, they
did not bother to go back to it. It became clear that real alternatives
fairly close to the original (e.g. solving problems of the same kind)
were acceptable, but the 'magic' solution was not. But in another
test situation, when the task itself was unrealistic—fetching an
object without moving from one's place—a 'magic' solution was
apparently found satisfying.

In general it appears that imagining as a means of finding solutions
to problems is not satisfactory—from the point of view of society or
educators—unless the imagined solutions are checked against
reality; or unless the problem is such that it can be solved by the
action of imagining itself. In some cases checking against reality is
not likely to happen; especially, perhaps, where self-concepts are
involved. Thus, if the child is troubled by feelings of inferiority or
rejection, imagining situations in which the child's true worth is
recognised will not necessarily prove incompatible with reality;
the child may think simply that recognition must come in future; real
behaviour by the child which doesn't agree with the imagined ideal
personality can be regarded as accidental or due to some peculiar
handicap in the real situation. So the child sees no need to seek a
further solution or to modify real behaviour. (Unless the child is an
existentialist; which few seem to be.) It is only if some kind of
objective criterion is introduced and recognised as valid that the child
(or adult) notices that the imagined solution is not good enough.

It is possible however that living a problem situation in imagination can help the individual to see it more clearly; and if the imaginary solution is communicated to someone else, useful insight may
be achieved or advice received.

Imagining and catharsis

To some educators and to some investigators it has seemed that if feelings can be expressed in imaginary situations—in words, or drama—or if we can even watch other people expressing these feelings, real action will no longer be necessary: the emotions have been satisfied, we are freed from them. This is the cathartic theory of participation in dramatic play, of being spectators at dramatic performances—the theory that by encouraging the child (or adult) to act out problems, to express emotion in drama, verse or other media, we offer a kind of safety valve. After the experience of emotion in the unreal situation, real emotional adjustment will be better and behaviour will be socially more acceptable. It is an attractive theory and has some evidence and arguments to support it.

Some of the enthusiasm for this theory has certainly come from the success of the psycho-drama as a therapeutic method. Here the individual, with the co-operation of the therapist and/or other members of a group acts various roles in some kind of relevant situation: emotional problems become clearer as the situation is acted. Various investigators have pointed to the success of this technique in helping people to form a more satisfactory relationship with others and to achieve some kind of reasonable solution to their emotional problems.

But it is sometimes assumed—by outsiders—that the expression of emotions in this imagined situation is all that is required to produce the happy results. Yet this is clearly an oversimplification and usually a misinterpretation. For example, where the individual has acted the part of other people in the problem situation and has expressed personal emotions appropriate to these other people there is scarcely a direct working-off of the individual's own feelings. (Though it may be argued that in some cases the problem arises because the individual has projected emotions on to the other people; so in allegedly expressing their emotions the individual is in fact expressing his or her own.) It may also be argued that the expression of any strong emotion gives relief from emotional tensions; yet this does not solve problems, even if reduction of tension is a step towards doing so. What does seem clear is that in many such situations casual observers overlook the part played by the social factors; the awareness of co-operation or approval from the therapist or from one or more members of the group. (Just as, in the classroom situation, the child basks in the teacher's approval or classmates' approval for playing a part vigorously, with passion.) There is also the important intellectual factor of achieving insight; if the individual realises, from the psycho-drama, how other people concerned in the problem situation probably react and feel, how the individual's own behaviour affects them, and if the performance is subsequently discussed, then the whole problem is viewed more objectively and possible solutions may be clearer.

But the theory is often said to be supported by Aristotle's statement in *The Poetics* about the purgative effect of drama. Certainly Aristotle asserted that the spectator can be 'purged of emotions'—notably of pity and fear—by the imagined occurrences of dramatic performances. (The purgation metaphor is possibly unfortunate; it deprecates the emotions in question rather neatly; but it implies that the emotional system and the digestive system work in the same way; which is not proven.)

But before relying on Aristotle's authority (if that can be done nowadays) we must consider the kind of drama Aristotle had in mind and the kind of drama which the modern spectator—or child in the classroom—is likely to witness. Classical drama conforming to the requirements which Aristotle laid down for true tragedy may well produce most beneficial insight. (Indeed, this is a circular argument, for on Aristotle's definition true tragedy must lead to insight into the way in which human destiny is determined.) By good drama the spectator is led to emotional acceptance of the power of the gods and realisation of this power; the spectator is being made aware of the human being's place in the scheme of things, perceiving human weakness and error leading to disaster, being convinced of a force leading to a final solution (whether that solution is happy or humanly desirable or not). Thus the emotions roused in the spectator reach a climax followed by calm.

But it does not follow that all kinds of drama will lead to this kind of insight or to succeeding tranquillity. Some do give insight into the human condition, awareness of a problem and a perception of how to react to it. Others do not. In the latter case, the effect on the spectator may be anything but cathartic; tension is built up without climax or outlet. Thus, for example, Anthony Burgess (1967), envisaging the future possibility of yet more television programmes which offer 'incomplete' drama or portray violence and cruelty without purpose or pattern, commented: 'Then I, for one, will go mad in my impotence to discharge the emotions aroused. I will rage, hit my head on the wall, or, more sensibly, go out and drink myself insensible.' And apropos of a play recently viewed: 'Oh yes, it was superbly done; it had the inarticulacy of true life; it was better than art because it was so *real*, etc. But, having aroused concern for a girl driven to schizophrenia, it failed to do anything with that concern. Ah (I will be told), but it's the job of you, the viewer, to carry off your donated sack of concern into the world of action. Go thou and be, for we have taught this lesson, more understanding and more charitable. What, at that hour of night? Or do I put that generated emotion beside my bed and fit it in, like teeth, in the morning?'

Similarly a film or a book can leave the participant in the same state of unresolved excitement; e.g. in the film *Kanal* two resistance fighters in the sewers of Warsaw come, after many dangers, to what could be a way out to safety by the river—only to find this exit blocked by an iron grille; and there the spectator is left, with terror, fear, sympathy unresolved. Or in Chamson's *Auberge de L'Abîme* the conclusion leaves a frail girl and a man suffering from a broken leg, their whereabouts unknown by the outside world, in a sub-terranean cavern from which the only safe exit is a path requiring exceptional physical strength. Such dramas leave the imaginer in a state of distress which can be dismissed only by the gradual working out of some solution; but, given the vividness of the circumstances, and the conditions set by the constructor of the imaginary situation in the first place, this may take much time and effort; and even then the result is not the same emotional calm as that given by 'true' drama in the Aristotlean sense. (A variant is offered by N. Freeling's *The Dresden Green* where the writer thought-fully provides two endings to the story—one happy and presumably satisfying to the reader, the other unhappy; but since neither ending has full authority the reader achieves neither the calm of a problem solved nor the calm of tragedy.) In this context it is in-teresting to notice that Himmelweit's (1958) survey of children's television viewing found that 'about one-third of the plays provide no solution for the problems raised, especially for those of personal relations'.

If then we are to attach any importance to the use of imagining to produce catharsis, it is obviously necessary to consider what kind of situation is being imagined or presented, and what scope is given for subsequent real action. Not all drama will be cathartic. Some groups may work through drama construction towards the con-struction of a satisfying solution, but the final satisfaction may be due not to undirected expression of emotions but to insight through verbalisation of the problem (with social reinforcement); and to some conscious direction of the imaginary situation. (We could also bear in mind that not all dramatists are renowned for their equable temperament and calm behaviour in real life—admittedly, they might be worse without the satisfaction of drama writing.)

Coming to more limited examples, we find some controlled experimental attempts to discover whether emotions like aggression are indeed affected by expression in imagination. Investigators have—daringly or unkindly, according to one's point of view—deliberately tried to provoke hostility in their subjects and then studied the effects of offering imaginary outlets for the hostility. One such investigation (Feshbach, 1958) studied the effect of annoying two groups of students by suggesting that they were inefficient, incompetent, and then getting one group to write TAT stories (cf.p.145) in which aggression could be expressed while the other group spent time in working through tests of a neutral kind. A control group (uninsulted) also wrote TAT stories. It was found that the 'insulted' group expressed more aggression in their TAT stories than the non-insulted group; a questionnaire and sentence-completion test showed that the insulted group which had written TAT stories subsequently expressed less hostility than the insulted group which had not written such stories: 'A significant negative correlation was found between the amount of aggression expressed in fantasy and subsequent aggression towards the experimenter for the insulted group which had engaged in fantasy.' But although the subjects expressed relatively little criticism about the 'neutral' activities it is possible that these were less enjoyable than writing TAT stories; the hostility may have been reduced partly by the pleasurable exercise of writing stories rather than by the content of the stories; though admittedly since the insulted group's stories showed more aggression than the control group's stories it does seem that hostility was also directly expressed through fantasy. One must also note that the differences in aggressive tendencies expressed in TAT stories by the non-insulted and the insulted group were not very large and not always significant; but it may of course also be argued that the experimenter was not very good at being insulting. This experiment does however suggest that a temporary and (presumably) not very serious feeling of anger can be lessened by expression in an imaginary situation—possibly because the distance between expressing verbal aggression towards the experimenter (which, one supposes, is what the insulted group wished to do in reality) and expressing hostility in stories is not very great; the substitute activity may be acceptable and effective because it is on nearly the same plane of reality.

Other studies of children's behaviour after 'aggressive play' in which physical and verbal aggression was encouraged showed no reduction in aggression—indeed these children were more aggressive than a control group who had enjoyed non-aggressive play (Bandura, Walters, 1964). Similarly Feshbach (*ibid.*) found no decrease in aggression in children after play with guns and other aggressive play activity. Some studies with adults found no reduction in hostility after a situation in which free expression of hostility had been allowed—and as Bandura and Walters put it, while it is suggested that aggression may be reduced by watching aggression acted, similar theories are not put forward for the reduction of sex drives.

An experiment by Wagner, Pytkowicz and Sarason (1967) similarly dealt with the writing of TAT stories as a way of reducing hostility which had been experimentally aroused; it also used day-dreaming as a variable (and day-dreaming is probably a more 'normal' method of coping with hostility). It was found that women subjects did not respond with anger to the experimental conditions—this is an interesting sex difference, which may account for differences in results of various investigations; for men: 'both daydreaming and TAT fantasy are effective cathartic experiences . . . and the cathartic effects were stronger for males describing themselves as frequent daydreamers.' But the experimenters also made the point that: 'When self-ratings of hostility are measured . . . fantasy results in increased hostility scores.' The use of imagining in this case did not simply offer a safety-valve but also added to the individual's picture of himself; this, if it happens generally, is an important factor. Even although no 'real' action has been taken, the individual who has imagined behaving in a certain way may subsequently feel as if this behaviour had really happened; so a change has been made in the individual's general personality (a change in the self-concept).

In general, the cathartic theory as tested in controlled experiment does not give simple answers; results do not support the view that by expression in imagination emotions can be wiped out, leaving no trace. If subsequent self-assessment is really affected when people have imagined themselves expressing hostility, there is some reason for Plato's concern about children dramatising unworthy behaviour (even if such children would have acted a part imposed from outside and not necessarily expressing their own feelings). It is also important to consider the depth of emotion for which catharsis is needed; if the emotion is superficial, as it tends to be in controlled experiments—if, for example, it is the response to some passing threat to the individual's self-esteem—then the appropriate real action might be relatively insignificant verbal hostility, and imagined expression of it could be sufficiently equivalent to give satisfaction. It does not necessarily follow that a more important emotion, an impulse requiring a different kind of action, not on the verbal level, will be equally well satisfied by the same kind of substitute activity. It certainly seems doubtful—on the basis of common observation—that a strong emotion can be removed by expression in an imaginary situation. The wish to obtain . something—e.g. an expensive car—is not satisfied by imagined possession of the car (or even by real possession of some other object), even if imagining can temporarily distract attention from the real dissatisfaction; an effort to obtain the real thing will be made if the opportunity occurs.

It is important therefore to ask precisely what kind of emotion is to be relieved. If it is really deep emotion there is a strong probability that imagining will not be possible; attention is fixed on the real problem and the real circumstances. If the emotions are trivial, substitute activity may be beneficial—provided the real stimulus causing the emotions is not renewed. Quite possibly there can be some improvement in the individual's general emotional state (as distinct from elimination of a specific emotion), provided that the imaginative activity has been of the kind which does leave good impressions. But if an external situation is causing trouble, and if it is not altered and the individual's perception of it has not been altered, then no amount of catharsis by expressing emotions in imagined situation, or by watching others express them in such a situation is going to be helpful.

Consequently it is absurdly naïve to act on the principle that any kind of imaginary experience, either as spectator or actor, in any dramatic situation chosen at random, developed at random, is going to lead to a happier real emotional situation. It is regrettable that too often precisely this kind of naïve assumption is made by teachers and writers on educational topics; unselective classroom acting, dramatising any piece of poetry, drama or any topic—or miming these—is assumed to be automatically good for the child's emotional adjustment; not because of the social activity or physical enjoyment of movement, but because of some vague but confident belief that emotions are in this way got rid of.

Forming attitudes and changing behaviour

Attitudes

Imagining, cathartic or not, has of course the merit of making life at least temporarily more exciting. But the excitement and enjoyment from the individual's point of view may be accompanied by the formation of attitudes and standards of value which eventually affect observable behaviour. In real life we assimilate attitudes from parents and others with whom we are emotionally involved; they feel certain reactions to some groups of people and some forms of behaviour and we feel with them—we develop the same attitudes. In imaginary situations produced by books or plays we become emotionally involved with the characters; we seem to experience with them the behaviour of people belonging to different social or national groups; and so attitudes to such groups or to their beliefs develop. Research in attitude change has shown repeatedly that to get people to change their opinion and their behaviour, rational, factual arguments are not enough (unless merely factual knowledge is concerned); emotions have to be appealed to, including social feeling. Imagination produces emotional experience; thus if in an imaginary situation the individual feels sympathy for a group of people, identifies emotionally with them, it is likely that an attitude towards them will be formed and their point of view shared. The situation can be like a real life situation in having lasting emotional results. So, at least, it is believed.

This belief in the effectiveness of imaginary situations in determining attitudes is certainly one which has been cherished by writers—

Yet we are the movers and shakers
Of the world forever, it seems.

The *roman à thèse* has been, and continues to be, written to convey an attitude, to change the opinion of society. Such books as *Uncle Tom's Cabin* are said to have been responsible for major social change. But such claims are unfortunately not proof of the exact effects of the imaginative experiences on attitudes. We cannot distinguish the extent to which such books simply embody ideas current at the time and clothe them in interesting characters; they may illustrate or reinforce current attitudes but not change them. But even this would be a noteworthy effect; it would mean that fiction provides, for those who have not the ability to translate abstract ideas into terms of human lives and feelings, an essential kind of experience; people who otherwise would be convinced only by personal experience (of a kind unlikely to occur in their real lives) become convinced by sympathising with imaginary characters. Nevertheless, other factors—awareness of social interest in the idea, of social approval for it—may affect the influence apparently exercised by a book or play. And past claims have tended to refer to a limited section of society, to those willing to read fairly serious books (and therefore possessing some general or verbal ability). It is also possible that the imaginative form does not transmit the underlying idea faithfully; the book may be emotionally exciting but convey attitudes other than those consciously intended by the author: or too much attention to the idea may make the book dull, with wooden characters—ultimately unread.

Children's literature, like television and films, has been accused of inculcating undesirable attitudes—though also used, at times, to inculcate standards of virtuous behaviour. The rather regrettable insularity of heroes of some popular stories for boys has been noted (and the same trait in heroes of stories for adults). Foreigners have so often been assigned the role of the villains, or have appeared as rather comic minor figures whose lack of skill in speaking English provides light relief. (Possibly modern science fiction can claim superiority in this respect since so much of it suggests future internationalism; and even if cosmic prejudices do intrude occasionally, we may postpone worrying about building up the wrong stereotypes of non-terrestrial beings.) In response to criticisms of stereotypes we find today a trend towards including 'foreigners' in sympathetic or heroic roles; this may be merely an attempt by producers to avoid protests (e.g. protests by Negroes in the USA objecting to the roles given to their race in the past) or a calculated bid to improve chances in the television or cinema export market, but it also seems to suggest that whether proven or not, some effect of imaginary situations on viewers' attitudes is expected. Similarly, the traditionally rather patronising approach to working-class 'characters'—their use for comic relief—is tending to give way to serious or normal presentation (*Coronation Street* is perhaps half-way to this state).

Has this kind of effect on attitudes really been proved? The effects are not always clearly demonstrated when objective studies are made. The Shuttleworth and May investigation (1933) tried to discover whether the attitudes of 'movie children' (who went to the cinema three or four times a week) and those of children who went less than once a month, or only once or twice a month, were different. They discovered that the 'non-movie' group and the movie group were different in some respects; e.g. movie children thought drinking more common than did non-movie children (which possibly supports the complaints of some television viewers that alcohol is offered and consumed so often in television plays that it must seem to children an inevitable accompaniment of almost all social situations); but the moral attitudes of the two groups of children towards drinking were not different; on other points—attitudes towards marriage and sex offences, for example—there was again no difference.

The investigation by Himmelweit and others (1958) did suggest that standards of value were absorbed by children watching television. Some evidence showed that children watching BBC television 'made more objective and fewer evaluative statements about the behaviour of foreigners or their characteristics'. The effects on attitudes towards foreigners seemed good, when viewers were compared with non-viewers. But the investigators were concerned that effects on other values were less good: 'Television stresses the prestige of upper-middle-class occupations; the professions and big business. It makes essentially middle-class value judgments about jobs and success in life. It stresses initiative and good appearance, and suggests that success in life depends not only on moral qualities but on brains, confidence, and courage.' But the tables quoted in the report show considerable overlap in value judgments between children of different social class, and considerable divergences in judgments. There is in any case some danger in this way of labelling values as distinctively the property of one social class (and by implication not the property of another). It is true that some ways of behaving may be valued by the majority of people in one social class and a minority of people in another—assuming that we accept the arbitrary methods used to decide membership of a social class. But it does not follow that values—such as 'courage'—are simply an attribute of social class membership or have no intrinsic importance. And if they have intrinsic importance, their transmission by television is to be welcomed, no matter which social class has a majority in favour of them. Nevertheless, television may well stress some values more than others, and so affect all viewers; but the evidence of this is not yet clear.

Some objective evidence on the effect of films was reported by Peterson and Thurstone (1933). In that study a deliberate choice was made of films and of the attitudes to be affected; the expected attitude changes occurred—for example, more favourable attitudes towards the Chinese resulted from viewing the film *Son of the Gods*, and a more favourable attitude towards the Germans after seeing a film chosen to show Germans in a favourable and sympathetic light. Similarly it has been found (McFarlane, 1945) that a 'story' film used in school teaching of geography can produce a more favourable response towards the people of the country studied, though 'non-story' geographical films may have no such effect. But the effects of such experimental manipulation of attitudes may be short-lived; the next film viewed by the group may cancel out the preceding one. And it is not always possible to cause the intended attitude change. It is also true that in such studies the measurement of attitudes is usually done by verbal questionnaires and we cannot be sure that real behaviour would necessarily correspond to answers given in this kind of situation. (This weakness is present in a great many assessments of attitudes.)

The cancelling-out effect seems to be highly probable in everyday circumstances; it is only when the same trend runs through many books, broadcasts or films that a real impact on attitudes would seem likely. Such a trend is probably of a subtle kind; but in some countries deliberate and consistent presentation of approved attitudes may be found.

There are also the effects of differences in age levels and sophistication which undoubtedly make some people more receptive to attitudes suggested in imaginary situations; real experience has been shown to be the most effective method of changing attitudes (more effective than talks, films, fact-presentation); where the individual's past experience has included a great variety of situations against which the imaginary situation can be assessed, resistance towards attitude formation will be greater.

In general, objective studies leave some uncertainty about the precise effects of imaginary situations on individual attitudes; some effects, at least of a short-term nature, have been produced; but too many variables enter into this kind of effect to make it possible to predict the results of a multitude of indiscriminate imaginary experiences.

Effects on behaviour

If attitudes are affected, we should expect behaviour also to change as a result of imaginary experiences; indeed it has been argued that seeing different kinds of behaviour in films, television, reading, will automatically produce imitation, reproduction of the actions brought to the individual's attention in this way. It has certainly been found on more than one occasion—for example, the investigations carried out by Lanz-Stuparich (1952) and Wall (1949)—that adolescents imitate styles of dress, manners, displayed by stars in films; the imaginary situations of stage and screen are regarded as sources of information, and this information is apparently assimilated painlessly —it is remembered as easily as parts of real experiences are remembered. Himmelweit's study found that one of the effects of television programmes was to give 'visual information provided by the dress and setting typical for people of different walks of life'. The emphasis which adolescents often put on the quality of 'realism' in films and programmes may be a recognition of this documentary use; the greater the 'realism', the better the knowledge of ways of behaving and dressing, or of love-making. (Though here it is difficult to interpret the appeal of the kitchen sink type of drama, or the dustbin play.) What worries many people is that adolescents and children will imitate not merely style of dress, etc., but any bad behaviour seen in the imaginary situations.

This concern has been perhaps unnecessarily reinforced by reference to experimental studies of imitation. Bandura and others (1964) found that children who had watched a film of aggressive behaviour, either by cartoon people or by real people, afterwards reproduced the kind of aggressive actions they had seen; watching aggression seemed to lead to imitation of the technique—but it depended on whether the aggression shown by the 'models' was punished or not. Further, the display of imitative aggressive techniques was produced when the children had been 'mildly frustrated'—i.e. the film did not cause the aggression, but offered the technique for expressing it when a real cause of aggression occurred.

The important factor does seem to be whether the behaviour is seen to be rewarded in the imaginary situation; and whether this presentation is strong enough to counteract what the individual knows as a result of actual experience. It seems improbable that imaginary situations would lead to misinterpretation of real consequences where clearly delinquent kinds of behaviour are concerned; straightforward imitation is improbable in such cases. But there are various other forms of behaviour for which the social consequences in real life are much less clearly foreseen. Imitation also presumably depends on how closely the watcher identifies with the model; it has been found in various researches that although young people can think of 'glamorous' occupations which they might like (and which they have seen others follow in fiction or newsreels) they are able to distinguish clearly between these and the occupations which they actually will follow; it is possible that a similar distinction applies to other forms of behaviour observed in imaginary situations.

But if imitation resulting from imaginary situations concerns us we have nowadays the even more worrying question of the effects of newsreels of aggressive behaviour (in war or civil disturbances); these non-imaginary situations (which are not 'really' experienced) may offer as much aggressive behaviour as the dramas so often objected to by critics. In such situations too, identification with the 'models' may be even more possible, since 'ordinary' people are seen in these situations; of course, it depends which side (victims or attackers) the viewer identifies with. Occasionally this violent behaviour seems to be rewarded, at least by the interest of the TV camera or the press; and 'rewarding' may lead to imitation. Those in control of the mass media should perhaps consider this aspect more carefully. Suppression of news is agreed to be bad; but presentation of events can be more or less biased; it might perhaps be made clearer that the consequences of anti-social behaviour are unrewarding. Certainly distortion could be avoided—the use of camera angles to give the impression of greater crowds than are actually present; the filming of parts of scenes only. (It is true that experience of reading about, or seeing newsreels of events in one's own locality does increasingly seem to be producing in some sections of the population of various countries scepticism about what is reported—or even 'seen'—in the news. Granted, such scepticism can be undesirable; but it is a protection against attempts by controllers of the media to construct their own version of what is happening.)

In considering imitation, we must further note that children do at times show reassuring ability to distinguish between the real and the imaginary; they can distinguish between behaviour which is acceptable in their real surroundings and behaviour appropriate in the imaginary situations viewed or read about, as the Himmelweit (1958) survey confirmed. The same survey found that children expressed different degrees of dislike for violence seen on television, and these seemed to correspond to the degree of reality of the situations—cowboys fighting on the ground, rolling in the dust, were popular, while rioters fighting in newsreels were decidedly less popular; similarly disasters in science fiction plays were more liked than newsreels of disasters: but the proportions expressing liking for the violence or disaster of real news scenes was depressingly high (from 46 to 20 per cent). Possibly, of course, there is a question of close-ups and realism again; some newsreel views are merely confusing; they are necessarily shot from a distance, at speed, so the amount of involvement of the spectator may be considerably less than in a carefully planned, unreal film situation. Again, it depends on how much imagination the spectator has—in the unimaginative the victims of real disaster will arouse little or no emotional feeling. This same lack of imagination should, however, be a protection against being led to imitate.

Some studies analysing the effects (whether through imitation or changes in standards of behaviour) of different kinds of imaginary stimuli have given reassuring results. One early study (Eisenberg, 1936) of the effects of radio programmes (not all of which were necessarily fiction) included some questions which seem naïve or even loaded: 'Have any radio programs ever led you to do anything good?' Yet the answers were of some interest; e.g. 44 per cent of the 3,004 school pupils questioned thought that the programmes did lead them to do good, and 30 per cent thought that desirable personality traits were helped by radio programmes; 11 per cent said that the effect of listening to the radio was bad, though analysis of the answers did not show any great amount of actual bad behaviour (staying up late at night was sometimes considered to be 'bad' behaviour). A large number however thought that other children might be led to do 'bad things' by the radio. (This tender concern for possible dangers to others seems a recurrent characteristic of groups investigated—and of critics of all kinds of stimulants of imagination. Lanz-Stuparich (1952) found adolescents saying that precisely the kind of film they themselves enjoyed most might have a bad effect on young people other than themselves.) On the whole, there was little objective evidence of either positive or negative effects on behaviour as a result of radio programmes; but it is refreshing to realise that even radio, which now (apart from pop music) tends to be regarded as innocuous, could be regarded as a source of corruption of the young.

The Shuttleworth and May study found some behavioural differences between their movie children and non-movie. The non-movie group was significantly higher on teachers' ratings of deportment, and on school marks; but not on conduct records; they were also higher on co-operation and self-control, but there was no significant difference in persistence or in out-of-school honesty. The movie group was lower in school honesty, but this was thought to be a symptom of conflict between pupil and school requirements rather than a genuine character trait. Reactions to movie children by other children seemed to show that they were mentioned—for good and for ill—rather more often than the non-movie group. They showed more emotional instability than the non-movie children but the conclusion arrived at by the authors was that 'the movies are drawing children who are in some way maladjusted and whose difficulties are relieved only in the most temporary manner and are, in fact, much aggravated. In other words, the movies tend to fix and further establish the behavior patterns and types of attitudes which already exist among those who attend most frequently.'

Investigations of the effects of television viewing on children give a similar impression that maladjustment leads to excessive seeking of imaginary experiences but it is not produced by these experiences; and that most children seem to avoid being adversely affected: thus one survey (ITA, 1958) reported that 'a substantial majority of parents with television say that television has positively improved their children's social conduct, while very few indeed say that television has a bad effect on it'.

Delinquency and imaginative stimulants

A number of surveys have attempted to find out whether in fact increases in delinquency can be attributed to increased cinema-going or to increased television viewing. Attending cinemas more frequently than the average adolescent is something delinquents have been found to do: e.g. Hargreaves (1967) found in his study of boys in a secondary modern school that delinquents showed greater frequency of cinema attendance than their non-delinquent classmates. Ferguson (1952) studying boys aged fourteen to eighteen did find that a group of sixty-four who were not regular cinema-goers at the beginning of the survey but acquired the habit during these years showed higher delinquency rates (22 per cent) than others; 113 boys who were not cinema-attenders showed low delinquency rates (5 per cent). But the majority of the group (1,083) attended cinemas throughout the period studied: of these 12 per cent were delinquent; but within this majority group cinema-going did not discriminate between delinquents and others. Other factors were much more clearly related to delinquency. Burt had indeed commented on cinema-going in his work *The Young Delinquent* in 1925 (7 per cent of his boy delinquents had 'an excessive passion for the cinema') but had pointed out there that the need for money to pay for cinema entrance was more potent as motivation for theft than the films actually seen: sheer imitation of crime was very rare. It seems in fact unwise to assume that the frequency of such enjoyment is a cause of the delinquency: studies of delinquency certainly do not produce any one clear cause, but indicate rather that the emotional conditions producing delinquent behaviour are complex and not to be explained as coming from one kind of leisure pursuit at a relatively late stage of development.

Studies taking larger and more balanced samples of whole populations have similarly not confirmed the view that this stimulation of imagination leads to anti-social behaviour. Bauchard (1952) quotes from Diana Scott's study the information that of 28,000 children coming before UK Children's Courts in a given year, only 140 delinquents and 112 children in need of care and protection seemed to show direct influence by the cinema. The Departmental Committee on Children and the Cinema in 1950 reviewed a wide selection of evidence and came to the conclusion that: 'The results do not in our judgment, fasten on the cinema any primary share of responsiblity for the delinquency or moral laxity of children under 16.' Bauchard (*op. cit.*) stated: 'It would therefore seem that the cinema only exerts a really harmful influence where the child himself is already, to some extent vulnerable.' Television admittedly may be more constantly available as an influence, but in less hypnotic conditions than cinema films. Various surveys, however, seem to lead to the same conclusion that 'heavy exposure is not a sufficient or crucial cause of delinquency' though 'some work suggests that criminals are heavy users' (Halloran, 1965). Halloran's later investigation (1970) of television's effects suggested that 'in so far as delinquents studied here did differ from the members of the control sample . . . their particular television preferences may well have been just as much a result of their drives, needs and social position as was their delinquent behaviour itself'.

Of course the point may be made that something harmful to vulnerable children (or adults) should not be allowed to continue— but this principle generally applied would restrict intolerably a great many popular activities. Vulnerable children are apt to be—literally and metaphorically—accident-prone; if we remove cinema or television as a means of possible damage they can still find books or—more effective still—bad company to lead them astray. We cannot really keep them from all harmful influences; idleness is equally dangerous for them. The constructive response is surely to try to make them less vulnerable (difficult as this may be), and provide acceptable other stimulants.

Thus, although Forman (1933) found that '38 per cent of the girls in a home for delinquents gave this pathetic succession of steps in their careers: wild parties patterned after what they had seen in the movies, then truancy, then running away from home', and Wertham (1955) making an attack on the violence shown in children's horror comics, found an association between addiction to comics and delinquency and maladjustment, and although the recently published report of the National Commission on the Causes and Prevention of Violence in the USA (1969) considers that 'a constant diet of violent behaviour on television has an adverse effect on human character' yet the solution does not seem to be to abolish these stimulants; so far as research goes, they do not act as the initiating cause—and indeed the National Commission appealed to parents to send in to television stations their criticisms of programmes showing violence: 'We believe that most families do not want large doses of violence on television'—which would seem to suggest that most people successfully resist the adverse effect of such stimulation on their characters. (It must be noted, however, that in the Commission's view violence was being shown as rewarded.)

It is unfortunate that an objective international comparison cannot be made of the effects of our own relatively permissive policy and that of the Soviet Union (and other communist countries). On the whole, young people in our culture can watch all kinds of television programmes, see a pretty generous range of films and books (though it is always possible for parents to exercise a more rigorous control); but Soviet policy is to control the production of books and films for young people. Judging by the moral so often preached in children's books and films in the USSR one might expect a very high level of character development; but one gathers that delinquency still exists. Admittedly we do not have data on the proportions and types of delinquency in the two cultures; and many other social factors would have to be taken into account in any such comparison. But it does seem a golden opportunity to compare the effects of different diets of imaginative stimulants on personality traits.

In general, the influence of imaginary situations on actual behaviour seems not to have been proved: influence on attitudes and self-assessment is harder to assess, but may to some extent be effective.

Controlling the use of imagination

So far we have considered mainly effects of imagination in everyday, uncontrolled circumstances. It is clear that deliberate attempts can be made to change or affect behaviour by the use of imaginative techniques; the psycho-drama already mentioned is one example, so is Thurstone's attitude change experiment. If in fact imaginative experience does affect attitudes then instead of bemoaning the results of television violence, the distorted senses of values shown in films, television and the rest, the obvious constructive step—since it seems unlikely that we can destroy or eliminate such stimuli—is to turn them to good account by deliberately presenting selected films, plays or situations (as, to some extent, Soviet society does). Clearly moral problems arise here: but what are the possible *methods* of controlling imagination's effects?

One is obviously to use films, broadcasts, etc., to try to develop attitudes which seem socially desirable; presumably the choice of set books and plays in schools is already made with some such end in view (though it is scarcely clear on what principle some of these choices have been made). But other techniques are being developed to direct the use of imagination, since not all children or adolescents or adults respond to imaginary situations in plays, books or films.

Increasingly popular is the technique of role-playing, or of simulation games. This is really an extension of the psycho-drama techniques, only now the aim is not to verbalise a problem—the problem is often well known to all those concerned, at the verbal level—but to give insight into the emotions involved, not for the improvement of individual personality but to improve social adjustment and make people more effective in working with others. For example, if the aim is to make people better foremen or supervisors the individual may act the part of the supervisor, possibly dealing with a persistent late-comer, while other members of the group act the late-comer or fellow-workers; or trainee nurses act the familiar situation of receiving into their ward a new patient, accompanied by a fussy relative, and so on. The use of this method has the advantage that the attitudes to be modified are limited in scope, and very relevant to the individual's real circumstances. To compensate for weakness of imagination in various individuals, instead of giving them a situation in words only, or even showing it as a film or play, one now puts them in a situation very similar to their own past experience and they themselves are the actors—they are thus as totally involved as possible, able to draw easily on relevant past experience, while, it is hoped, they experience new emotional reactions which will influence their future real behaviour. Of course some demand on the individual's imagination is still being made; indeed it is sometimes remarkable that people can become actors so readily in this kind of situation. Dialogues may not always be true to life; but at least the additional sensory perceptions help to create the situation and other people's emotional reactions can be emphasised as other members of the group speak. The technique seems to be effective for many people, though it does not produce equally good results for all.

Similarly some training courses present trainees with a dossier to be discussed as at a committee meeting, or with an 'In-tray' (including often full details of the imaginary people referred to in its contents); a plan of action or development has then to be prepared; for example, future headmasters may be asked to indicate the action they would take on a Monday morning, when confronted with this In-tray; their proposals for dealing with the delinquent accused of stealing from another pupil must, of course, indicate their knowledge of relevant legal facts as well as an emotional understanding of the people involved in the situation.

The increasingly popular 'War Game' is another example of the same kind; participants are fed information and identify themselves with those holding responsibility in the countries engaged in the imaginary war; results of their actions are transmitted to them and further adaptations have to be made. Apparently emotional involvement in this situation can become considerable, at times to an embarrassing extent; so some degree of realism is achieved. (Unfortunately it is not yet clear how this device could be used with the people really likely to conduct wars. Nor is it always clear in what direction it is intended to modify the behaviour of the players.) In these techniques there is the paradox of using imagination to give the individual's imagination as little to do as possible; real cues are provided, real people respond to the individual's actions in a fairly realistic way. Yet since emotional involvement develops, some effort of individual imagination is clearly made; and this emotional imaginative response is essential to the success of the technique. Presumably such techniques are most important for people whose reaction to words is limited; people who do not respond fully to all that words are intended to convey. Administration is often badly done because the response to words is too abstract —words and figures are no longer associated with human beings and the decisions arrived at consequently fail to allow for human feelings; in such cases a wider use of imagination-stimulating techniques should be valuable.

But even for those whose imagination works spontaneously the techniques can be helpful. Their final effectiveness depends on the sufficiency and relevance of the information supplied when the imaginary situation is presented; so they show the need to conduct imagining on a basis of relevant data. Organisers of such simulation exercises have to think carefully in providing data and giving further information about the results of 'imaginary' actions; if insufficient, irrelevant, incomplete data are given, the solution arrived at experimentally will not be valid and the insight which the participants think they have achieved will not work in the real situation. (If fellow trainee managers don't really respond as the delinquent workman would, future behaviour towards delinquent workmen will probably be ineffective.) This means that there is an important difference from normal imagining or day-dreaming; in the latter it is the responsibility of the individual to determine what is relevant, to choose what to include. (Admittedly in presenting a play or novel the creator can decide what data to offer; but the readers or viewers can overlook some of the data supplied.) In role-playing technique, failure to notice relevant data is one of the things which can be brought to the individual's attention; the consequences of such omissions can be shown and realised. This is a point of considerable importance for the educator.

Use of imagination in planning

It is often claimed that imagination helps successful planning since courses of action can be tried out in imagination. This may be so if we are good at imagining, for then we do not simply have an abstract idea of possible results of our proposed course but also feel the emotions which are likely to result, or we can call up some sense perceptions of the details of real situations likely to develop. If we have had experience of role-playing technique—or have spontaneously evolved it for ourselves—we should be able to plan in a way which pays attention not only to what we propose to do but seriously considers what other people are likely to do, say, feel in response. Planning in this way should lead to more successful and more acceptable behaviour. But the snag is precisely this question oɪ selecting the relevant data; if, for example, we do not correctly foresee the physical circumstances, the plan can be unhelpful; if, for instance, in planning a talk to be delivered the speaker imagines a large hall, only to find in reality that the talk is to be given to a small group of people seated round a table, the imagined plan is not going to work well. Similarly if the personalities of the audience are not accurately judged—if the speaker prepares an erudite talk and discovers that the audience consists of unsophisticated people who are not used to attending lectures and are distracted by the young children whom they have brought along with them, the planning will not work successfully. Or even if a speaker has prepared a talk—or a committee member has prepared a fairly detailed comment on an item of the agenda—and the opportunity for speaking comes at the end of a lengthy session, the preparation made with a fresh audience in mind is not going to be adequate. (Better provision of data by organisers of meetings would of course be better than the speaker's unaided imagination; but relatively few organisers have the imagination to realise this.) Thus it becomes again important to have had a wide range of previous experience, so that relevant data—or something reasonably relevant—can be used to construct in imagination the situation for which the plan is needed; though even then the wrong selection from the varied past experience can be made. (The experienced teacher can plan a lesson rapidly and find that it frequently develops as expected. Knowledge of past classes enables such a teacher to 'see' how classes will probably respond and which activities will succeed with them. The inexperienced teacher who has not tried out such kinds of activity before and who constructs from data given by childhood experiences in an entirely different kind of school may form a horribly misleading plan and fail utterly to foresee the riot that will develop.)

The same problem of imagining on a basis of relevant data occurs when understanding of other people is involved. It is a good thing in the modern world that better communication has made us more aware of circumstances in other places and the problems of other social groups. But the sympathy resulting from an attempt to imagine what life is like for such people can be misplaced or wrongheaded if it is built on only partial knowledge. Protests then may be based more on a projection of individuals' own feelings of being oppressed, and on the individual's own experience, than on an accurate estimate of what the situation is in another country and what should be done. Reactions to racial policy in South Africa, for example, may be based on memories of extremely intolerant, sadistic characters in plays or books, and on lack of knowledge of the behaviour of uneducated Africans; thus leading to total incomprehension of people who, judging from *their* limited experience, cannot see uneducated Africans as their equals but wish to treat them with kindly paternalism; thus reasonable communication with the people whose policy it is hoped to change becomes impossible: the two sides are talking about two different situations. (This is not an argument in support of racial inequality; simply an example of a case where sympathetic imagination is not enough, if it is based on inaccurate data.)

Hence the planning of future action depends on imagination fed and sustained by a good selection of relevant data; the modification of attitudes and behaviour similarly depends on providing relevant information in the construction of situations calling for emotional involvement and imaginative responses. To ensure the relevance of the data the opinion of a group can sometimes be much better than individual judgment; thus in the role-playing situation some members of the group may point out that the situation would not develop in reality as it has just been developed in imagination; they can affirm that they themselves would certainly not have responded as some of the participants clearly imagine others would. In this way individual weakness in selecting data can be corrected. Naturally there may still be a problem of communication—members of the group with relevant experience may not be good at explaining it or at convincing the group that they are right; or their emotional response may not be clearly understood by others in the group. But at least individuals gain by noting gaps in their own experience or comprehension.

In such appeals to group opinion there is another advantage which aids the learning process; attitudes are reinforced by group approval. Individual weakness in value judgments may be corrected by discovering how the group feels about some forms of behaviour; this in turn may affect both real future behaviour and also future planning in imagination. Whether such changes are beneficial depends obviously on the quality of the group's attitudes—and possibly on the ability of the group leader (or teacher).

Controlled use of imagination in therapy

Imagination can be used in therapy when the aim is to decrease or remove anxiety about some particular object or situation; or possibly to affect behaviour of a specific kind—e.g. to help smokers to give up smoking. The method is to induce a relaxed state, either by drugs or other methods, then to tell the patient to imagine (to 'visualise, picture or somehow make present') a situation resembling the one causing the phobia but far enough from it not to be disturbing; then gradually to bring the patient to imagine situations nearer and nearer to the problem situation, but maintaining the relaxation so that eventually the hurtful situation can be imagined in this relaxed state and emotional calm can gradually be associated with it (Graham White, 1967). If in the course of the series the patient's reaction is so strong as to destroy the relaxation, a return is made to a milder situation until the stronger one can be accepted. (Some physiological measures can be used to determine the state of relaxation; and also to show the correspondence between the imagined situation and the subject's reactions to it; skin resistance has been found to increase notably when a crucial situation is imagined (or is said by the subject to be imagined) whereas only slight increase is noted when a 'neutral' situation—for example a television view of the Royal Family, with corgis, on the lawn at Sandringham—is imagined.) If an addiction is to be removed the technique calls for imagining more and more unpleasant consequences of the action. This aversive imagining has not yet been proved to be generally effective, but some success has been shown for the de-sensitising imagining. In such work it has been found that even people of relatively low intelligence seem able to produce strong imaginative responses; and although individuals apparently differ in their ability to imagine, this ability does not necessarily correspond to differences in intelligence.

In such cases people are being asked to imagine something very relevant to their own experience; indeed to some extent they could be said to be remembering or recalling actual events. But while relevant sensory impressions or memories would be used it is remarkable that in this instance what people are ultimately trying to do is to dissociate the emotional components of these past events from the sensory impressions; so that instead of imagining in order to produce a certain kind of emotional response or instead of enjoying the emotional response an imaginary situation produces, they are trying to destroy the dominating emotional association with it and substitute another. (Possibly the compulsion some people feel to re-enact scenes of anger or other emotional events where they feel dissatisfied with their performance is an attempt to change the emotional loading of the events in a similar way—i.e. to change from a situation in which unsatisfactory emotions were present to one in which more satisfying emotions are felt.)

If such a process is possible, it may be a highly beneficial technique for common use: if in fact experiences can be re-lived (in imagination) and associated with relaxed or happier emotional states; or similarly if future situations could be associated in advance with chosen emotional calm. Yet since imagining in normal circumstances is in response to emotion or has as its purpose the continuing or experiencing of emotions, the habit of imagining *without* the usual kind of emotion (but with calm contentment) might be difficult to cultivate. In the therapy situation there are external aids to relaxation; encouragement from someone else, exercises to induce relaxation, even drugs; in normal situations these aids might not be easily obtainable. (Some people are certainly more able to relax than others; for them this technique might be more accessible.) In any case, this remains a fascinating line for further study.

It is also found that not everyone so treated can imagine the situation at will; in such cases pictures of appropriate scenes are used; so again individual imagination is helped by providing actual sensory cues. Possibly in other cases weak imagination is helped by drugs and relaxation.

One exponent (J. G. White) of this therapeutic technique has argued that the method shows the real danger of stimulation by the mass media, since children or adults watching television violence experience these events in the relaxed circumstances of their own home; thus they might become equally de-sensitised to such events since they experience them in emotional calm. But different types of relaxation are involved here; although the relaxed feeling of being safe at home is somewhere in the consciousness of the child watching television, this calm is not associated directly with the imaginary situation seen—the feelings of horror and pity which the imaginary situation (or the real situation of television news bulletins) evokes are still powerful—if they are not, there is little fun in watching. The individual in the therapeutic situation remains emotionally unmoved by the frightening scene imagined because it is not really a frightening scene (for most people) and because definite means are used to preserve relaxation. The spectator who is unmoved by an imaginary situation will probably stop watching. (Some children have been observed to stop watching also when a situation becomes too frightening or horrible; this does not suggest that they watch in an emotionally relaxed way.)

But admittedly all imagining, of whatever emotion, is carried out against a background of at least relative tranquillity or with the possibility of immediate return to calmness; yet it is not usually considered a de-sensitising activity, one which makes us increasingly unemotional and relaxed. If it were really de-sensitising possibly it might de-sensitise (or remove) the impulse to action as well as the emotion appopriate to the action: so its consequences might be beneficial—in so far as apathy can be beneficial.

An individual technique of imagination control

To conclude this survey of methods of using imagination to modify behaviour we may note an individual do-it-yourself technique proposed by Rousseau in *La Nouvelle Héloïse* (lettre 37), though we have no evidence of whether he himself tried it, or with what success. His hero has written sadly to inform Julie, whom he loves, that he got involved in bad company and so spent hours which he now regrets—and which he knew at the time he would regret; but he failed to act as he knew he should. Julie writes back to suggest that on such occasions he could use his imagination to better effect; instead of foreseeing and imagining merely the immediate and unpleasant stage of taking the right course of action—foreseeing the mockery of his companions at his decision to leave—he should have instead concentrated his imagination on a more distant stage; on the relief he would feel once he was out on the street and free of the bad company, on the pride and satisfaction he would experience on telling Julie of his victory and on her delight in hearing of it. It is possible that Julie was overlooking some important psychological factors—the dominance of the immediate present, and the changing balance of vectors of attraction and repulsion as the individual approached the centre of repulsion (the difficult action)— but the idea is interesting.

Conclusions

In spite of the claims often made for the effect of imagining on behaviour—whether for good or ill—we have to recognise that the evidence is not conclusive. Some evidence suggests that imaginative experiences do affect attitudes: but there is much less evidence than would be expected to show that they have bad effects on behaviour. There are promising techniques for trying to control imagination (it is indeed possible that some individuals have long since discovered them and have been using them effectively) but here also there is not really enough firm, experimentally obtained evidence. It is also clear that so many variables are present in the circumstances of everyday life, so many imaginative stimuli affect the individual, that reliable evidence is difficult to obtain, if indeed not impossible to obtain: the multitude of influences may result in cancelling out.

Thus although there are indications of some lines of action which seem worth following, the educator cannot find detailed specific guidance about practical daily problems of trying to control children's imagination or use it to affect behaviour in what seems to be a desirable way. On the other hand, the educator may take comfort from the more negative evidence; the behaviour of children is not so adversely influenced by television and other mass media as at times seems probable and as is often asserted. If effect on attitudes does occur, there is still comfort in considering how readily the attitudes induced by many imaginative productions seem to fade when brought into contact with reality, or to cancel each other out. We can also note possibilities of improving the ability of individuals who are weak in imagination: additional cues may help them to enter into other people's position, to some extent. There is also the very important point that the data on which imagination works must be as reliable and relevant as possible—so that the application of intelligent thought (traditionally the domain of the educator) appears as an important factor in what is sometimes regarded as a purely emotional activity. So to our earlier questions:—does imagination affect behaviour and can it be developed by education? —we return uncertain answers. We are as yet unable to trace all the imaginative stimuli and all the imaginative activities which have produced spontaneous individual behaviour. We can see possible methods of helping imaginative behaviour; but there are clearly individual differences to contend with and we have no guarantee of complete or lasting success. Nevertheless, the survey of the existing techniques and research findings gives some foundation for further effort in education: and it may clear away some hallowed but mistaken beliefs.

Chapter 6

Measuring and assessing imagination

Much of our information about imagining comes from people's reports of their own experiences, though some of it has come from studies of answers given to questions about behaviour. It would be extremely helpful if we had some accurate and reliable way of measuring and comparing imagination in different people—or even in the same person at different times, or after educational attempts to change imaginative ability; but there are two main difficulties; one is that 'imagining' is used to describe different kinds of behaviour, so that tests allegedly measuring imagination often measure what seem to be different things. The other difficulty is that some of the most interesting kinds of imagining do not have measurable effects; they do not lead to overt actions, observable behaviour; they do not affect the outside world. Hence the only way to find out about a great deal of imaginative activity is in fact to ask people about their experience; but—as we have pointed out earlier—people's accounts are not always reliable and they are not easy to compare. So a considerable variety of tests has been used in the last hundred years or so to try to give more objective indications of some kinds of imagining and to produce some comparable measurements. Considering these tests throws some light on what people mean by 'imagination' and on the kind of activities that have been described by this word.

Early tests of imagination concentrated on (1) the ability to recognise and reconstruct sense impressions gained from previous experience, and (2) the ability to make new creations from these. From sense impressions investigators have gone on to consider (3) the ability to make similar constructions or reconstructions using words (stories, poems, descriptions of scenes or situations) and (4) the ability to construct new ideas or theories. Investigators have also been interested by (5) the degree of novelty of the new creations, (6) the sheer quantity which some people can produce, especially in a limited time, (7) their aptness or beauty. Such tests focus on active or creative imagination, imagination which produces some object or effect; they leave aside imagination which is simply participation (e.g. reading or watching) or whose purpose is just the production of an emotional state.

Running through the diversity of tests which have been employed there is one constant theme; the use of past experience to form new constructions—whether these constructions are expressed in sensory modes, as objects or drawings or sounds, or whether they are expressed in words conveying situations or ideas. This characteristic of recombining data coming from past experience is the reason that such a variety of tests and performances have, at some time or another, been referred to as tests of imagination; yet it is often difficult to accept that all these tests are dealing with the same thing, or difficult to expect that people who are good at one of these tests are necessarily going to do well in others. It is possible that in fact several abilities are involved—this is still a matter of controversy; nevertheless we can see a unifying concept in the variety of tests and theories. Emphasis has changed, however, during the development of different tests so that we are now less concerned than before with construction from simple sense impressions and much more concerned with constructions using words, ideas and situations.

Interpreting sense impressions

A cluster of tests has been concerned with the ability to use past experience in interpreting present sense impressions. The theory here has been that imagination should enable the individual to draw on past experience to complete a present impression which is actually incomplete; the more incomplete or the more vague the actual stimulus the greater the imaginative ability needed to draw on past experience to supplement the present sense impressions and so form the perception of a complete object; i.e. a lively imagination is thought able to construct an object when only a few clues to its nature are given by present sense impressions. This clearly stems from some of the older definitions of imagination, and the association with memory is evident. If one has clear and accurate impressions of things noticed in the past one is able to recognise them with very little help from present impressions; one cue leads to total reproduction or reconstruction; though if the memory is too specific (recalling the object only in precise circumstances) imagination will not work. An example of this type is the 'window' test; a picture is covered by a sheet of paper in which various flaps have been cut so that they can be lifted to show part of the picture underneath; the test is to discover how quickly the picture is recognised as one flap after the other is raised; expert 'imaginers' can recognise the picture with very little assistance of this kind; others may need to have all the flaps raised—and still not know. Similarly there is the test in which people are shown a very schematic picture of a familiar object; then a series of increasingly more detailed pictures is presented until the whole object is normally shown; again the test is to discover at how early a stage the object can be recognised. Similar tests, oddly enough, have been used as non-verbal tests of intelligence and to discover effects of brain damage. (Magazines or television tests of this sort show photographs of objects in close-up or from unusual angles. On a verbal level, tests calling for the completion of words of which only some letters are given—or even anagram tests—would seem to demand the same kind of ability.)

The same idea seems to underlie other tests in which very slight clues as to the form of an object are given, and it is left to the individual to decide what the object is. But here the ability to recognise or reconstruct any one object is less restricted by the test situation, since it is possible to give a number of 'correct' answers rather than the one correct answer of identifying the 'real' object. We find here tests like the 'four dots' test, when four (or another number of dots) are to be joined together to make pictures of objects or designs; and the sticks test, in which fifty small sticks are provided and designs or patterns are to be made, each taking not more than six sticks. Similarly a starting line or curve may be provided as something to be incorporated into a drawing of an object or pattern. (Popular magazines love to present this kind of exercise as a personality test.) In the same way a sheet of fibrous paper with flecks and marks on it is presented so that outlines can be drawn of the objects which can be 'seen' on it (Hug, 1952). There are also numerous tests of the 'Clouds' variety (where the stimulus is shading of a cloud-like kind, with no clear outlines; and outlines of what is 'seen' are to be drawn (Stern, 1937)) and of the 'ink-blot' variety (with Rorschach probably the best known) in which again it is a question of 'seeing' various objects in the vaguely defined visual stimulus offered by an ink-blot or something of the kind (Binet, Henri, 1895; Dearborn, 1897). (The latter tests of course have become tests not only of form recognition or reconstruction—imagination in the older sense—but of the emotions which, in addition to sensory memories, determine what is perceived—imagination, perhaps, in the more modern usage.)

When such tests are used to discover personality factors leading to the imaginative response new considerations are involved and new problems in measurement develop. It is possible to measure accurately and objectively the number of 'windows' which must be opened before someone perceives a concealed picture, or to note at which stage the distorted or schematic photograph of a familiar object is recognised. When a number of responses are possible one can simply count the number given and award credit accordingly. But where a stimulus can be interpreted in a number of ways, some interpretations will appear to fit the stimulus better than others; at the lowest extreme it may be uncertain how anyone could 'see' what someone is claiming to see in the stimulus; at the highest it may be marvellous that someone could perceive something so original and yet so well fitted to the stimulus, once it has been mentioned. It is possible to make an objective measure of 'originality' by counting the number of people who give a certain interpretation; thus whoever 'sees' something no one else has thought of can be given a high mark, and so on; but when using this technique we may become uncertain whether some of the more unusual interpretations deserve a high mark for originality or a low mark (or none) for being totally unsuitable (and possibly given at random, simply because some response was required). There is also the question of quantity versus quality; who has performed better in such a test—the person who has thought of a great many interpretations or the person who has thought of rather fewer but very good ones? It all depends what we are trying to assess; and it is not clear which of these qualities—if either—should be regarded as imagination. If we take imagination as being the ability to deal efficiently with past sense impressions to construct new perceptions, there is something in favour of the person who can produce a great number of interpretations; but more popular interpretations of the word 'imagination' would probably stress originality; in this case the person giving the more unusual responses is due the higher marks (though with some hesitation about the more bizarre responses). Originality in using past sense impressions was of course by no means excluded in older definitions of imagination. In many people's responses the two qualities— quantity and originality—may be combined; but this is by no means invariably the case.

It has been found that when the stimulus is deliberately vague and therefore open to many interpretations, what people 'see' shows not simply their ability to deal with sense impressions past or present but their own interests, the subjects with which they are pre-occupied. Consequently the assessment of responses to such tests may be based not on the number of responses or their originality but on their relationship with different emotions and different types of personality; thus a number of unusual responses in ink-blot tests— e.g. 'seeing' white shapes on a black ground instead of the more customary black shapes on a white background—may indicate contra-suggestibility. Scoring of unusual responses may depend on the examiner's skill and experience in interpreting: so the test becomes less objective than other kinds of test (although accumulated knowledge of 'typical' responses can reduce this problem; much has been done to make the interpretation of some such tests, notably the Rorschach, independent of the personal bias of the interpreter). But we are then assessing the whole personality, not one aspect of it like imagination.

Construction of new designs and objects

Before considering examples of tests which have been used to assess both personality and imagination, we may note some other tests using sense impressions and involving objects rather than words.

Tests of spatial relations offer drawings of shapes; they set the problem of deciding which shape would result if some or all of these shapes were fitted together; or they set the problem of deciding which shape would fit into another, possibly three-dimensional, shape from which a piece is shown to be missing. In such cases the shapes might have to be placed in positions or at angles other than those shown in the picture before they would fit; thus there is possibly a need for 'mental manipulation' of these sense perceptions, moving them about, as it were, in the mind; and this ability to transform images, change them in some ways, seems to resemble imagination as described in earlier times. (Here admittedly there are also actual sense perceptions; but as they have to be flipped over or moved round abstractly—i.e. the actual perception is of the object fixed in one position, but to solve the problem a perception in another position is necessary—then it is not purely a matter of interpreting the present sense-perceptions, for some people at least. Conceivably abstract analysis of the properties of the shape can also lead to a solution; it is true that the tests can be done by people claiming to have no imagery. So the test does not necessarily involve imagination even in the old sense of the word.) It may be because of this variety of possible response that spatial ability tests have not been widely included in assessments of imagination, though they are often thought relevant in the assessment of some kinds of creative ability, e.g. in architecture.

Another test of the same type is the Art Form test (Stephenson, 1949) in which variously shaped pieces of coloured paper have to be put together to form a pleasing kind of design. This again can be considered a measurement of ability to deal with present sense impressions rather than with past data; yet past impressions can affect the present arrangement; and this test also has been thought relevant to ability for creative work. In much the same way the mosaics test, in which a design has to be formed from variously coloured pieces, has been used. In both these tests it is difficult to arrive at objective assessment of good and less good designs.

Markey's test for children (1935), using five blocks which have to be put together, gives also some scope for judging the artistic merit of the child's response, though in this test the ingenuity with which the blocks are employed is more important: this test can be used to discover how many solutions the child thinks of as well as how ingenious the solutions are. (The house-keeping game, also by Markey, gives the child actual dolls, models of chairs, tables, etc., to construct with, and so perhaps fits better into a later category of tests.)

A very straightforward kind of test, which most people would accept readily as a test of imagination, is to ask for designs of every-day objects; for example, the test used by the Industrial Fatigue Research Board (1926) proposed designing (1) a teapot, (2) a pillar-box, and (3) a postman's uniform. Again there are problems of assessment since the attractiveness of the designs produced may vary in different individuals' judgments. Another possible criterion is whether the object would be functional (though strangely enough the I.F.R.B. did not seem to take this into account). On much the same lines was another test used by the Board, asking for plans or designs of a room as the children would like it to be (possibly a greater number of personality factors would enter in this test).

The Village Test, discussed by L. R. Bowyer (1970), seems also a test of imagination as the word is often understood. The requirement is to 'make an imaginary village where you will live'. Yet investigators' interests here lie not so much in the skill with which the village is constructed or in the pleasing appearance that results (or does not result), as in the expression of personality traits; this is indeed the main purpose of the test, though it does require using past experience and creating something new from it. Similarly the 'world' test of Lowenfeld (Bowyer, 1970) calls for a construction based on past experience (using miniature models of people, animals, etc.); but it also is intended to discover personality qualities rather than imagination.

Tests of artistic judgment

Before leaving the tests which involve the use of objects or designs we should perhaps mention tests which mainly aim at measuring artistic ability and judgment, since these are held to be imaginative activities; for instance, the Meier-Seashore Art Judgment test offers two versions of a picture and the problem is to decide which is the 'right one—i.e. the one which is as the artist produced it (the other version having been changed in some way, e.g. by moving some object in the picture to another position). In a similar way, tests of poetic judgment often offer two versions of lines of poetry, the one 'correct', the other having suffered modifications from the original; or people may be asked to choose between examples of 'real' poetry and verse constructed simply for the purposes of the test (the authorship being concealed, of course): an alternative is to use poems written by 'good' poets when still children and not yet fully inspired. There are some additional problems in this kind of testing, since in matters of aesthetic judgment there are no fixed standards; we could argue at times that the modified version or the *ad hoc* construction is 'better' than the original. (It does help in testing if one can be sure that one answer rather than another shows ability.) But this kind of test does have some kind of objective criterion; the original work has been considered the 'right' answer by a great many people, so there is one way of distinguishing between people's judgments (even if this does not give credit for originality). Unlike other tests considered so far, these are not tests of active imagining but rather of response to someone else's creation or imagination. But it is assumed, perhaps wrongly, that artistic judgment corresponds to some extent to artistic ability. 'Expert' creations can also be offered for ranking in order of preference, whether the choice is of poems, pictures or other works; this gives some indication again of the standard of individual judgment; but this technique is probably more often used to discover what qualities are valued in the expert productions—e.g. romanticism, colour, form.

Verbal tests

Testing by giving people part of a sentence and asking them to complete it, or by giving them words which are to be made into a sentence, is one of the more traditional techniques. Binet (1903) found the sentence-completion test useful both for assessing intelligence and for giving insight into what he described as different kinds of intelligence (or different kinds of personality): one of his daughters, for example, tended to complete sentences in a practical, realistic way while the other preferred general, more abstract sentences. This kind of test of course measures also the ability to use the language correctly; to that extent it is a sort of test of scholastic achievement—and indeed a good many teachers of the more old-fashioned kind consider that getting pupils to construct sentences using certain words (words which have been new to them or whose spelling they are learning) is a useful technique: they would probably be rather astonished to learn that they were testing the pupils' imagination or personality (though they would concede that some pupils show considerable ingenuity in such exercises). And yet this kind of test has been used for precisely these purposes: it can be regarded as testing the ability to integrate data, to make new constructions from what is known.

Similarly, one word or a phrase may be given as the test stimulus and a count made of the other words which can be produced in association with it (Stora, 1946). There are two ways in which this kind of test can indicate the individual's abilities: answers can show what kind of resources from past experience the individual has available and so indicate the probable limits of new constructions. Or the test can show ability to make constructions using these past experiences together with the present stimulus. (It can be argued that if the associations produced all centre on one theme a new construction is actually made in the test situation.)

For example, one experimenter (Pickford, 1938) found that when people are asked to learn nonsense syllables (as part of a learning experiment) some embody them in a kind of 'story' which links the nonsense syllables with words they resemble; and this story, while showing ability to construct situations, can also indicate something of the individual's personality and problems. This, the experimenter suggested, shows the interpretative type of imagining as distinct from appreciative or creative imagination.

Similarly the Brook Reaction Test, which asks for verbal associations with words which have more than one meaning (e.g. check/cheque) but leaves it to the people doing the test to decide which meaning is used, indicates ability to recall past material but also indicates people's interests and personality (Heim, 1967).

Quantity or quality problems in testing

As in tests earlier mentioned, we can find two main lines of development in verbal tests; one emphasises the wealth of material available, the other the use made of it. In the former, fluency is tested, the task is to think of as many responses as possible to the stimulus word (as, formerly, as many responses as possible to a drawing or object were required); responses may be limited by the demand for a certain characteristic—e.g. the words given must all begin with the same letter, or they must all be in the same category —e.g. all describe 'something round' or 'something to eat' (Cattell, 1936). These tests are easy to mark, if sheer number is taken into account—and when the requirement is words beginning with a certain letter of the alphabet, this is really almost all that can be taken into account, though one can still see, if some time is given for the response, individual differences in association groups of responses —some associated through verbal form, others through meaning (e.g. minor, minority, minimum, midget; or mean, miserable, maladjusted; or meal, mean, mead, meek, me). But even in fluency tests an attempt is sometimes made to distinguish the number of ideas represented and to give marks for these rather than for single words; then it is difficult sometimes to know where one idea ends and another begins, and thus to know exactly how many marks should be given for a series of responses.

When the other line is followed and the use made of the material is considered important, marking becomes even more difficult; marks can still be given objectively for word frequency or for formal correctness in the use of language; but in assessing the content and meaning it is a problem to find ways of ensuring that the same standards of assessment will be used: that a given response will be assessed in the same way by all markers. There is also the problem of deciding whether the interest now lies in the originality or creativeness of the response or in the personality revealed by it. Different experimenters tend to produce their own schemes of classification: for example, Ley and Wauthier (1938) using tests of (1) sentence construction from three elements, (2) sentence completion, (3) construction of 'metaphors' ('red as . . .' 'fragile as . . .'), assessed responses on a four-point scale: 0 = most common: 1 = banal, concrete; 2 = rare, personal or metaphorical; 3 = an original metaphor or one showing philosophical, poetical or humorous thought; whereas Binet and Ebbinghaus in similar tests gave credit simply for logical, formal adequacy.

This problem is very evident in one of the most commonly—but not most methodically—used techniques of testing children's imagination, that of asking them to write stories, compositions, essays. This test is probably most common in the school situation but many psychological investigations have worked with the same kind of material, analysing the choice of themes, or the structure and the length of the productions. For instance, early in the century, Hall (1914) made a large-scale analysis of adolescents' stories; more recent studies have been made of children's compositions from the point of view of development of intellectual ability, skill in handling sequences of ideas (e.g. M. Vernon, 1948). And again, with the emphasis mainly on discovering different kinds of themes, Pitcher and Prelinger (1963) analysed stories told by relatively young (pre-school) children. An additional complication in this kind of assessment is that often a sex difference is found; girls tend to produce longer compositions than boys—though this may depend partly on the subject; there may be other sex differences in type of grammatical structures, sequence of ideas, etc. In large-scale public examinations the problem becomes one of routine marking; but various examining bodies have found it difficult to decide how much value to allot to such formal qualities as grammatical accuracy, spelling, punctuation, and how much to give to the qualities more often thought of as imaginative—i.e. the qualities of ideas, vividness and originality. The present trend in such testing seems to be to assess on impression, and investigators have found that this method is no less reliable than that of using a detailed marking scheme; but even so, examiners have to know what they are looking for: and it is easier, perhaps, to get agreement on formal accuracy than on quality of invention, or 'imagination'.

Another verbal test producing the same kind of difficulty of assessment is that in which titles have to be provided for stories, or captions have to be supplied for pictures. This seems to deal with much the same abilities as the other verbal tests, though the stimulus here controls and directs possible responses more closely: here the possible attempts at humour can make the problem of standards of assessment even more acute.

Projection tests

Story-telling has also been widely used in the assessment of personality: principally perhaps in the kind of tests of which the TAT (Thematic Apperception Test, Murray, 1943) is the best-known example; in these a story has to be composed, in speech or in writing, in response to a picture (or series of pictures) and the pictures are selected to evoke important aspects of personality. Problems in classifying responses occur here also, even although careful schemes of analysis have been worked out; it is also possible for two judges to assess stories independently and find out to what extent their conclusions correspond; and there is by now a fair amount of evidence as to the responses most commonly given. (It is of course also possible simply to compare responses from two groups of people—or from one individual on different occasions, or in comparison with the rest of the group—without referring to a wider response from a large number of people: this can be done where some specific trait is important.) One of the curious features of this kind of test is that although originally the TAT was presented to those taking it as a test of 'imagination' (with the encouraging addition of a statement about imagination being closely related to intelligence) the one variable which does not seem to have received attention in analyses of results is precisely this one of imaginative ability; which seems to indicate something about the moral or psychological beliefs of the investigators. Admittedly, considering the wide variety of activities which—even at this point in our discussion— 'imagination' has been seen to cover, it is probably simpler to stick to such simple things as dominance, 'nurturance' and the rest.

The stimulus for such projective stories need not be a picture, though many series of pictures have been devised by various psychologists to cater more adequately for different age ranges and social groups. Some tests use a more indeterminate stimulus than a picture, since occasionally the stimulus given by typical pictures is considered to be too directive—the picture may set rather narrow limits to plausible interpretations; e.g. the observer may consider that the person shown in the picture looks stupid and must therefore behave stupidly in the story; consequently the story-teller does not identify with this character; or the unattractiveness of the people in the pictures may lead simply to lack of co-operation in the whole enterprise. There is probably something to be said for trying less loaded beginnings like lines or cloud shapes.

One of the basic problems of this kind of test must be noted, since it is relevant to the wider problem of imagination and behaviour; it is the problem of interpreting the relationship between what happens in the stories and the individual's actual or potential behaviour. Symonds (1949) discussing results from early use of the TAT, expressed this problem very clearly: 'If a person works out his problems in overt behavior, he does not find it necessary to work them out in fantasy; and if he works them out in fantasy, he is not bound to express them in reality. It is for this reason that seldom were the characters in a person's stories replicas of the person himself in real life. More often the story characters represented his otherwise unexpressed longing and fears, the person he would like to be or the person he fears to be, the neighbor or school mate whom he has secretly admired, the gangster, criminal, or adventurer that he has secretly longed to be. In short, adjustment methods are not mutually exclusive. What the person dreams of being, he need not be; what he is, he need not dream of being.' Yet later, Symonds also stated: 'Fantasy is the impulse toward action.' It is clearly not possible to know without reference to other data whether the story represents the aspirations of the individual or gives a fair description of the actual self; and this would seem to limit its value to some extent. Yet the stories often are most revealing. It is also possible, looking at some of the written responses (where the time available has made reasonable length and structure of stories possible) to perceive differences in creative ability—even if this is not often done, and even if assessment of such creative ability is not explicit or taken into account: some stories actually sound interesting and real. To devise criteria for assessing such qualities would be difficult—especially as in appreciating a story a great deal depends on the reader's contribution, the reader's own imaginative participation in what is told. (And this may well depend on how much the story happens to accord with the reader's personality; the reader, as well as the story-teller, projects emotions. This is the case with so many aesthetic judgments.) At times it does seem as if vividness or zest in TAT stories might be as useful a predictor of behaviour as the more commonly measured traits; even when the themes of two stories produced by different individuals are the same, different modes of presentation may make one story banal, the other readable and interesting: an assessment of such differences in imagining would be useful. (Measurable features like frequency of use of proper names for the characters have been introduced in some schemes of assessment, but they seem unlikely to cover all the differences perceptible in these cases.) The stories may also by their vocabulary and sentence structure, their coherence of ideas, reveal academic ability; this also tends to be neglected when personality traits are regarded as being what the test reveals.

It is worth remarking here too that story production in response to an outlined situation, although now a test procedure, has been much more often used in the past—and still is used—as a *teaching* device; at present a popular teaching method is to show a picture or short film (or play a recording) which begins a story and then ask children to construct their own story from this beginning.

This brings to our attention the fact that along with the use of projective techniques in psychological testing there has grown the tendency to bring to the teaching situation a psychologist's interest in the projection of personality. More and more teachers of English seem to be analysing pupils' prose and verse in this kind of way, finding in children's drama and classroom writing evidence for all kinds of psychological traits, repressions, latent hostility, inferiority and the rest. But this kind of analysis can be dangerous if it means that imperfectly understood psychological theories (or the less reasonably established psychological theories) affect the teacher's estimate of the pupils and the teacher's attitude towards the pupil. This can happen if the teacher arrives at a 'psychological' diagnosis of pupils without taking the customary professional psychologist's care to include all possible relevant data and assess all data carefully. (Granted, of course, that teachers can arrive at biased opinions of pupils by various other undesirable routes.) One can sympathise with the teachers in this case: pupils' creative writing does show fascinating aspects of pupils' personalities, even if we are not always in a position to know what has led to writing about a certain theme—whether it is imitative, casually chosen or arising from some strong emotion or important real experience. But 'instant interpretation' can lead to regrettable misunderstandings.

Possibly one efficient safeguard against an extreme development of this kind is the speed with which knowledge of current psychological theories filters down into the general knowledge possessed by pupils; so that anyone invited to compose a story in response to a given stimulus, or to produce poetry for public consumption, will be well aware of the analytic process which may be applied not only to the style but also to the content. We might in fact expect a swing in pupils' writing towards carefully formal expositions of conventional themes, of only those aspects of experience which the pupil feels willing to communicate to the teacher or a wider public—except of course in the case of pupils who may still think teachers shockable. An alternative evasion would perhaps be pure nonsense-writing—though it has to be very pure to foil the ardent interpreter.

Situations tests

One of the curious features of the testing of imagination is that those tests which to the ordinary person seem most likely to involve imagination are likely to be infrequently used: this seems largely due to the problems of marking, or assessing. As we have seen, the analysis of story composition has tended to turn very largely towards consideration of the personality revealed in the story; which is not really the same as the assessment of the individual's power to imagine. The same kind of difficulty arises in further tests which, on face value, seem particularly good tests of imagination; they are the Probable Situations Test and the Imaginary Situations Test which were described in Hargreaves' monograph of 1927. In the Probable Situations Test what is required is to list (1) all the things one could do and (2) all the things one would do in a given situation. (A four-minute time limit was set in Hargreaves' use of this test.) It is in fact a kind of Predictions Test (this alternative title is sometimes used) or in some ways it could be said to resemble a test of intelligent planning. In the Imaginary Situations Test initially what is required is to write down all the things that might happen, if, e.g., everyone had wings and could fly. Both this and the Probable Situations Test seem fairly close to everyday imagining or even day-dreaming (or even to traditional school compositions—'If you had £1,000, what would you do with it?'). When it comes to marking the results, the quantity-quality problem recurs, especially if, in the

Probable Situations Test, people are asked to give reasons for their chosen actions. We can count the number of proposals for action and see how many are produced: but in assessing fluency of ideas it is difficult to decide where a new idea begins—how slight a variation should really count as a new idea. Again, we may feel that the novelty or brilliance of one of the responses suggested should receive more credit than the large number of commonplace proposals made in other cases. It is of course possible to assign separate marks for the qualities of novelty and of rational originality—possibly on the lines suggested earlier for the Metaphors Test; but classification of this kind remains tricky.

Rather akin to these tests is the kind of test now often included in 'creativity' test batteries, the Multiple Uses Test in which the problem is to state as many uses as possible for some fairly commonplace object like, for example, a brick. This again may show differences in personality types, between those who give various uses fairly closely associated with building or the purposes for which, presumably, bricks are normally manufactured, and those who give more unexpected responses—of the 'ash-tray' or 'tombstone for a mouse' type. It is in many ways an attractive test and does seem to correspond to the remarkable ingenuity of many people in real-life situations (a study of the uses to which paper-clips are put showed that the collective ingenuity of human beings really is astounding; and recent advertisements of a cellophane sticky-tape firm, asking people to compete in stating possible uses for the product make a clever appeal to this ingenuity). This test also shows a quality perhaps less clearly called for in earlier tests—that of being able to detach oneself from commonly received ideas, able to put one's past impressions into a new framework or see them as associated with entirely new circumstances. Admittedly, in other tests impressions have had to be dissociated from their past associations—words have had to take new associations or be seen in new groups; so also has the behaviour attributed to imagined people: in designing objects also a breakaway from previous uses and associations (the teapot in the shape of a cottage) may be made. But perhaps this quality of flexibility is more clearly seen in the Multiple Uses test.

It is important to note that the Multiple Uses test, like many tests of imagination, has been used as a test of intelligence; but it does clearly have some relationship to a kind of imaginative ability—certainly many people think that finding an unforeseen use for an object is an imaginative act; it is also imaginative on traditional definitions, since it requires a new construction of the data of past experience. Possibly the fact that the test uses objects rather than words or ideas emphasises the need for flexibility; we are rather more used to employing words in new associations, and words, being abstractions, are less closely linked than objects to specific situations in the past.

At the same time it should be noted that in this particular test situation the words of the instructions may make considerable differences in responses; fluency will depend on the definition which the individual gives to the word 'use' when asked to think of 'uses' for an object. Liam Hudson (1968) found that when examples of possible responses were given in the test situation boys who previously had been less fluent than others were able to respond with greater fluency than before; he takes it that their 'creativity' was inhibited by personality factors, since they assumed, evidently, that 'use' ruled out some responses; when examples made it clear that 'use' could be very widely interpreted (indeed, could refer apparently to almost any quality of the object, to anything that might be done with it, whether what was done was utilitarian, practical or probable —e.g. 'using' a piece of elastic to make a bad smell) then they offered more responses. This raises the question of whether the test really discriminates between two types of thinking, two levels of imagination, or simply discovers differences in interpreting words used in instructions. It is possible that originally some boys could not think 'creatively' to any great extent, or were emotionally inhibited about giving some responses in the test situation; it is also possible that some were simply more selective about the responses they thought worth communicating—i.e. both sub-groups might have the same frequency of response but one would allow a greater proportion to pass through the selective net since it is less concerned with the meaning commonly given to the word 'uses'. This is an important and interesting difference; but it is not necessarily a difference in flexibility or imaginative ability. (A rather similar situation may be found in judging the 'brain-storming' technique by which members of a group trying to solve a problem or produce new ideas utter any idea—no matter how absurd or seemingly irrelevant—that comes to mind apropos of the topic; they 'defer judgment' on the ideas, and it is argued that this can lead to better problem-solving, and better creative ideas, than situations where ideas are judged before presentation and some possibly excellent possibilities eliminated too soon. As Freeman, Butcher and Christie (1968) point out, while there has been much favourable reporting on the brain-storming technique's results, there is still a great need for more careful analysis of the other conditions which affect such groups and of the effect of the instructions given in such sessions.) The question of the point at which it is best to judge the relevance or usefulness of an idea is still unanswered; clearly different individuals choose different points for inhibiting ideas; but their choice may be influenced by the circumstances in which they are working and the instructions they receive. Yet presumably individual differences in flexibility and creativeness are not entirely due to differences in inhibition.

The same kind of test as the Multiple Uses is what P. E. Vernon has described (1967) as the Tin Can Test; instead of presentation in words, this problem was set with an actual object—'an empty, clean, baked-bean or dog-food tin (large size) was presented with the top still attached. The suggestions were: "Now here's an empty tin can. Suppose you had one just like this, tell me some things you could do with it." And later: "What else? Tell me as many different things as possible you could use it for." ' In such circumstances it would seem probable that some of the more extreme non-utilitarian responses given in verbal test situations would be eliminated; it is also possible that actual sense-perceptions of the object could limit the range of possibilities—or possibly stimulate more the practically-minded individual whose response to the abstract word might not be very good. In the particular investigation described—a cross-cultural study—there were clearly merits in avoiding problems of translation by using an object which could be more or less the same in all countries studied.

Creativity test batteries have recently added largely to the frequency of use of many of the tests we have considered; from being tests of intelligence or imagination they have become tests of this new, and still controversial ability. (The relationship between 'creativity' and 'imagination' is something to be discussed at another point.) It is encouraging to note that some investigations of creativity have also included kinds of assessment other than tests—e.g. school performance or ratings by observers who know the individuals well. This is a line of research which is highly important since it is easy to forget, when looking at the variety of tests available, that the test situation is abnormal, and that observer error and distortion of individual behaviour by the test situation are easily overlooked. For both creativity and imagination tests there is certainly a continuing need to validate tests by relating them to actual performance in normal conditions—if this can be done.

Assessing imaginative behaviour in normal situations

Another defect of the test situation is that the activity is deliberately provoked by the investigator: the stimulus to imagine is determined externally; thus the tests may not give a very good idea of how the individual would normally behave, or indeed whether the individual would normally use the ability which is being tested.

It is possible to avoid some of these difficulties with young children because they often show by observable behaviour of a spontaneous kind that they are imagining; they move objects; they gesticulate; they speak about their imaginary situation; so objective evidence is possible. (As one writer (Bossence, 1967) reminisced: 'I used to conduct cowboy and Indian battles, gang warfare and baseball games in my mind and the only drawback was that they involved me in a lot of arm-swinging, skipping and other actions, which, when they were carried on in the street, convinced the neighbours that I was as nutty as a fruit-cake.') To make estimates of the frequency of such behaviour more objective, the time-sampling method can be used. For example, Markey (1935) observed a group of fifty-four nursery school children for sample periods of fifteen minutes on ten occasions; the children were playing normally and two observers recorded the 'imaginative' behaviour (playing with objects imaginatively) of each child during the observation period. (Thus having a check on individual errors of interpretation.) In another study a complete record of the conversation of each of seventy-five pre-school children was made; this admittedly gave 'spoken' imaginative behaviour only. Such methods are not wholly objective, since in such cases it is necessary for observers (or those analysing the records) to agree on what they will accept as evidence of imaginative behaviour and sometimes arbitrary decisions may have to be made here; but (even if observers diverge slightly) they do seem to give reasonably reliable results.

The long-term records sometimes kept by parents or friends of children give some information about the occurrence of types of imaginative behaviour but unluckily they are not usually kept objectively or systematically enough to be useful for comparisons between children, or even to be a fully reliable record of individual development. Yet they do give some kind of external assessment of the part played in normal circumstances by imagination, and comparisons between them can be illuminating—it is also reassuring to find that in many cases they do concur. In the same way, auto-biographical statements, on which we have drawn largely earlier, can be useful, although they also are liable to errors of memory and other kinds; one can at least see some common pattern in many of them—though again this pattern may be characteristic only of the kind of people who write autobiographies which get published.

Day-dreaming can to some extent be noted from outside; but again, this is not a reliable method, and confirmation that day-dreaming is actually going on can be obtained only from intro-spective reports. And in such observations, what is noted is only the occurrence, not the content or quality of the day-dream.

Thus even these possible ways of observing the existence and use of imagination in normal circumstances are restricted and have serious possibilities of error; but since tests have similar weaknesses it is important to consider more often the advantages of using a variety of modes of assessment, and especially trying to make sure that observation in the test situation is supplemented by some information about behaviour in normal conditions.

The emotional aspect and tests of imagination

This balance is the more important because if we consider the tests outlined, they seem to omit in a really remarkable way one of the main qualities of imagining—the quality of emotional involvement and emotional response. It is true that some of the tests described do try to discover the emotional state of the individual, and that more or less direct expressions of emotion in test productions are considered highly important; but the success of the individual in creating an imaginary situation which is emotionally satisfying, the individual's delight in imagining, the emotional involvement of the individual with what is created, the extent of this involvement— these factors are irrelevant; they are certainly not assessed though they may be subjectively noted in individual testing. Yet this is one of the main attributes of imagination—the emotional satisfaction it can give; people imagine in order to enjoy emotional responses; but in most, if not all of the tests described, this aspect is irrelevant; emotional enjoyment indeed would probably be a handicap in many test situations. In most of the test situations the individual is motivated to carry out the required activity mainly by the investigator's request; there may well be a general emotion of wishing to do well in comparison with others, or in trying to co-operate with the investigator; occasionally the stimulus offered may appeal to the individual being tested—e.g. projective tests may bring to mind some theme that has strong emotional interest; but the test circumstances are not likely to allow the dwelling upon it, the repetition and embroidering of the theme which would be the normal imaginative response. The activities demanded are quite often unlikely to lead to emotional enjoyment or involvement; forming designs may give aesthetic pleasure; there may be pride in one's ingenuity in analysing shapes, in recognising forms; there may be excitement and exhilaration in producing a large number of responses, or a neat title or caption; there may be scope for some amusement and a feeling of self-satisfaction; but these are not the normal feelings of imagining. Emotional enjoyment cannot really flourish in a timed test situation, where a new stimulus is about to be offered and there is awareness that an assessment is being made.

It is true that some investigations have recognised the importance of the emotional state of those studied. Wallach and Kogan (1965) very admirably took great care to avoid the possible anxiety that test situations can produce; their 'tests' were introduced as games in a play context (though as they recognised, a child who has been conditioned to try to perform well in tests, can bring this anxiety feeling to any situation which seems to offer a similar challenge, even if it is said to be a game). But this does not dispose of the major difficulty. The emotional impulse to imagine or to construct imaginative products cannot often be produced at the time convenient to the investigator.

It may be argued that some of these objections are similar to complaints made earlier about intelligence tests—it was said that intelligence test items differed from anything met with in normal circumstances, but such an objection was reasonably disposed of by pointing out that in intelligence tests the operations involved are precisely the same as those involved in normal situations; the difference is simply that the operations have been analysed and are now tested in smaller units, in a deliberately formal way; but since the operations are the same, the test is a valid measure of the ability demonstrated in other situations. It is true that in a test situation we have to accept some artificiality; analysis of the activity may make testing by smaller units which at first seem unrelated to the large-scale 'normal' situation quite reasonable and satisfactory. But this kind of argument does not apply to tests of imagination: they do possibly use smaller units: but they omit an essential element —emotional response: even if they do allow scope for emotional response and emotional involvement, the marking scheme normally gives credit for the form only, for the non-emotional aspects. Emotion is not merely an accompanying condition of imagining in normal life, a condition which could be dispensed with while the essential operation goes on: emotional response is the basic operation in imagining, so far as the imagining is part of normal experience; an unemotional response is not an exercise of imagination.

Mackinnon (quoted by Freeman *et al.*, 1968) makes an allied and important point apropos of Guilford's creativity battery: 'It is not that tests of this sort fail to tap the kind of psychological processes involved in creative thought ... It is rather that they fail to reveal the extent to which a person faced with a real life problem is likely to come up with solutions that are novel and adaptive and which he will be motivated to apply in all of their ramifications. Much more promising as self-report predictors of future creative performance are autobiographical questions concerning past and present manifest activities, competencies, and achievements, as are found, for example, in the American College Testing Program.' While he considers that the creativity tests do deal with the same kinds of process as are required in real situations he emphasises the importance of the motivation necessary for real creative activity. But in imagining (which does not necessarily, or indeed often have 'real' products) the discrepancy between test performance and real behaviour can be even greater.

Other means of assessing imagining

Can anything be done to try to assess the exercise of imagination in normal circumstances? We find occasional illustrations of this kind of approach which indicate that the imagining tested by formal tests can differ from imagining in everyday life. The investigation carried out by the Industrial Fatigue Research Board (1926) tried to discover the presence of 'purposive creative imagination' in the children they were dealing with—i.e. imagination spontaneously used, apart from the artificial stimulus of test situations or classroom demands. Admittedly, some of their tests and questionnaire items may be unreliable; but their questionnaire did ask whether the children had written stories or poems, made paintings or drawings, played with meccano and similar toys (boys only!), or made up dresses 'in their heads' (girls only!) or tried to invent things. Scoring of the responses to these questions was arbitrary; two marks were given if it was judged that there was 'decided imagination shown', one mark for 'slight imagination'. The correlations between marks awarded in this way and marks gained on the formal tests of imagination were 0·75, 0·21, −0·09, 0·11. (The groups were taken from four schools, and the correlations are presented separately for each school.) It would seem that in only one group was there a high correlation between the formal test situation and the spontaneous use of imagination. (Unluckily it is not at all clear why there should be this striking difference between one group and the others.) The relationships between Binet-Simon tests and the formal tests of imagination, performance tests, teachers' ranking for imagination and teachers' ranking for intelligence were all very much higher than this. It would seem therefore that the spontaneous use of imagination (as indicated by self-reports) had not been efficiently discovered by formal tests of the kind used here. It is a pity that so few other investigations have tried to validate the formal tests against introspective reports of imagination. (In the study of pre-sleep imagining reported earlier (Sutherland, 1962) there was for girls a significant correlation between pre-sleep imagining and teachers' ratings for school composition and school dramatisation—the latter are possibly 'tests' of a less formal and less restricting kind than the tests discussed earlier in this chapter; even so, this relationship was not found for boys.) We return indeed to the point that intro- spective reports are the only adequate indication of the existence of imaginative activity: and they give no way of assessing its quality— though frequency may be of interest.

Conclusion

In general, looking at the tests which have been used and which are continuing to be used to test abilities which at various times have been described as 'imagination' we can be impressed by their ingenuity and interest; they show some fascinating differences in performance and they demonstrate how some kinds of intelligent and even creative behaviour can be measured or predicted; they also afford insight into the structure of personality: in fact, they test a great many intellectual and personal qualities. But they do almost invari- ably show this blind spot, this astonishing failure to include attention to the emotional component. Consequently, they do not really advance us materially in the attempt to discover what effect imagina- tion has on behaviour, what contribution it makes to the develop- ment of the individual; and they really do not offer guidance to the educator who is concerned about the part that imagination should have, and the influence that education should perhaps bring to bear on imaginative processes. Worse still, it too often happens that as a result of some such testing, psychologists throw out unconsidered proposals for future classroom work which would amount more or less to practising exercises similar to fluency test items or to cultivating the interpretation of sensory stimuli; or even propose that deferring judgment should be encouraged by classroom practice, without any particular control of the circum- stances in which it may be appropriate. Here we have again to be careful about the blanket use of such terms as 'imagination' or 'creativeness' or 'creativity'; we may be told that such and such an exercise will improve children's performance in these respects, when what is meant is that possibly they might make higher scores in a test of a small and not necessarily essential part of a productive process, a process which itself may have little resemblance to the real activity of imagining.

Chapter 7

Imagination and other kinds of thinking

It has been clear in the discussion so far that imagination is closely related to other abilities or other kinds of thinking; the tests described as tests of imagination have indicated this entangled relationship. It is a relationship worth considering more closely. It is possible that there is no such thing as imagination—that it is simply a mixture of other activities or another name for some other kind of ability. What are the other activities to which it is most closely related and which it could consist of?

Remembering and imagining

The association that has been most discussed in the past is the association between remembering and imagining. At various times investigators have tried to distinguish at the most elementary level between the memory image and the image produced by imagination. Earlier philosophers thought that the difference was simply that memory images related to one particular, identifiable impression or experience while imagination images were more general, using a combination of past experiences to form an image of something never actually experienced—in the example we noted earlier, having a memory image of grandparents who have been seen but an imagination image of great-great-grandparents who have not been seen. At other times it has been argued that this is not a real difference; in Dürr's supplement to Ebbinghaus's *Grundzüge der Psychologie* in 1913 this point was made: 'The oft-repeated attempt to make a distinction between memory- and fantasy-products was foredoomed to failure; for the products of fantasy are nothing but functions of memory . . . In so far as the reproduced contents of consciousness appear in a different combination from that in which they previously were, in so far as the dispositions of memory are so set in motion that objects which have never been seen before appear before the inner eye of the subject, in so far one speaks of creative fantasy. But naturally there is nothing creative about this. The combination of already-rehearsed elementary functions in a form which did not previously exist, is by no means always (indeed perhaps only very rarely) the result of a set purpose, so that the term 'creation' which usually implies thinking of a voluntary action, is misleading. Instead of the creation, one should rather speak of the originality of fantasy productions. But one should not think that all fantasies are distinguished by originality. Many objects of fantasy are nothing more or less accurate copies of what has already been seen, and their fantasy character is conditioned only by the fact that the subject does not remember having already perceived such an object, or a similar object before. . . .' This statement at least indicates the kind of relationship which has been noted between memory and imagination but it also suggests we cannot say that the two are identical.

From the point of view of everyday experience it is perhaps difficult to see why people should be concerned about such differences. As a rule, when events rather than images are concerned, we do not feel any doubt e.g. as to whether we actually faced an attack by nineteenth-century Zulus or not—and most problems of distinction seem to us to come into this kind of category. We would however probably agree that in remembering we can think of how things might have developed differently; indeed, when a situation has not developed quite as we wished, we can improve on what we remember by constructing a day-dream in which things do go differently; but we do not—at the time—find it difficult to distinguish what actually happened from what we imagined happening; and even after day-dreaming we are reasonably sure what did actually occur, as distinct from what we would have liked to happen. Our main impression is then that we know when we are remembering and when we are imagining; so that this quality of awareness would, in everyday experience, be one of the most obvious and most accepted ways of distinguishing between the two activities. We can see the similarities; we can see that imagining may be made up from memories of what we have experienced, and that in imagining we are using past experiences; but the differences seem equally clear.

Yet experiments and observations have shown that memory is by no means simply a matter of reviving past impressions, of taking them out of storage and re-presenting them exactly as they were. It certainly evokes past impressions; but—according to the event, and possibly according to its time of occurrence or the way we felt about it—memory also constructs from past impressions. Hence the inaccuracy of memory, as it has been demonstrated in Bartlett's

(1932) experiments and many others, an inaccuracy which can be present in spite of our feelings of belief that we are remembering exactly. What is initially recalled are one or two cues, and an attitude of mind; and what is finally remembered is something which fits in with these but need not be exactly the same as the original experience. Experiments show that even having a vivid visual image of an object is no clear proof that the memory is exact. It is, all the same, astonishing how few people accept what has been proved repeatedly in such experiments; they tend to be confident that when they themselves are remembering, what is remembered is accurate, even though they agree that they do not remember everything. Yet it is not only a matter of experimental evidence; studying other people's recollections of everyday events we know that other people do sometimes get things wrong when they try to remember; at times the subtle, or not so subtle, changes their memory makes are amusing since the reason for them is clear.

In clinging to the belief that they know when they are remembering something and when they are imagining, people are probably—however unconsciously—accepting Hume's view of the way in which we can deal with any confusion between fiction and fact. Confusion, he agreed, there may sometimes be; but he asserted (*Essays and Treatises*, vol. 2) that there is a feeling of belief which cannot be explained or defined accurately but which makes us distinguish between the two; and this belief means that our idea of the factual occurrence is 'more intense and steady' than our idea of what was imagined. Even if experiments have shown that we can have an 'intense and steady' conviction of something which in fact did not happen, this conviction is probably what makes many people decide that something really happened; and even if this guiding feeling is not infallible at least they have the comfort of thinking they perceive a difference. People believe, when they have this confidence, that they are remembering accurately what happened in the past; in imagining, in normal circumstances, they have no such confidence, they know that they are not dealing with what actually happened; and they are unlikely to believe that they are imagining something when in fact they are remembering something which did happen. So at least the criterion works in one way: they can be misled about memory: but they are unlikely to think they are imagining when they are really remembering.

A rather similar way of distinguishing is described in a comment in the book by Miller, Galanter and Pribram (1960) on the problem of distinguishing between perceptual images and imagined images: 'There has been much written by psychologists about how a person can tell his perceptual images from his imaginative images. By and large, criteria of vividness have not proved satisfactory. The basic difference between the two types of images concerns the conditions under which they will change. The imaginative image can be altered by an act of will, by creating a Plan for changing the image into something else and then executing the Plan. Such subjective Plans normally have remarkably little effect on perceptual images. However, perceptual images can usually be modified by moving or adjusting the receptor organs themselves. Thus it seems likely that as children we must all learn a set of subplans for testing the plasticity of our images, for distinguishing between imagination and perception.' The reference to forming plans in childhood so as to be able to make this distinction is important; we may indeed develop early in life some system of checking, to ensure that we are right in recognising some impressions as coming from memory while others are produced by imagination. (Though the strategy described does suggest that everyone has easily controlled imagery.)

Even in normal circumstances there are some occasions when it may be difficult to disentangle memory and unreal occurrences, and when strategies of some kind or another have to be employed. For example, dreams may sometimes be so vivid that on first waking we have the impression that their events have really happened and are being remembered as part of real experience. Then can come the happy—or on some occasions depressing—realisation that the dream situation was not real. For children, this sorting-out of the two kinds of impression may take longer. When we come to think of it, it is difficult to see how in some cases we can confidently distinguish between what occurred only in the dream and what really happened, since both are a kind of remembered experience and may have deeply affected our emotional state—first meeting someone after a strongly emotional encounter in a dream can be trying; we know that the encounter did not really take place and the other person knows nothing of it; but a change, even if temporary, has been made in our attitude. (Such a difference in attitude could be due to a new awareness of previously suppressed feelings which have found expression in the dream; but it does not always seem that this is the whole reason.)

Malebranche (*De la recherche de la vérité*) used this uncertainty as an explanation of how belief in witches and their activities had become accepted in his time; the kind of reality test by which we consider whether events fit into the ordinary sequence is one which we would normally apply; but he pointed out that as witches' activities are said to take place by night, people—in his time—could dream of themselves attending a witches' sabbath and come to believe that they had actually done so, because there was no good objective proof that they had not; such activity would not interrupt the continuity of their ordinary behaviour and might not leave material traces; consequently they could not prove to themselves that the dreamed-of events did not actually take place; a vivid impression made by a dream could be accepted as belonging to real experience, since it was believed that such things did happen. Whether many people of Malebranche's time did really face this particular problem is not known; but the reference to the problem and a possible strategy for determining whether things really are being remembered is important.

Does all this really matter? It does matter, because it is important that people should know when they are recalling what really happened and when they are constructing an unreal situation; life would be even more difficult if our versions of what happened or what was agreed and planned generally differed widely—people who seem less capable than most of us in distinguishing between imagining and remembering do cause a lot of trouble. And it is important to know whether imagination is more than rather careless remembering; and whether we do base our present behaviour on what really happened or what we imagined happening.

Life in fact becomes very difficult on those occasions when people diverge widely as to what they think happened or was said on a given occasion. Both sides then tend to feel that while they recall accurately, the other side imagines—or tells lies. Hence the admirable custom of minutes of meetings (written up promptly after the event). The situation is even more impossible when it is a matter of remembering not merely what was said or done, but people's attitudes or feelings, for these are not so easily checked against objective criteria and do not have to fit into the known sequence of events. Interpretation even at the the time may differ according to the different people involved. Hence, for instance, if someone says: 'Remember how annoyed you were!' we may indignantly deny that we were annoyed; either because our reaction was misinterpreted at the time or because we have forgotten how we really did feel, or because we now feel differently about the whole episode. (All this should warn us against the 'gentleman's agreement' which assumes that both gentlemen have infallible memories and are in perfect communication at the time of the agreement. It is also a warning against situations in which 'it is understood that' something will happen in future, but not explicitly stated that it will happen.)

A further complication emerges when we consider that we also remember imaginary events. We remember experiences which have been enjoyed through imagination. Consequently as well as using our own real experience to make constructions in imagination, we can also use material gained by imagined experience; we can read or hear about someone else's real experience and imagine it as if we were experiencing it; then this experience can be used for future imagining. This process has been beautifully illustrated in Lowes' (1930) study of the sources of Coleridge's *Ancient Mariner*—of how Coleridge weaves into the narrative, with what sounds like the vividness and reality of personal experience recalled, experiences described in books he had read—phosphorescence against the side of the ship, and details of such a kind. This process is more remarkable than is generally realised. If the other experience is communicated in words—as it often is—then we have to understand the words; this we do by using our own past experience and learning. But if the communication is to make much impression we must feel that we are actually experiencing the situation described, we do not simply understand it abstractly. Thus, taking the example Malebranche discussed, we may know superficially that witches gathered together for their sabbath; but to realise it and to use it for future construction we have to 'see' the ceremonies, feel as if flying through the air, be aware of wild exhilaration amid the fire flicker and the dark shadows; in this way the situation is fully realised although we have not in fact experienced it. (It will be remembered, as we noted earlier, that complete imagery is not an essential part of this process; there may be more or less of visual, tactile, auditory impressions; but some degree of emotional response is essential.) In future then we would have a kind of memory of what it was like to be at a witches' sabbath. (It might, of course, be a most inaccurate impression, depending on the authenticity of the account we have been given.) We do not always absorb information in this way; in some cases we simply accept facts without identifying ourselves with the situation, or realising it. But some people can accept communications so fully that they can later use the imagined experiences as effectively as if they had occurred in reality. Thus impressions received through imagination become available for use much in the same way as impressions received from reality. We have in fact a second or third order imaginary construction; constructions of the first order being based on our own real experience, the second based on hearing or reading about someone else's experience; the third based on someone else's construction of an imaginary situation. (Again one is reminded of Plato's concern about the reality of knowledge through imagination.) Yet although we may use memories of imagined experience we usually can distinguish them from memories of our real experience.

But the most interesting problem here is the kind of distinction that can be made between memories of imagined emotions and memories of real emotions; indeed the problem is whether this distinction can be made and does exist. Perception of objects can be attributed to external stimuli (if we discount some philosophical arguments); sense impressions are generally produced by things which are outside us (though admittedly some come from within— e.g. pain, awareness of position, various physiological changes). But the origin of emotions is more difficult to define; they would seem to come from internal stimuli, from an internal perception or interpretation of an event which is happening or has happened externally; or they come from anticipation of future events—possibly from imagining them; or from information received that certain events are happening or have happened (even if these are not physically perceived). Thus, for example, someone speaks insultingly; the words are a stimulus coming from outside; the words are understood, the insult is perceived; anger is felt (whether it too is a perception of physiological change doesn't matter here). But a feeling of anger also results when the insult is remembered; the recall or memory—or a report from a third person—of the words is as effective in producing the emotion as the direct external stimulus. Or the thought of the probability of criticism, of opposition, can produce a feeling of anger also. Thus what stimulates or leads to the emotion is the internal perception—the thought process. So that whether the starting point is a present event or information about a present event, memory of a past event, anticipation of a future event, the emotion is prompted by the same kind of stimulus by our perception in thought; the emotion prompted by a perceived, a communicated or anticipated situation is the same. Anger at a remembered insult is real anger; anger at an actual insult, equally real—and anger at an imagined insult, real too.

Vygotski (1930) has a rather neat illustration of this kind of common quality; he states that there is a 'law of the emotional reality of imagination' and points out that a child scared by a shape seen in the twilight may imagine it to be a brigand; the brigand is not real, but the emotion of fear is real. Hence, he points out, the deep effect of books, plays and music; for even although we know the cause is not real the emotion produced is real.

(There is also, for many people, a kind of memory of having 'lived' in the atmosphere created by a book; this is the feeling of a real past experience; at times one wishes to return to that atmosphere as one would wish to return to a place in which one had formerly lived.)

Thus the memory of emotions experienced in an imaginary situation may be a memory of real emotions. Can we then distinguish between this part of imagining and remembering? We know whether memory is referring to real or imagined events, normally; but our awareness of past feelings, our memory of emotional experience does not seem to have possible distinctions between real (provoked by real events) and imagined (provoked by unreal fictions) emotions. We have said earlier that our criterion for distinguishing between what is remembered and what is imagined is our feeling of belief. It is possible that those emotions caused by a real situation are more vivid and steady, more intense than those caused by an imaginary situation. It has indeed been suggested by various writers that one of the merits of books and plays is that the emotions aroused by them are less intense than those aroused by the same situation in reality; that there is an underlying awareness which muffles any acute reaction and prevents the stimulation from reaching a painful level; so that while the emotions caused by the actual event would be unbearable or extremely unpleasant, the slighter emotion caused by the imaginary event is agreeable. In short, we are aware of our suspension of disbelief: we can alternate between feeling for the imaginary people and reassuring awareness of our own real circumstances. (Yet at times this awareness is lost—temporarily. Hence, for example, dislike for realistic forms of violence on television, in which this awareness of true reality is presumably threatened.) If we always remained partly detached, the emotions caused by imaginary stimuli might be remembered as less deep and thus, possibly, be distinguishable from emotions caused by real situations (though real situations don't always cause deep emotions). But there does not seem to be any certainty that personal involvement in the imaginary situation always remains at the comfortable level; especially as the imaginary situation may stimulate real anxieties or real ambitions in the individual. We know, finally, that some events are unreal—but can we have unreal emotions? If we try to trace the emotions to events causing them, we can probably make a distinction; but the emotions themselves are indistinguishable.

This has the important consequence that, e.g. we may feel guilty about the emotions felt in response to imaginary experiences; or simply feel that we have experienced some situations—e.g. enjoyment of cruelty—since we have felt them though not acted in them: and our emotional tone may be determined not by any actual experience but by the experience we have imagined. Seeing a gloomy play may leave us discouraged and depressed; if in our identification with the hero or heroine we have experienced achievement or triumph we are left exhilarated as if we had achieved something worth while.

In memory, then, recollection of what was imagined and what did happen is much less distinct and easy than at first seemed to be the case. Nor can we, when it comes to emotional states, use the criterion of appealing to others to confirm or deny the accuracy of our memory.

Nevertheless, where events are concerned, we do have a further criterion; in many instances we can make an initial choice; we consciously try to remember or we decide to imagine—not necessarily explicitly, but with a definite 'switching-over' attitude; in some cases we take the decision to enter into imaginary situations by picking up a book or switching on a television programme or going to a play. We therefore feel confident that we know which activity is going on because we made this kind of decision and know we made it; though sometimes we can later move over the boundary of remembering or of imagining without a conscious decision.

But in spite of such strategies, it looks as if the distinction which we confidently assume we can make between memory of real events and imagination of unreal happenings is much less clear than was expected. We have some ways of discriminating; but as the experiencing of emotion is part of our real experience it seems improbable that we can always discriminate clearly among remembered emotions. Consequently imagining can leave in memory a kind of trace very similar to that left by actual occurrences: at this level, remembering what was real and what was unreal (i.e. imagined) can blend: our self-concept may be affected by both.

Nevertheless, though memory may contain both what happened and what was imagined, we use our judgment confidently for events: we know the normal sequences; we have a feeling of conviction as to what did or did not happen; we can make quite different decisions to remember or to imagine; and we seldom trouble to make distinctions of this kind among past emotions.

Thinking intelligently and imagining

In rather the same kinds of way we can see that the distinction between imagining and other kinds of thinking may be difficult to make. It is clear that both thinking and imagining make use of what has been previously experienced. It is also true that various psychological investigations have used the same tests both as tests of intelligence and as tests of imagination. The closeness of the relationship becomes even more apparent when we consider the kinds of abilities which have been thought of as intelligence. Spearman's (1927) classical theory of intelligence referred to the eduction of correlates—which involved making constructions from past experience; it referred also to the awareness of experience (though this aspect was rather neglected in subsequent discussions of his theory). Awareness of experience and construction from past experience are activities very closely related to imagining.

But in considering Spearman's theory we can note the rather important point that construction is not equated with creation of something new in the sense of something not previously existing: the construct made from the data need not be a creation in the sense of being an original, novel construction even although it is a new rearrangement of the data; thus, e.g. the question of finding the missing component of the analogy '*black:white* as *night*:?' means that the respondent has put together past knowledge in a new association to construct the appropriate fourth term, 'day', but has not produced something not previously thought of, something unexpected. In the case of genius, the relationships perceived or the construction from the data will be original, unique, unforeseen; but in many operations of intelligence in this sense the relationship or product is already known. The individual does construct—but in the majority of cases comes to the same end product as many others have done and will do. It is possible that a similar situation obtains in much imagining; the construction is new for the individual, and thus created by the individual; but it does not necessarily differ from constructions imagined by other individuals—except in the cases when unusual ability is at work.

In more recent discussions of intelligence, however, there has been considerable emphasis on the ability to give an unforeseen answer, to produce something new. At times, the word 'intelligence' has seemed too prosaic to describe creative thinking: and at this point many people find it more satisfactory to talk about imagination— especially in science, where they want to emphasise inventive ability, making new discoveries. Hence the ability described as 'scientific imagination'. Is it the same as the imagination with which we have been concerned?

It has of course now become a cliché to say that scientific discovery is not always a matter of methodical, logical construction; intuitive leaps from one point to another, flashes of insight, the perception of relationships between things previously thought of as separate— all these processes which have been commonly associated with imaginative ability are now commonly accepted as normal characteristics of scientific thought and discovery; and, as we saw earlier, a whole mythology has developed about some of the most noteworthy scientific discoveries made by imaginative or dream processes. More recent statements have however suggested that the process of scientific thought is a little more complex. Thus, in P. B. Medawar's

(1967) description, the scientific process 'consists of or makes use of a rapid alternation, a rapid interaction between an imaginative episode of thought and a critical episode of thought. In the imaginative process we form an opinion, we take a view, we frame a hypothesis, we make an informed guess, about what the truth might be. We invent a possible world or possible fragment of the world. We tell a story that might be a story about real life—and of course all this lies outside logic. But then we subject these imaginative conjectures to ruthless criticism to see if our imagined world corresponds to a first approximation to the real world'. And again: 'In science this critical process—the critical element of this twofold process—is normally an experimental one. . . .'

And further: 'What I think one can say is that the imaginative process as it occurs in science is very much like any other intuitive or inspirational process, as it occurs perhaps in the creation of a work of art . . . It is whole, it enters the mind suddenly, and it's the result of some process that goes on below the surface of the mind. But we know nothing at all of the internal circuitry.

'The line of demarcation between the imaginative and critical components of scientific thought isn't really as sharp as I've represented it to be. Some critical process must go on in the mind before a hypothesis is framed, because the hypotheses thought up by an experienced scientist are reasonable or plausible—they're not silly or far-fetched. So some censorship process must be at work before the hypothesis comes to the surface of the mind, and this built-in process of censorship is at least a part of what one means by "judgment" . . . Science is an exploratory process. It's an exploration guided by, given direction by, an imaginative preconception of what the truth might be; but the imaginative process is always under critical pressure, always under the threat of refutation.'

Accepting for the moment (though many would not) the view here given of artistic creative processes, we have various interesting points to note. There is, for instance, some confirmation of the view that the scientific mind does not readily defer judgment; that some kind of selective process goes to work before the imaginative theory is produced. This would support the views of Liam Hudson and others as to the lesser fluency of the scientific type of mind. But this is not necessarily an indication of less freedom in thinking; it may well be that in working with their material and data, a process of judgment is imposed on scientists—some far-fetched hypotheses are destroyed by elementary observation or by knowledge of what is possible with certain materials. (Admittedly in some cases such abandoning of a hypothesis can occur too soon—apparent limitations can be accepted too readily. But this is a common weakness of human thinking.) The limitation is possibly that referred to by Francis Bacon in *The Advancement of Learning*, talking of the non-scientific formulation of theories: 'For the wit and mind of man, if it work upon matter . . . worketh according to the stuff and is limited thereby; but if it works upon itself, as the spider worketh his web, then it is endless, and brings forth indeed cobwebs of learning, admirable for the fineness of thread and work, but of no substance or profit.' The spider may be highly creative—or at least fluent.

But the important point made by Medawar is this process of checking the imaginative theory. Medawar's analysis suggests the kind of checking process which we have already discussed in talking about role-playing situations and the use of imagination in planning. There is also a similarity to the check sometimes applied to memories —whether a remembered situation will fit in with other events which are known to have happened; or, in the case of the scientific theory, whether the hypothesis agrees with the properties of the material with which the scientist is working, and with what happens in reality if the theory is applied or acted on. In intelligent scientific thinking the checking process is an essential; in imagining it is by no means so—as we have noted, a great advantage of imagining is that it can disregard consequences. Thus we have an essential difference between the two activities. (It is only when imagination is to be used for rational planning, or to help understanding, that the checking process is essential.)

It is to be noted also that although this intuitive view tends to emphasise flashes of insight in scientific thought, imagining is not necessarily speedy; it can be a deliberately prolonged construction or a construction begun again and again, repeated for pleasure many times. Here also everyday imagining distinguishes itself from scientific thinking; the latter is directed towards some solution; in imagining the activity itself gives pleasure and satisfaction—it is the solution.

There is a further distinction between the two—and again, one which is amazingly frequently overlooked: Bronowski (1963) stated that: 'Reasoning is constructed with movable images just as certainly as poetry is. You may have been told, you may still have the feeling, that $E = mc^2$ is not an imaginative statement. If so, you are mistaken. The symbols in that master-equation of the twentieth century—the E for energy and m for mass and c for the speed of light—are images for absent things or concepts, of exactly the same kind as the words "tree" or "love" in a poem. The poet, John Keats, was not writing anything which (for him at least) was fundamentally different from an equation when he wrote

Beauty is truth, truth beauty—that is all
Ye know on earth, and all ye need to know.

There is no difference in the use of such words as "beauty" or "truth" in the poem, and such symbols as "energy" and "mass" in the equation ... Imagination is the manipulation inside the mind of absent things, by using in their place images or words or other symbols.'

But—apart from the use of the word 'images' here to express, presumably, something other than recalled sense impressions—this statement conceals a major difference. Words can and do refer to absent things or concepts; but words do more than simply bring these absent things or concepts into mind, or revive sense impressions; some words also produce emotional reactions. It depends, probably, on one's own background and training whether the word 'mass' arouses any kind of emotional feeling or even sensory images; for many people (taking it in a scientific though not in a religious context) it does not produce emotion; it is a statement of abstract fact. 'Energy' similarly (in a scientific context) does not normally rouse personal associations; 'beauty' may easily do so—'truth' is more doubtful. 'Love' is strongly associated with personal feelings; the emotion evoked depending on the state of one's affections at the time.

Thus there are the two major distinctions between scientific thinking and imagining; the first is that the scientific hypothesis is concerned with 'manipulating' elements which represent concepts but do not arouse emotions (apart from feelings of enthusiasm, curiosity perhaps) whereas the elements of imaginative constructions are chosen precisely for their emotion-provoking powers. The second is that if the scientific hypothesis is to survive it must, as we have noted, fit with observed events.

It is of course a matter of convention whether one describes scientific discovery as an instance of imagination; the use of the word has some justification. But if the word 'imagination' is used too widely there is a danger of forgetting that it applies especially to a distinctive kind of thinking and that this kind of thinking can play an important part in individual behaviour. If we focus on the encouragement of scientific discovery (and even of artistic creation) it is easier to overlook the much more important part of human experience which is devoted to the less spectacular but more common kind of imagining. And if, further, we give the impression that there is little difference between 'scientific imagination' and the other kind, we confuse people who want to find methods of education which will encourage the more common and important kind of imagining.

12

A rather similar distinction arises if one considers Guilford's (1964) analysis of intelligence. In some ways, intelligence described by his model including divergent production of relations, systems, transformations, with possible varieties of content (figural, semantic, symbolic) sounds very similar to imagination on some of the older definitions—producing from various units new combinations, transforming them, etc.; it even allows admirably for the inclusion of different types of imagination—creating new products with artistic content of various kinds, or scientific systems, or verbal constructions; and the divergence aspect fits well with older emphasis on the originality of the poet or other imaginative worker. Yet the model is cognitive—it does not (except possibly in references to 'unconscious development') include the stimulation of emotion and the use of emotion to form and enjoy the new structure.

Verbal ability and imagination

While imagination has been said to enter into creative work in all the arts, it has fairly generally been accepted that some kinds of artistic creation require other special aptitudes as well, and that these special aptitudes are unevenly distributed. But when it comes to artistic creation which uses words, there is a less clear distinction between people who have an unusual gift and the rest of the population. Creativeness through words seems one of the simplest forms; words are so accessible; they require little in the way of material —books are easily transported, they are sold in vast numbers of copies; the human voice can produce this kind of creation so quickly and easily. Consequently, the relationship between imagining and using words seems particularly close—at times, it seems as if creative work in verbal form requires simply verbal ability, rather than a special ability of imagination; whereas creative work in other forms clearly requires some other distinctive ability (musical, spatial) whether there is such an ability as imagination or not.

Words and imagining have been found closely associated. Many of the most imaginative people have had notably high verbal ability; and imaginative play in childhood seems to develop with the ability to use words. Imaginary companions are important when speech apparently becomes internalised. Sartre and others have claimed that words alone are enough when we are reading with enjoyment. Pre-sleep imagining is said (possibly because language is inadequate) to be a matter of 'setting oneself to sleep with tales'—i.e. with word cues. (Admittedly Miller, Galanter and Pribram (1960) suggest that in falling asleep we switch off inner speech; but there may be an intermediate stage in the use of this inner speech.)

It is consequently tempting to identify imagining with the development of verbal ability, especially if we accept the view propounded by Luria (1969) and others that the formation of programmes of behaviour is associated with the development of speech—that the child, by speaking aloud words which describe its actions, develops the central nervous system mechanisms which control conscious actions; that this speaking aloud of the words serves to internalise the appropriate concepts; it enables the child to acquire control of its actions and understanding of them. But the child, having discovered the use of words, and having acquired the ability to plan behaviour through them for practical purposes may then also discover the usefulness of words in producing responses in its own mind. In this way we should expect the child or adult with high ability in using words to have high ability in organising real behaviour—and also to have high ability in co-ordinating and evoking the resources of past experience in the mind to produce enjoyment in imagination.

In many cases this does seem to be what happens. But there is not always a close correspondence between verbal ability and imagination. As we have seen, there is some evidence that other kinds of impressions enter into imagining; imagery (of the various sensory modes) may not be essential or constant or complete, but it does seem frequently to be present. We have seen too that some people who cannot readily imagine when words alone are used, can do so when helped by other forms of experience—by seeing and hearing other cues. Further, there is the evidence of various researches that internal speech is incomplete; that when it exists it is not logically ordered, nor fully descriptive. So that ability in internal speech would seem at least to be different from skill in the deployment of a wide vocabulary or construction of sentences in proper and appropriate form. Imagining can proceed by other methods, even although for some individuals words are the most important cues and are much used, internally, in imagining.

Nevertheless, when it comes to controlled imagining, or to planning behaviour, verbal ability may be highly important. It is undoubtedly important when we are attempting to check the limits of individual experience or individual imagining by talking to other people, or when we are trying to enter, fully and imaginatively, into what they are trying to communicate about their experiences. (Though some degree of communication of experience by non-verbal methods is of course possible.)

But the association—or apparent association—between imagination and verbal ability frequently noted in the past does depend a great deal on the kinds of test that have been used. If the existence of a factor of imagination is investigated by tests which demand high verbal ability, it is not altogether surprising that the results indicate a verbal factor though possibly not an imagination factor; especially if, in marking the tests, credit has been given mainly for the number of words, or the originality of the words used. (On the other hand, if it is decided that appropriate tests of imagination are a mixture of tests requiring verbal ability and tests apparently requiring visual or spatial imagery, it is not altogether surprising that intercorrelations are low and the existence of an imagination factor again appears doubtful.) In any case, though verbal ability may play a large part in imaginative activity, it is clearly not identical with it: it may be important for imaginative work which is to be communicated to others: but not so essential in individual imagining.

Imagination and divergent thinking and creativity

The situation has become even more complicated in recent years since many of the tests formerly used for imagination or intelligence-testing now find their way into batteries of tests of 'creativity' or of convergent versus divergent thinking. Certainly in the past, when imagination has often been associated with the creation of original work, it would have been accepted that imaginative ability coincides with divergent thinking of some kind. It would seem therefore a favourable omen for the future education of imagination that in so many current writings there is considerable enthusiasm for divergent thinking and so little enthusiasm for convergent thinking: (we may even perceive a certain chilliness towards pupils who score highly in the kind of intelligence test said to measure the latter ability; which is a more doubtful omen.)

Let us consider briefly some of the attitudes towards the 'new' abilities, for this devaluation of convergence is interesting. Certainly one can sympathise with the belief that non-conformity is important; the prospect of a society composed of people who accept—unthinkingly—the same views on all matters is unattractive. It is a constant danger in human thinking that we may accept conditions as unalterable—assume that it is natural for large numbers of children to die in infancy, accept that childbirth has always been painful and always must be, etc. It is dangerous to society as well as to individuals if the child or adult who thinks differently, who proposes new solutions or has new ideas for making or using things, is ignored, discouraged or forced to conform. At the same time, some degree of convergence is necessary; language itself demands acceptance of conventions about the meaning and use of words— calling an object by a nonsense syllable popular in a small family circle will lead to a breakdown of communication with people outside the circle (even if language does slowly change). Two and two must be accepted as making four in some contexts, if not in all; if experience and experiment have led to a convergence of knowledge about the breaking point of materials (in a lift, for example) it is unwise to diverge. Communication and dealing with the physical environment do demand some degree of convergence.

But the strength of the emotional enthusiasm for divergence is interestingly shown in the amount of attention paid to Getzels and Jackson's investigation (1962), and especially in subsequent accounts of it, to the 'discrepant' cases—to the people said to be high on divergent ability or creativity but low on convergent, conventional intelligence tests. It is reasonable to be worried if children able to contribute new ideas and objects are likely to be neglected by the educational system and not given a chance to develop their abilities: but at least in theory the educational system tries to give all children a chance to develop their ability fully—it does not, in theory (and even in practice) devote its attention only to those doing well on tests of convergent thinking. In practice one has the impression that it is mainly the child who does well in school attainment who is most favoured (and certainly this may indicate the child willing to conform to some extent): yet Getzels and Jackson's work seemed to indicate that the 'discrepant' divergent-thinking children of their group did better in school attainment than would have been expected from their performance on conventional intelligence tests. This and other investigations certainly did not offer clear evidence that such a group was being neglected—only that they might be, if attention was given purely on the basis of conventional intelligence test results. Further, the attention given to this discrepant group seems to obscure the much larger numbers of children noted in other investigations whose scores were not discrepant; i.e. who made high scores on both types of test or low on both or moderate on both. It looks as if occasionally a reasonable desire to protect children's originality develops into a romantic protest about society's lack of appreciation for the unrecognised genius—without proof that the genius really is talented.

It is true that society, as represented by teachers, has seemed relatively unenthusiastic about some of these discrepant-divergent children—a point confirmed by Wallach and Kogan's (1966) findings as to the maladjusted behaviour in the classroom of some such children (though some high-intelligence high-creativity children also caused classroom problems). This reaction by teachers, if it is indeed found generally, need not necessarily be interpreted as an attempt to restrain creative and original thought. It is again a question of deciding when to defer judgment on comments or observations. If a group is working on, say, appreciation of poetry or prose, the 'off-beat' comment by the diverger can be of little or no value but may very effectively break up the interest and concentration of the group and destroy the atmosphere which the teacher has been at pains to create: if in other lessons the immediate purpose is to follow a logical sequence of arguments, to work out a satisfactory solution to a problem, then having to go up various blind alleys with the child who cannot inhibit such proposals or who has not bothered to consider them before voicing them, can be a frustrating waste of time. The teacher may make mistakes in discriminating between the enlightening and liberating divergence and the disturbing and silly deferred-judgment throw-in; but for those parts of the curriculum which include transmission of basic knowledge the teacher is probably right on many occasions. (It depends, of course—and this is inescapable—on the personality of the teacher; an extreme converger will frustrate even the highly intelligent divergent pupil; an extreme diverger will frustrate the whole class.) Creativity indeed is itself said to depend on a combination of convergence and divergence: Mackinnon (1962) emphasised that it must be 'adaptive to reality'.

The problem of the correct attitude for teachers as well as the problem of establishing the relationship between imagination and creativity is further complicated by the uncertainty which still exists as to whether ability on creativity tests and ability on conventional tests of intelligence really differ. Some researchers have suggested that there is in fact little divergence between creativity test scores and conventional tests; others that the two correspond generally but that at the higher end of the scale differences between divergers and convergers become more important. Thus Barron (1963) stated: 'Where the subject matter itself requires high intelligence for the mastery of its fundamentals, as in mathematics or physics, the correlation of measured intelligence with originality in problem-solving within the discipline tends to be positive but quite low. Among artists such as painters, sculptors, and designers, the correlation between rated quality of work and measured intelligence is zero or slightly negative. Again, however, it must be remembered the commitment to such endeavors is already selective for intelligence, so that the average I.Q. is already a superior one. I would suggest a generalization based not only on my own studies and those of my colleagues at the Institute . . . Over the total range of intelligence and creativity a low positive correlation, probably in the neighbourhood of ·40 obtains; beyond an I.Q. of about 120 however, measured intelligence is a negligible factor in creativity, and the motivational and stylistic variables upon which our own research has laid such stress are the major determiners of creativity.'

Much of the confusion as to the nature of 'creativity' has probably arisen because of the different selection of sub-tests; but a major problem does seem to be whether the ability to do well on the kind of sub-test usually claimed to measure 'creativity' is equivalent to the ability to be creative. Increasingly it is recognised that test performance of this kind is not in itself enough to predict important creativeness (as high scores on conventional intelligence tests are equally not enough for such prediction): motivation is essential. As Barron continued: 'Among these motivational variables must be included what I shall call simply "the moral attitude". One finds in creative writers a profound commitment to larger meanings of an aesthetic and philosophical sort. ...' And various studies (cf. Freeman, Butcher and Christie (1968)) have now begun to investigate the various personality factors which apparently determine creative performance, and the environmental conditions which may be associated with the development of this essential motivation.

So far as creativity as measured by test performance is concerned, we can note various points of contact with the ability of imagination as we have defined it so far. Fluency in using words and ideas is frequently required in creativity tests; as we have indicated, fluency seems to be associated with making constructions from past experience, recalling past experience readily: and this can be considered an aspect of imagination. Fluency similarly can influence the results of verbal tests of imagination—e.g. writing stories. But it is doubtful whether the kind of ability tested with visual stimuli— ink-blots, shape completion, etc.—is as relevant to imagination, though it may have some relationship to artistic creation (which has been claimed as a form of imaginative performance); it is however interesting that such tests seem often to show negative correlations with other kinds of creativity tests. Performance in tests like thinking of uses of objects could be related to scientific imagination.

There is certainly an important difference between creativity and imagining in the stress on both quantity and originality. Creativity tests tend to stress originality; imagination, as we have considered it, does not have to be original. There are many situations in life which are by no means original or unique but which are intensely important to the individual—in whose experience they *are* original, novel, unique: thus in imagining the imaginary situation need not be new—it may be a copy of someone else's experience (though with such individual touches as may be contributed by the individual's own past experience). Originality in imagining becomes an important factor only when communication is intended, when recognition of artistic merit, an audience for the creative work is sought: if creative work in the arts is to stimulate others and enrich their experience, originality is desirable. Imagination for individual enjoyment, or even for planning or dealing with real situations does not need this quality; though if novelty cannot be achieved by taking additional data from books, plays, etc. the individual's ability to produce original variants spontaneously would undoubtedly enhance the activity. Similarly with quantity; creativity tests set a premium on numbers of responses; but an enjoyable imaginary situation can be repeated with no variations or very slight ones; there is little need for a large, changing series of constructions, though these may sometimes be welcomed from outside sources. Thus, two qualities much emphasised in creativity tests—originality (or novelty) and fluency may be unimportant in imagining. Flexibility, however, is common to both activities.

The relationship with intelligence as measured by conventional tests may also be a point of difference; there is some indication of a correlation, even if a moderate or low correlation, between creativity test performance and intelligence test performance. As we saw earlier, there is no clear evidence of an association of imaginative ability with conventional intelligence test performance; there may certainly be some link through the verbal factor; but the distribution of imagination does not necessarily follow that of conventional intelligence test ability—or creativity test ability. This is, however, a point on which certainty is impossible since, as we have recognised, there is at present no reliable indication of the frequency and quality of imagining in the population generally.

The growth of interest in the motivational factors associated with creativity or with creative work may cast light on some of the emotional aspects which are so often omitted or overlooked in research dependent on tests. The study of behaviour, of observers' assessments, of self-assessments and self-reports, may lead to much greater knowledge of the essential activity of imagining as well as of creative production. Wallach and Kogan (1966) indicated that they found symptoms of withdrawal in their high-creativity-low-intelligence group; this might well be compatible with refuge in imagining, with avoidance of what was going on in an unsatisfactory classroom situation; yet in other cases, high creativity scorers have been a nuisance in the classroom situation because of extrovert behaviour— which would scarcely seem necessary if they had the available refuge of imagining. Again, Wallach and Kogan expressed concern that the high-creativity-high-intelligence group were valued in the classroom situation more for their intelligence than their creativity; if creative activity is not allowed scope there, one would expect concentration on imaginative pursuits out of school—or day-dreaming in the classroom situation, with high intelligence available to avoid the consequences and enable the pupil to retain the teacher's approval: further evidence on such points would be valuable.

Another interesting point in creativity studies is that some have suggested a sex difference, boys being more 'creative'. In studies of imaginative behaviour girls and women have often appeared to be more imaginative than boys and men; and yet there is a fairly wide-spread belief—indeed there is evidence—that girls and women are more conformist in their behaviour. This again may suggest a distinction between imagining and creativity. Wallach and Kogan's work suggested that there may be important differences in anxiety and defensiveness when boys and girls are compared, and that this could account for the different reactions of boys and girls, especially in the high-creativity-low-intelligence groups. The same work indicated that part of the differences observed (differences in assessments of classroom behaviour) might also be due to the different cultural expectations of boys' and girls' behaviour in the classroom; and that the boys find a more straightforward situation, giving more scope for the expression of unrest.

In all, if we take imagination as an activity discovered and enjoyed by many individuals mainly for its emotional appeal it differs in various ways from the kind of activities discussed under the title of creativity or regarded as divergent thinking; at the same time there are several ways in which the same kind of ability could affect performance in tests of creativity or of intelligence (conventional or less convergent) and success in imagining.

Imagining and thinking

Imagination has some possible relationships with creativity and is also possibly linked to intelligence, verbal ability and inner speech; it is also closely related to memory. Can we therefore reasonably think of it as a specific ability or activity? Or is it simply an aspect of normal thinking? When we imagine—are we simply thinking?

It is true that the ordinary kind of imagining would seem to enter into a great deal of our thinking. Partial or incomplete images, the appearance of sensory images—these are processes common to both thinking and imagining. References to what we remember, to what we recall of past experiences—these too are a part of normal thought.

When it comes to planning, similarly, we may try to foresee a situation as realistically as possible—and so we perhaps imagine it; even in thinking about our programme for the day we may anticipate clearly, and so find ourselves imagining what we will be experiencing later; or, thinking back over the day's activity, we may re-live it, with perhaps some alterations and quite notable emotional responses. And at any time, if we are not concentrating on our actual activity we may find ourselves moving into a day-dream, imperceptibly, and returning just as smoothly and naturally to the former train of thought. Indeed so far as our thinking is conducted by internal speech it may be called imaginative, since speech supposes an audience, and even if this audience is only very vaguely present to our awareness there is some degree of feedback—some emotional atmosphere is created by the imagined attitude of this hearer, who may well be ourselves or part of ourselves. Miller, Galanter and Pribram (1960) put this view at its extreme: 'Suppose that under ordinary conditions a waking person is constantly constructing and revising more or less coherent Plans for his own behavior. Suppose that some of these Plans are visualized, some are felt kinesthetically, etc., but the more elaborate voluntary Plans involve a self-conscious exploitation of language. Inner speech is the kind of stuff our wills are made of. When we will to do something, we may imagine doing it and we repeat our verbal command to ourselves, subvocally, as we concentrate on the task. It is a familiar fact, emphasised by nearly all behavioristic psychologists since J. B. Watson that most of our planned activity is represented subjectively as listening to ourselves talk.' Granted, there are limitations on the amount and coherence of such inner speech (as many investigators have noted): but quite a lot of thinking, for many people, does seem to be conducted in this way, especially in planning. Or we may 'think things out' by mentally explaining them to someone else—an imaginary companion (whether the original is real, contemporary, historical or fictional). (Though there are also awareness states, thoughts which move much too quickly into and out of consciousness to be expressed in words.) In our thinking then there is a great deal that can be described as imagining; and the use of language, the effort to understand other people's communications, may demand imaginative effort—re-experiencing what we are trying to say ourselves, calling up our own past experience and reconstructing it in order to understand fully what someone else is relating.

Is the identity complete? Can we say that all thinking is imagining? Or that all imagining is thinking? There is a lot to be said for either form of the statement of identity; yet most people would reject both statements. We can distinguish. Admittedly it is difficult at some points to decide whether we are thinking out a plan or enjoying an imaginary conversation, but we can usually tell—if we think (not imagine) about it—whether our activity is realistic, referring to actual conditions and events, or imaginative. We can take a conscious decision to imagine or to think rationally or intelligently; we can, e.g. take the decision to devote our attention to imagining by beginning to watch a play or read a work of fiction; we can decide to think rationally or intelligently by settling down with a non-fictional book or the elements of a problem (even if concentration on the thinking activity may for many people be harder to prolong than concentration on the imaginative; and even if some rational thought enters into the fiction and some imagining into the non-fictional situation).

To some extent it is a matter of arbitrary and individual choice, which word we use for these various activities. The use of the terms 'imagining', 'thinking rationally', 'thinking intelligently', or 'creative thinking' implies a greater separateness and exclusiveness than are found in normal human consciousness. Normally we experience a rapid, mixed sequence of what are inadequately described as sense perceptions, emotions, concepts, memory traces in the form of, or interspersed with images, inner speech, 'states of awareness'. It is by taking a kind of time sample of this process, by knowing very approximately the frequency of some such occurrences as compared with the frequency of others during a given period, by knowing that we have been making an effort to increase one frequency and decrease others that we decide which word to use to describe the process. Thus when we claim to be 'thinking rationally' or 'thinking intelligently' we are probably trying to ignore emotional reactions, to exclude present sense impressions, to keep attention focused only on those memory items which are relevant to the topic, to recall relevant information and form concepts which are in accordance with reality and will be so recognised by competent people. But during the process of this 'rational thinking' we do continue to experience the other processes to some extent; and their frequency may increase to the point where we recognise that we are no longer 'thinking'; or we may attend intermittently to other reactions, experience briefly emotions of despair, triumph or aggression, be aware of sense impressions—move to a more comfortable position—or recall information on some other topic and decide to act on it. Similarly when we are 'imagining' we may interrupt the imaginary situation by real action—switch off some machine, fill a kettle, recognise that it is time to leave to catch a train; or we may change the imaginary construction because it has occurred to us that it conflicts with an objective fact which has just come to mind—we may even check whether it is in accordance with such facts. In creative work similarly, when an idea or emotion or impression is to be communicated to other people or given perceptible form, attention is focused on the use of the medium, the way in which the communication is taking shape—in some creative artists the mastery of the medium may be so great that this attention can be shared with strong emotional reactions; in others, emotion may be less, or may intermittently relate to the foreseen reception of the created work rather than to the theme itself; there may be moments of desisting from the creative activity to return to the original concept; here also a mixture of other impressions can be intertwined with the dominating activity. The differences thus are differences of frequency and choice of dominant reaction, choice of focus of attention. Such choices cannot be totally exclusive nor indeed long maintained by the great majority of human beings. (Individual differences in excluding other reactions can be a source of irritation—the lack of attention to 'practical details' of the creative artist; the lover who is aggrieved to find that in moments of passion a partner can still note the chiming of a clock and make a quick readjustment of future plans accordingly.) Referring to differences in frequency and choice of conscious processes by distinctive words is however a convenient way of indicating a real if loosely defined difference in experience; though at any time we may mingle the various activities, move from one to the other and back again, or combine them. At times, there may be no conscious choice of process, the alternations may be so frequent, that we would not refer to our state as being one or other of the activities; it is when a sustained choice of activity is made or perceived that we normally use the distinctive word.

Similarly emotions experienced during the processes described by the terms of 'thinking intelligently', 'thinking rationally', 'thinking creatively', 'imagining' differ apparently not in kind but in duration and strength. Imagining cultivates emotional responses, repeats them, has them as an aim; but emotions aroused by imaginary situations can to some extent be switched off (though not always) when attention is called back to, or returns to real circumstances, while emotion provoked by actual circumstances is dependent on other people's reactions or on objective external circumstances—that is, the stimulation and duration of the emotion are then less under the control of the individual. In rational or intelligent thinking emotion tends to be cut out; it is often irrelevant to the data considered, even if it appears intermittently in the thinker's consciousness; though some intelligent thinking may call for deliberate attention to emotional implications, to imagining them. In creative artistic work the aim is not the creation or enjoyment of emotions within the individual alone but expression and production—though individual emotion may inspire, accompany and result from the creation. Again, emotional states may be determined not exclusively by any one activity but by a sequence of different activities.

These are obviously speculative considerations; yet considering popular usage and many analyses of thought processes we can take it that differentiations are made and reasonably made between these various kinds of experience. Confusion arises because we do not always make these differentiations consistently—we use words to describe activities which differ in dominant qualities but also have common elements; we then at some times emphasise what they have in common (using the words interchangeably) and forget the differences—forget the need for appropriate forms and skill in artistic creation, the need to satisfy objective conditions in scientific creations; we overlook the fact that popular assessments can exaggerate differences, create differences of quality where there are simply differences of quantity. Further, when our attention is rightly claimed by the perceptible products of intelligent scientific thinking or artistic work it is easy to overlook the imaginative thinking—the creation of imaginary situations, the emotional response to these—which occurs in normal experience but is not perceptible; we imagine so much that we tend not to notice that we do so. Thus we begin to reserve the word 'imagination' to describe special kinds of imagining combined with other activities, applying it to producing artistic, scientific, original results and communicating them to others; or we take it so much for granted that it seems the same as normal consciousness, normal 'thinking', not worth distinguishing.

In human experience, imagining is distinguishable from the related kinds of conscious behaviour which we have been considering. Individuals differ in their conscious control, their enjoyment of it, the frequency with which they imagine systematically, their ability to respond to other people's imaginative constructions. But the construction of imaginary situations (more or less lengthy and complex), emotional responses to them, shaping them to produce the desired emotional result is a much more universal, much more pervasive activity than creating products to be shown to or used by others. We are not all artists, scientists, great thinkers; but we all (probably all) to some extent imagine. Education, therefore, while reasonably concerned about developing the creative abilities linked to imagining and the skills by which imagining can sometimes be expressed, while concerned with fostering scientific ability and intelligent rational thinking, has also to be concerned with this wider general activity and its development, to some extent at least, for the benefit of the individual in relationships with other individuals.

Chapter 8

Education and imagination

Now that we have reviewed various aspects of imagination can we arrive at conclusions as to what education should do about it? In some important aspects the evidence is inclusive; some of the most interesting examples of imagining occur independently of school education, and there is little or no controlled experimental evidence about this kind of activity. Nevertheless there are some conclusions which we can reach and some ways in which education might encourage a better use of imagination—ways, that is, by which education might try not simply to increase artistic or scientific production but to encourage use of the general activity of imagining for socially valuable purposes. In considering this project for education we have to realise the uncertainties of present knowledge, the precise aims of educating imagination, and so arrive at the methods likely to be effective.

First, what are the areas of uncertainty? We do not know (1) whether every child can imagine and to what extent imaginative ability can be improved: (2) we do not know whether there is a real sex difference in imagining: (3) we do not know to what extent attitudes and standards of value are permanently affected by imaginary situations.

What effect do these uncertainties have on educational policies?

Individual differences

Let us consider this problem of individual differences in ability to imagine. Clearly, imagining is spontaneous in some people; many children use it freely, without any conscious direction from outside and without any instruction in technique; they transform what is available to them from their own experience. Admittedly, many of these children may be greatly influenced by encouragement from parents or other people who tell them imaginative stories, approve of their attempts at imaginative play. Even so, a great deal of use of imagination is made independently, privately; the amount of time spent in reading or watching television does not by any means show its full extent. But from the evidence of children's play it seems that some children do not spontaneously imagine in this way; and from observation of adult behaviour it is clear that some individuals do not feel any attraction in the usual kinds of imaginative stimulus—they prefer to talk to people, to be active in some other way, rather than read or watch plays on television or on the cinema screen. (Even among adults who read there is a difference between those who enjoy fiction and those who read it little if at all.) Consequently there seem to be great differences in the amount of emotional satisfaction which people seek and obtain through imaginary situations presented in these ways. Yet it is clear that everyone does remember, and that most people can think of some kinds of hypothetical situation (though with what degree of realism is uncertain): it therefore seems likely (though not proven) that some ability to imagine is present in everyone, that the general activity of imagining is universal, though more cultivated by some people than by others: and possibly more easy to cultivate in some than in others.

Attempts made in schools to increase imaginative activity and improve imaginative powers do not as yet seem to have achieved spectacular results—though schools differ in achievement here. Lack of success may often be due to the use of methods not ideally adapted to the purpose and lacking in appeal to those being taught— some pupils see no point in the cultivation of literary skill in 'imaginative' essays, or appreciation of unfamiliar situations or sensations. Some undoubtedly go through school remaining impervious to the attractions of fiction and poetry; more seriously, some apparently remain unable to enter into the feelings of other human beings sympathetically, though even they may engage in day-dreams of their own success or enjoyment. Where methods have been tried which give more help to a weak imagination—where situations are well acted or where role-playing and discussion are well used, there does seem to be improvement in perception of the situations and of how other people may feel in them; to this extent imagining has been improved. But we still do not know whether there is then a general transfer to other situations, whether the technique will be used widely; and if it is generalised, whether it will work for other situations and eventually lead to wider enjoyment of the imaginary situations found in books or elsewhere.

It is also unclear how many people systematically enjoy imagining; to what extent some abandon the habit as they grow older, and divert their attention to more real activities; and to what extent people who outwardly would not be considered imaginative are in fact devoting a great deal of their thinking to this kind of construction. The quality of individual imagining remains equally undetermined; it is obvious from the sales of various books and from the popularity of various films and plays that the range or type of imaginative experience most sought after may not be what the educator would wish. Thus on the one hand the immense popularity of fiction—and for this one has only to look at the growing provision of paperbacks, and the huge audiences for various programmes, films and plays—makes it clear how eager people are to enjoy imagining; while on the other hand, the level of situation provided, the monotony of themes emphasised, raise some doubts as to the quality and vividness of the activity. Certainly emotional satisfaction does not seem to depend on the originality or the complexity of what is offered (though it is true that even the most hackneyed cheap stories may contain their own minor variations); nor does the fluency or even the vividness of what is offered seem great enough to attract such enthusiasm. (Since one characteristic of some of the cheaper forms of literature is the flatness of the writing, the inadequacy with which the situations seem to be presented, we are left wondering whether the readers of these have unusually powerful imaginative ability which can make good the deficiencies of the writing, or whether they merely react strongly to a few very simple cues and ignore the rest. Or whether, possibly, they read on doggedly, unaware that other literature would offer much greater nourishment for their questing imagination.) The flood of fictional writing is astounding: it seems to show an insatiability of demand for the stimulation of imagination, which is all the more remarkable when we simultaneously remember that in so many homes no books are read (though these homes in our country now, presumably, receive some imaginative material through the increasingly omnipresent television set).

It is true that not all reading of fiction is necessarily a quest for emotional satisfaction. Yet if the quest is simply for knowledge of other human beings and other kinds of human experience there are other sources—factual studies in anthropology, history, biographies, psychological and sociological studies (all possibly fictional to some extent at some time) which would provide more reliable data about more people and more varieties of human existence; whereas the fictional source presents—as we have argued earlier—only one view; though it may give a greater depth of information about that one. On the whole, the enthusiasm for fiction does not seem motivated by the search for knowledge.

We are thus uncertain about the frequency and quality of the spontaneous use of imagination by the majority of people: but we can still decide what we want to achieve. We may not know how much success can be expected from the education of imagination, but we can try to use effectively the methods which seem likely to be appropriate.

Sex differences in imagining

Similarly, we do not know whether there is a real sex difference in imagining. If we consider everyday imagining rather than artistic or scientific creation, there are grounds for supposing that girls and women are more likely to practise it than boys and men. Various investigations show a greater frequency of occurrence of imaginative activities among girls; in school work girls' essays are often more fluent—the novel, which is the art-form most closely related to such writing, is the one field of artistic creation in which large numbers of women have achieved success (though one cannot say more success than men); in childhood, there is possibly a greater frequency of imaginary companions for girls. There is also the earlier development of language in girls and relatively greater skill in using language, and language ability may be importantly related to imagining. Women are also said to be more interested than men in human relationships, which again would suggest a greater readiness to enjoy imaginary situations exploring these relationships—but there is clearly considerable overlap in sex interests here, as in other skills and interests. However, there have been investigations where a sex difference in imagination has not been found; when it comes to essay writing, a great deal depends on the subject given; and verbal fluency may not be as closely related as we have assumed to imagining ability.

Even if there is a sex difference in performance in tests closely related to everyday imagining, and even if there is a sex difference in everyday imagining, it would not necessarily follow that there is a biologically determined difference. The evidence relating to imaginary companions, and to day-dreaming or pre-sleep imagining, suggests that external conditions considerably affect individual interest in imagining. Where outside interest is absent or where external conditions are unsatisfactory, day-dreaming or imagining of a more systematic kind is likely: where there is not an outlet for enjoyable activity, recourse to imaginary living becomes more attractive. The way of life offered to girls and women in some social groups may still mean that they are more likely to suffer from dissatisfaction with the immediate environment. Routine household work, carried out in solitude—or even in the company of young children, whose conversation does not necessarily provide intellectual stimulation—probably provides ideal circumstances for imagining, since it may make few demands on thought and be not very rewarding in itself. (There are of course many occupations followed by men which are equally routine, and which make equally few demands on thought or attention. But they are perhaps more often carried out in company.) Of course in some societies and social groups the amount of hard physical labour required of women may be such that they are too exhausted to enjoy simultaneously any imaginary activity. At present in our own society it is less likely that girls will be kept to a more restricted round of activities than boys; our schools probably offer equal opportunities; but there is still a lingering tradition that girls spend more time in or near the home, in quieter occupations or in routine housework.

To discover whether there is a sex difference and if so, whether it is due to social conditioning, requires considerably more research and cross-cultural studies. From the point of view of education, the results would be important not so much for aims as for method. Educators would presumably hope to achieve the same results for boys and girls, whether both sexes begin with the same initial handicaps or advantages or not. But if boys in fact are less likely to enjoy imaginary activities than girls are, more specific methods of supplementing their imagination are needed—more appeal to films, dramas, more nearly realistic situations. If women are more imaginative than men, their treatment of subjects taught in school—indeed their choice of emphasis in teaching a subject and their expectation of pupils' response—will be different. (Some sex differences in choice of subjects and methods of teaching have been found—e.g. Shanks (1964)—though there is evidence of considerable similarity in the average approach by both men and women.) All this could be a further argument for co-educational schools, or at least for mixed staffing of all schools, so that the benefits of teaching by people with different approaches to imagination may be enjoyed by both boys and girls.

Effects of imagining

Thirdly, there is the problem of the effect of imagining on other aspects of behaviour and personality. Living in imaginary situations obviously has created personality problems for some people or has, in some cases, arisen from such problems. The individual who prefers an imagined situation to the real situation is not likely to get on well with others, to make and retain many friends (assuming normal conditions); though some people manage to combine quite successfully intense enjoyment of imaginary situations and reasonable adjustment to ordinary life. (There are of course some circumstances in which refuge in imagined situations is the most satisfying and even the most useful way of dealing with harsh reality.) But a child should not be forced into preferring the imaginary situation because of loneliness, lack of occupation and lack of sympathy in the surrounding world; yet we cannot ensure a sympathetic home or neighbourhood environment for every child.

It also seems probable that some attitudes and values are derived from imaginative experiences presented by books, plays, stories: but the exact effect of these on behaviour is one of the points on which evidence is uncertain. A great deal depends on whether the same values and attitudes are consistently presented in these situations, and in many cases this will not happen; e.g. a play showing a given racial group in an unfavourable light one evening may well be cancelled in its effects by one showing them more favourably the following evening—unless the society as a whole is determinedly prejudiced; in which case the attitudes in question will have been firmly transmitted by real life situations already. Further, the effects of these imaginary experiences may be cancelled out by real life experiences—the latter have priority in establishing attitudes; so attitudes derived from imaginary situations may be obliterated by attitudes more effectively transmitted by the immediate group—by friends, the neighbourhood; the imaginary situation has less reality than these, and so has less chance of implanting an attitude. What may be more influential are more subtle attitudes and values, not clearly defined or contradicted in real situations; information about ways of behaving, casually acquired as part of the fictional situation; an impression of inevitably happy endings; identification with a central character, a hero who will survive and who deserves to prosper; belief in a comprehensible pattern to human experience; belief that the virtuous tend to be rather stupid or at least dull.

The vexed question of the contribution of imaginative stimulation to delinquency is not clearly answered. Large-scale surveys in different parts of the world have failed to prove that seeing undesirable behaviour on television or at the cinema develops delinquency in people who would otherwise remain normal well-adjusted members of society. It also seems true that the existence of these forms of enjoyment provides an attraction for people who are not well-adjusted to their real existence, and this may become for them an addiction. But the evidence suggests that this excess of attention to imaginary enjoyment is a symptom rather than a cause of delinquency and maladjustment. Certainly techniques of delinquency may be assimilated from such sources; but motivation comes from other sources. Yet many members of the general public and even of the teaching profession show strong resistance to believing this. Possibly it is a kind of indirect expression of their own shock or repugnance at the sight of violence or crime. Possibly it is a kind of evasion. It seems simpler to prevent people from going to the cinema or watching television, it seems—oddly enough—simpler to ban some films and some plays, than to cope with the complex factors which combine to produce anti-social behaviour. But such behaviour has existed where the stimulus of television and cinema was non-existent (though quantitative comparisons between different eras and societies are unfortunately too complex to make). But while there is uncertainty in this respect there are some conditions about which there is no uncertainty; over-crowded homes, parental apathy, bad schools, ill health. If these conditions were attacked with as much vehemence as occasional films and plays there might be further progress in removing them, and we could discover then whether the remaining imaginative stimuli have a large or small or negligible effect.

It should in any case be more widely recognised that the level of satisfaction offered by imagination is essentially less than that offered by real experience; greater satisfaction can be given by the real people in the child's environment or the adult's environment; these people control the standards of behaviour of the individual and are—initially at least—the most important in the individual's life. Attempts to reduce maladjustment and delinquency should therefore centre on these factors rather than on the fringe circumstances of television, cinema, books. It may of course be argued that to lessen even a little the influence of an adverse factor would be good; but treating a symptom usually means that others come in its place. To impose general censorship, to limit viewing or reading, would be socially unpopular, restrict everyone's freedom—and probably be unworkable in our society. And all this would be for the sake of a result which is not at all confidently to be predicted. (Parents of young children may however feel more competent to censor and more justified in doing so. But for them, as for society at large, the best method seems to be the provision of more attractive alternatives rather than arbitrary deprivation.)

Looking then at these three areas of uncertainty we can conclude that they do not prevent educational attempts at encouraging the use of imagination in ways which parents or teachers, after due thought, consider desirable. Fuller information, more conclusive evidence would be helpful in developing methods; but unless later evidence runs contrary to the partial evidence so far obtained, it does not suggest that imaginative activities should be excluded or suppressed; rather that there should be discrimination among them.

Defining objectives

What kind of imaginative activity is to be encouraged? We have emphasised that in individual experience the most important is the pervasive imagination for emotional satisfaction, imagination as the construction of unreal situations; but education is of course concerned about other uses for it and concerned about other activities sometimes described as imaginative—scientific imagination, invention, artistic creation. Some methods appear to have the admirable quality of providing conditions in which all these kinds of activity are apparently favoured; but there are some methods to be avoided, or at least to be recognised as probably unproductive, and some aims which are unrealistic.

There is, for example, the method of image formation, the aim of encouraging the habit of forming clear images; as we have seen, though it is interesting and attractive, it does not really seem conducive to worth-while development of abilities. There is, further, the possibility of cultivating 'creativity' as defined in contemporary tests. But again, as we have noted, present studies in creativity do not offer real guidance to the teacher; it would be sad to begin practising exercises of the test type before the existence and validity of the ability said to be measured by the tests have been established; and before proof is available that such practice would improve any kind of important performance. It is certainly interesting to discover that pupils of one school do better than pupils of another on creativity tests (as in Haddon and Lytton's (1968) study of primary schools' approaches), but the evidence for the tests' value is not yet strong enough to lead to the conclusion that the one school is therefore giving its pupils a better education than the other. (It may be doing so; but creativity test results are not yet a reliable criterion.)

Further, although education should certainly try to develop the creative abilities of all pupils, whether in imaginative creation or intellectual or practical creation, we must be aware of the difference between creating something for individual enjoyment and creating something which is to be communicated to others or offered to them. In the latter case, originality is important; other people want something new and preferably better, something to add to the variety of their experience. But for individual enjoyment there is no particular need for originality; the most commonplace theme can be emotionally enjoyed. Granted, new twists to the plot are agreeable; but there is no need to be a creator in the sense of producing something that has not been seen or heard of before. It is indeed the difference between making an apple-pie and making a work of art. The former is a creative activity; it transforms the basic ingredients; it gives (well carried out) considerable satisfaction—but it does not astonish the people who enjoy it or make them salute the creative ability of the baker. (Even so, it probably has some individual characteristics or novelties—the amount of clove flavouring, the twist of the ornamentation, if any; but it is not really the sort of thing to be expected of someone scoring high on creativity tests.) Yet it does give the individual the emotional satisfaction of making something, and it is highly enjoyable, even if someone else's recipe is being followed. (And one has to recognise that a lot of minor work in crafts and arts is on much the same level—especially as more and more people take up painting, pottery, poetry.) Further, we must recognise the level of creative ability (or of practice in trying to create) which does not reach originality, but helps to make individuals appreciate others' work.

Schools then should be clear about their expectations; original work worthy of presentation to a wider audience is probably not going to be frequent (after all, there is a point at which the audience becomes satiated). It is unwise to try to encourage efforts at this kind of work by people who clearly do not want to attempt it and have not the ability to do so; but it is reasonable to give scope for creating what is new to the individual and satisfying to the individual—and of course essential to give scope to the truly gifted. Generally we can recognise and admire the occasional good line in children's verse-writing without rushing to publish a class anthology; and without fretting that not all the pupils write the kind of thing appearing in so many published anthologies.

Similarly with scientific creation or scientific imagination. Again, certainly, education should give scope for original work and the development of unusual individual talent; but without expecting all pupils to be capable of original discovery or anxious to work constantly in a creative way.

What should be cultivated in all pupils is the ability to use imagination in dealing with other people and in planning for future activities: and this is by no means easy—to form the habit of controlling and using constructively a kind of thinking which naturally tends to be used only for emotional relief or enjoyment.

Methods

Assuming then that educators know what kinds of creative ability or ordinary imagination are to be cultivated, what positive action can be taken at present?

One which tends to be overlooked is encouragement of the self-discipline and discrimination essential to creating anything of value; to acquire these, there must be practice in handling the raw materials of creative work, especially in the arts and sciences—handling leading to intelligent recognition of the qualities of the material. Similarly with the more ordinary use of imagination; if imagination is to be creatively or valuably used, experimental work on role-playing, simulation techniques, etc., suggests the need for some addition of intelligent control. This control applies to the selection of data; if imagination is to be constructive in science or in human relations, data must be accurate and relevant. Control applies also to the construction or the solution: these must be checked against what is intelligently known about the qualities of the data or the normal course of events. In some cases this intelligent control, this selection of data and checking process can come from outside—whether from a therapist, parent, director or teacher or from members of the group; in other cases it can come from inside, from the individual's own reflection on what has been imagined, from reference to past experience; and this control can lead to rejection of solutions and qualities which, though tempting, are clearly not valid. So that, assuming that in other respects scientific imagination and ordinary imagining may have something in common, they certainly do have in common this need for control by the exercise of intelligence: and, as usual, the school has the task of encouraging this precision without discouraging enthusiasm.

Experience and realism

Very clearly, if such checking is to occur, basic experience is needed. All kinds of imagining and creating need the raw material for construction. These materials need not always be first-hand experience; as we have noted, children, especially those with high verbal ability, can build on what they learn through books or other reports. But there is a danger that what is acquired indirectly may be inaccurate and misleading; the advantages of first-hand experience, especially in the early stages, are considerable; and where pure first-hand experience is not possible, experience as close to the real thing as possible should be provided. Verbal description can be supplemented by sight, sound or touch; similar, if less exacting experience can at times be organised. The range and variety of real experience clearly set limits to the scope of imagining: and skill in creating, accuracy in scientific judgment, are more likely to develop during long periods of work with the appropriate materials and concepts than to spring into existence on a minor and superficial acquaintance. Thus the first line of action is the provision of wide first-hand experience. This indeed is already generally advocated in schools for a variety of reasons. It is recognised that the chances of learning, remembering, understanding are greater if the child is able to experience situations rather than read about them or be told about them; if the child is able to examine material, play with it, experiment with it rather than work initially with words or abstract symbols representing it, cognitive learning is favoured. In the teaching of various subjects more and more effort is being made to let children acquire this kind of experience, to visit their own neighbourhood and others, to see different occupations, to talk to people, to discover how public services function. This kind of activity not only lays the foundation for better understanding of civics, occupations, town planning, it also gives the data from which imaginary situations can be better constructed. Similarly by studying plants, rocks, other natural phenomena, by school visits abroad, children acquire not only knowledge but the necessary relevant, accurate data for future constructions and interpretations.

There has in fact been—as often before, but it seems recurrently necessary—a move towards greater realism in education; it is admirable that the more realistic education is, the more it can help imaginative ability and enrich imagining. Only those who have not thought clearly about imagining deplore the probability that in future children are more likely to be able to recall some of the real experiences to which poetic or other verbal descriptions refer instead of struggling to imagine: that children will no longer be in such incredible positions as being asked to appreciate lyrical references to a snowflake when they have never seen, touched, felt, stared at falling snow, or to imagine the terrors of storms at sea when they live far from the coast and have known such storms only through words. Charming as some of the naïve interpretations may be that children construct when inadequately informed, it really is rather pointless to force on them the making of guesses which are bound to be inaccurate. There is of course the protest that their imagination might somehow atrophy if not used in this way; but if imagining is merely making inaccurate guesses and forming misleading concepts, it is scarcely worth while preserving it. It is improbable in any case that human beings could ever have no need to use imagination, to go beyond actual experience, or that they could lose the habit of forming new constructions. Real imagination is highly unlikely to die out through want of stimulation.

This realism in teaching method is especially desirable when it gives more first-hand experience to children whose home background has been greatly limited, so that they have missed even the opportunities of the average child to acquire extensive knowledge of the properties of the world about them; children who do not have play materials, and who do not travel beyond a few streets. If schools enlarge the experience of these children they are—apart from the obvious benefit of enabling them to enjoy life and education—also giving them greater possibilities of enjoying imaginative experiences. (And this ultimately might provide the missing evidence on the question of the extent to which imaginative behaviour depends on cultural environment.)

Education in using words

It does not follow that in giving children more and more opportunity to see, touch, work with materials, schools should give less attention than before to improving children's ability to use words. Methods here also may change; but using words remains of primary importance. For one thing, it has been clearly shown that words are helpful and at times essential if what is seen—e.g. in a film—is to be fully understood; visual impressions without words can sometimes convey nothing; visits which are not discussed may be fun at the time but quickly forgotten, and the knowledge that might have been gained from them can vanish rapidly. Words used in talking about an activity or visit lead to improvement in vocabulary and also—since other people probably contribute their impressions also in words—lead to noticing what the individual might have overlooked; they can at times lead to realising misinterpretations an individual has made. Words too are a particularly useful device for more efficient storing of what has been learned; they increase freedom to work with concepts and they are an admirably succinct way of recalling a variety of past data. Where imagination is concerned, it has seemed probable that children with high verbal ability are particularly good at profiting from other people's experience as conveyed by writing (though also liable to being misled by other people's mistaken views or by inadequate comprehension); more skill in word-using might help. It would indeed improve so much the smooth running of society if more people understood what is conveyed by words; if they could progress beyond partial understanding of, and partial attention to what is said; and if they could interpret words in terms of the human situations to which they refer, behaviour might be more helpful generally—there might even be less maddening inefficiency of the kind produced by simple failure to communicate.

It is also by using words in group discussions that imaginative situations can sometimes be better appreciated; individual points of view are balanced by discovery of other people's reactions; general standards of behaviour, value judgments can be formulated. (This implies enough verbal ability on the part of the teacher to see where the discussion is going and to distinguish the occasions when the wrong conclusion is being reached because words are being used carelessly, misleadingly, emotively.)

A major task of education is to prevent the misuse of words, especially in the propaganda widespread in the modern world; to make more people able to recognise when words are evoking an imaginative, unreal situation (in advertisement, in political argument) which does not stand up to rational checking and does not fit into the real course of events. The essential control of imaginative activity which we have emphasised must often come through the use of words.

At the same time the deficiencies of words have to be recognised. They act as a set of signals, but only by a process of abstraction which may cut out some of the important parts of the things for which they stand. They do—as Francis Bacon (*Novum Organum*) and others have pointed out—create an environment which does not completely correspond to reality; they provide the stage setting in which we plan; and this can be as unrealistic as even the most realistic stage scenery is bound to be. To some extent, communicating with other people lessens the dangers of words; the individual's own overtones, the individual's freedom to manipulate words are necessarily limited by the reactions of other people. But there are also possibilities—as Plato and other Athenians discovered and pointed out—of intoxication by words in a group situation; it may be precisely those who are most skilful in using words who are most likely sometimes to move entirely on the verbal plane and forget important aspects of the real situations to which words refer. This is where the checking process is necessary; where it is necessary to recognise the emotional components, if they are the element left out by verbal descriptions, or to recognise when factual components are being omitted because words are being devoted to the stirring up of emotional responses.

Educators should therefore have very great skill in cultivating children's ability to use words: thus, the teacher needs good verbal ability. It is possibly one of the greatest dangers in education today that this skill is not so often as before recognised as essential. There has, justifiably, been a determination to recognise that teachers can have many kinds of ability; that their ability to create good relationships with other people is important; that their ability in artistic creation is valuable; that practical skills are important. The danger is that with this recognition, and with the attempt to escape from pedantic teaching, to escape from the emphasis which in the past has too often been laid on merely verbal knowledge, we should come to believe that verbal ability is not important. But what was wrong in past or present systems of education was not the value set on verbal ability but the attempt to cultivate the wrong kind of verbal ability by the wrong methods; words were misused because they did not correspond to clear concepts and because they were learned unintelligently by children who were not given the necessary foundation of experience and interest before being required to use the words. These faults have been pointed out frequently in the history of education—Comenius and others stressed *res non verba*; but too often the conclusion has been reached that the one aspect of learning can be effective without the other. At the present time there is an alarming readiness on the part of educators of teachers, and employers of teachers, to assume that the verbal skill of the teacher is relatively unimportant. But failure to develop subtle and complex use of language may mean failure to develop skill in thinking. If fine discriminations conveyed by the right use of words are not perceived, thinking is conducted in ignorance of some relevant data and is less efficient. If reservations and qualifications are not expressed in words, they will often be overlooked in thought. If complexity of structure does not encourage perception of complex stimuli, thinking may oversimplify, omit relevant data. Thus an impoverished environment—impoverished so far as language skills are concerned—can mean failure to develop the ability to think well, no matter what the child's initial potential: and poverty of language development can exist in classrooms as well as in homes. (In both cases access to books may be the way of escape for children; but it is not clear, as yet, why some children determinedly seek this escape through reading and learning while others, even in the same family, do not.)

Possibly the increasing amount of sociological studies bearing on the use of language in different social classes will rehabilitate the teacher's verbal skill (though initially such studies tended to suggest that the teacher's command of language could be a barrier to communication). Certainly if one observes communication between teachers and pupils one realises how constantly verbal skill is needed—to offer a model to the children, to explain, to stimulate their thinking and experimenting; and to understand in turn what the children are trying to report and what ideas they are—sometimes vaguely or perplexingly—formulating. The teacher's skill with language enriches vocabulary, introduces good structures; and it does make a considerable difference to the kind of relationship existing between the teacher and the pupils—even if sometimes this relationship is best fostered by the teacher's ability to use the appropriate catch-phrase or the regional dialect. Verbal skill is by no means the only ability required in good teaching—some bad teachers may have it; but those teachers or intending teachers who have other essential qualities should certainly develop what ability they have in using words and in being aware of what words mean and do.

Freedom to think

As important as providing first-hand experience and words to deal with it, is provision of freedom to think about it. But freedom of this kind has different uses for different types of imagining. Children who are taught that they must not depart from the textbook formula are unlikely to discover new solutions or form new theories. Children who use formulas or languages which they have learned without understanding cannot turn them to their own purposes. Lack of freedom thus inhibits the scientific kind of imaginative discovery. But children whose freedom in school is greatly restricted can always seek refuge in everyday imagining—and come to prefer it to the restricted real activities of daily work at school: this excessive imagining can be guarded against by giving freedom to act.

Freedom to think and to experiment seems a simple requirement, but it takes considerable skill on the part of the teacher to create the conditions of this freedom. There is a limit to what the individual child can discover—in some cases, children must be guided to what has been found to be a good solution (given, as it were, the recipe for the apple-pie); the solution is new to them, but not original; some experiments are profitably indicated by the teacher and the solutions learners 'find' are theirs in the sense of being personal experience even though foreseen and known by the teacher. What is important is that if a child finds an alternative solution the teacher should be able to recognise whether it is valid or not, and should not automatically reject it because it is not the accepted solution or explanation. The ease with which this can be done varies; it is possibly easier in scientific subjects than in literary (and of course in language teaching one has in many cases to make the point that the alternative is not possible because it departs from accepted structures, and languages, being a matter of convention, do not allow much freedom here).

But if freedom of thought is to be encouraged, a great deal depends on the way in which children's solutions or comments are accepted;

it is so easy for the teacher to build up in the child the fear of making mistakes, or of saying something which will be found ridiculous by others in the group or by the teacher. Occasionally the child's solution is absurd; but the teacher has to control the situation so that the child who on one occasion does put forward an unworkable solution or a wildly wrong answer does not feel that conformity is essential in future, if the horror of being laughed at is to be avoided. Fear of being laughed at, fear of making mistakes, can encourage withdrawal into imagination's satisfactions; since real action is not satisfactory, it will be avoided in future. (Of course the teacher cannot prevent some experience of failure from occurring; it is part of human life that some answers simply are wrong; and however hurtful or damaging this may be to our self-esteem we have to incorporate this fact in our concept of our own performance. The ability to accept laughter when we do make a wild error is a good thing. But the teacher has to discriminate again as to whether the learner is ready for this learning.) Even if there is not deliberate discouragement, it is sadly easy for a teacher to discourage through blank incomprehension the child's novel solution or thought; unhappily we cannot expect all teachers to be intelligent enough to avoid this kind of situation completely.

It is not clear to what extent such freedom in thinking, in the sense of lack of inhibition about trying unorthodox solutions, can be cultivated by offering models for imitation. It seems probable that the teacher's approach to authoritative (or authoritarian) statements in books and elsewhere (e.g. by television commentators) will have some effect in building up the belief that (1) such statements are gospel, not to be examined critically or (2) any statement can be submitted to critical study. Again we need discrimination—a perpetual reaction of contra-suggestibility, unwillingness to accept any statement without challenge, is not really a helpful result of education. But the basic principle, that what has been affirmed or is being affirmed by another human being can be mistaken, should be made clear. Again, a great deal depends on the teacher's own habits of thought; the teacher who thinks flexibly, who approaches a topic so as to leave open the possibility of treating it in a new way— or who, from time to time, clearly has a new perspective on the subject under discussion may encourage this kind of flexibility in pupils. It is not, unfortunately, possible for people to become flexible in their thinking on demand; we must again be resigned to the fact that some teachers have been so conditioned by their own early training that they cannot offer for the benefit of pupils examples of flexibility. Yet even those who are not themselves likely to leave the worn path can be encouraged to develop an attitude of tolerance for those who—whether as colleagues or pupils—are able to find new ways for themselves.

Possibly too the kinds of heroes offered for study in history or literature may build up the idea that unconventionality in thought, questioning of accepted views, are sometimes rewarded and rewarding. And, for older pupils, there is the example set by some writers; and even by some of those speaking in broadcasts.

The positive steps we have just been looking at are by no means easy to ensure; they depend so greatly on the personal qualities of individual teachers. But if schools are willing to approve them, some progress can be made. And of course many schools already do try to provide as rich first-hand experience as possible, supplement experience with verbal information where appropriate; they do try to build up language skills; they encourage freedom in thinking. As do some parents. There is not yet sufficient experimental evidence on the effects of different home or school attitudes on creative skills but Mackinnon (1962) reported that parents of creative architects were characterised by 'an extraordinary respect for the child and confidence in his ability to do what was appropriate. Thus they did not hesitate to grant him rather unusual freedom in exploring his universe and making decisions for himself.' Other researches however are less conclusive as to how scientists and literary creators respond to different types of parental attitude; e.g. whether the over-protective mother may favour literary creation; and whether an absence of close emotional ties to parents is a correlate of creative freedom. Similarly there is not enough evidence to show how school atmospheres have had an effect; especially as it is true, as one relevant research report (Lytton, Cotton, 1969) pointed out: 'Teaching approach in a secondary school is uniform for a department rather than for a school'—or indeed may depend on individual teachers who create atmospheres not found in colleagues' classes. And again, we have seen that imagining for private enjoyment may be little affected by school work.

On all counts, though, it is clear that the fewer barriers set to freedom in thinking, the better (assuming that we can discriminate between thinking and pseudo-thinking).

We must note also that these positive approaches tend to deal mostly with scientific work; they must certainly be supplemented by others if the more social uses of imagination are to be fostered and imagination is to be used in building up attitudes towards other people and other groups of people, and if the ability to understand other people's reactions is to be cultivated as far as possible.

Educating the emotions

The motivation for scientific or artistic creation may well develop in circumstances where freedom to experience and discover is provided: the motivation for emotional imagination is more difficult to encourage and assess. The situation is certainly not simplified by naïve acceptance of the view that all that is needed to stimulate this kind of imagination is complete freedom of emotional expression, or any kind of dramatic performance—or artistic work—which will express some kind of emotion. A negative prescription for educators is consequently to be selective in encouraging dramatic performances or other exercises of that kind. Possibly, too, to consider more carefully the kind of emotions expressed in the literature presented to learners; not with a view to censorship but with some kind of discrimination, so that the possible effects of this specific stimulation of emotions can be considered—what values are implied by a story set for study. At least we could avoid giving the impression that all forms of emotional behaviour are equally valuable, interesting and deserving of sympathy.

In fact we arrive here at the problems of a kind of education which from time to time is mentioned as supremely important—the education of the emotions. But the introduction of the emotional element in this aspect of education seems to have had the same kind of obscuring effect as it has had in discussions of imagination; people are aware that it is present; it is stated to be essential; and then, somehow, the discussion moves on to other things. (Or if the emotion is kept in view, the educational element is forgotten.)

Herbert Spencer, for example, pointed out with his customary lucidity in *Social Statics* that if we hope by education to produce better members of society, people who behave well, we must have an education which works on the emotions rather than on the intellect—but he evaded further discussion in one context at least by praying heaven to defend us from legislative attempts at such an education—i.e. from such education in publicly provided schools; and in other contexts, e.g. his essay on *Moral Education*, he confined himself mainly to proposing discipline by cause and effect—which undoubtedly involves some emotional education but is by no means the whole answer. Other more modern writers on education have pointed out the neglect of the emotions in formal educational work; they have very rightly indicated that a curriculum which provides only for intellectual development is unbalanced; but then they merely prescribe subjects which are excellent enough in their way but which do not necessarily do anything further for emotional development as distinct from emotional expression. There have been attempts to give greater recognition to the child or adolescent's emotional needs; but how are they to be *educated* once the expression of the needs has occurred? There have also been very admirable discussions of emotional response to literature and art, a kind of response which can be evident even when the learners are too immature for intellectual response (e.g. M. Hourd's work, *The Education of the Poetic Spirit*, 1949). It has been convincingly stated that there are great dangers of inhibiting enjoyment of art and literature by demanding an intellectual response too early, by overlooking the emotional impact or smothering it in verbal questioning and analysis, enforcing the learning of stereotyped formulas of appreciation; but once the emotional response is there, how is it educated? Is its simple existence enough? Or even its existence enriched by analysis of the details of the artistic creation and technique?

It has also been asserted that the education of the emotions is more effectively carried out by other means—by the experiences of the sports field, where a valuable control of emotions is said to be achieved. (Spectator sport and televised matches and competitions have possibly weakened this argument.) Here we find emphasis on developing group feeling, by belonging, by participating in group activities; but again it seems to be a matter of considering that if the feeling is there, the emotions have been educated—not simply been allowed to develop or to exist. There is also little precise prescription of how to develop enjoyment of togetherness in those who do not naturally appreciate it—or who find themselves in the wrong group.

In all this, the main source of weakness is evasion of the central problem—the aim to be achieved. The trouble is that when we come to the education of the emotions we don't know exactly what we are trying to do. Emotions come from past as well as present experience (so of course does most knowledge); we cannot be sure of producing at a given moment exactly the emotional response we want; and above all we are not certain what the ideal end-product should be. Some educational theories have defined the 'good' emotions, the ones which we should cultivate; Soviet education, for example, is fairly explicit about co-operative feelings and unselfishness and cheerfulness; but even this definition may concern overt behaviour only—internal emotion is assumed to correspond to overt behaviour, but it may not inevitably do so. In our own educational system we have less clear definition of the good overt behaviour to be produced by emotions and little clarity as to what emotions we hope individuals will experience, or as to what the individual's general emotional state should be. We have some traditional clichés about keeping stiff upper lips, not weeping in public (if male), not exulting over the defeated (unless possibly in some competitive sports); possibly a vague feeling that emotions should not lead to excitable behaviour, nor, of course, to neurotic behaviour. But how does the individual *feel* (and express feelings) if a successful education of the emotions has taken place? Sunnily optimistic? Serene? Dispassionate?

There are various possibilities, if we consider types of ideal results. We could say that the ideal product of a good education of the emotions is (1) someone whose emotions do not produce anti-social behaviour; i.e. who is sufficiently in control of emotional reactions not to express them in actions disapproved of by society; (2) someone who does not feel any undesirable emotions and has therefore no problem about suppressing impulses to undesirable action of any kind—i.e. someone in whom every situation produces the 'right' emotional response; (3) someone who can switch off emotions—possibly experience them in retrospect, but at the time of action follow simply the reasonable course; (4) someone who may initially feel what could be considered wrong responses but who can, through controlled imagination, come to feel the right response and therefore act on that.

It may be argued that (2) is impossible for a human being; there is indeed a common view that it would be undesirable to be like this; but it must be noted that what is presupposed here is not a cold, unemotional human being, but a warm, emotion-feeling, responsive —if saint-like—human being. (The type described under (3) might come nearer to the unimpassioned, controlled reasoner who seems to provoke a great deal of animosity.) But perhaps there is some foundation for the belief that any human being living with other human beings is bound to be provoked to some feelings of hostility or dislike at some time or another: i.e. must experience undesirable emotions. Thus the human being who has no unpleasant emotional responses seems unthinkable.

We must also note that so far as action is concerned, all four might *behave* in an identical way. But it is important to know which type we consider ideal—which kind of emotional response should lie behind the 'right' action. Certainly it can be agreed that whatever else education does, a minimum goal is the achievement of type (1)—the individual whose emotions are sufficiently under control for anti-social behaviour to be inhibited; or even one whose emotions are sufficiently under control to produce the polite forms of be-haviour like smiling cheerfully and congratulating a winning oponent, being friendly to people who are disliked. But is this minimum enough?

From the social point of view, emotional control which keeps behaviour within socially acceptable limits is certainly a desirable aim—even if minimal it is considerably beyond what we can at present achieve. But from the point of view of the individual and ultimately of society it is possible that another aim could make for greater happiness; suppressing emotions is not really a happy activity, even if it leads to acceptable behaviour: it would be much more pleasant not to have a discrepancy between feelings and behaviour.

It can be argued that feelings of anger and despair are useful in stimulating better performance on future occasions; yet they do seem often to have no immediate use—especially if better perform-ance is not within the individual's capacities. Does modern education really wish to perpetuate the situation in which these emotions have to be denied outlet? In the past, religious training gave clearer directions as to what the individual should strive towards; there should be sufficient unselfishness to rejoice in another's well-being, even in another's victory—though even then it was not altogether clear whether some grief on one's own behalf was totally ruled out: but confidence in a benevolent and comforting deity was presumably to be great enough to prevent too anguished a feeling of regret for one's own suffering or that of others. It cannot really be said that this ideal of emotional control is widely emphasised in educational writings at the present time; more often we accept the existence of 'normal' human feelings; even psychological theories which seem to imply that more free expression of emotions would lead to greater mental health do not assume that all emotions will be pleasing to the individual or society: and in many psychological theories (even the Freudian) it is assumed that some emotions cannot be expressed in action—so the human being is left with some kind of inappropriate emotional response to struggle with and to deny outlet to, as well as possible. Thus education of the emotions is generally thought of as encouraging ways of behaving which will conceal or inhibit the expression of some emotions; but there is little suggestion that education should develop the individual to the point of reacting with pure rejoicing at other people's success and feeling no frustra-tion, sorrow, anger or aggression when experiencing failure or lack of recognition or perceiving injustice which cannot be remedied. As illustration, take the classical example of the candidate defeated in an election who rejoices that others better qualified than he to serve the community have been found. Now, assuming that the emotion of rejoicing is genuine, and not simply an elegant verbal gesture—is that the kind of reaction which today we should expect as a result of an ideal education of the emotions? Or would we expect concealed bitterness, dismay, even in the educated?

There is also uncertainty about the extent to which the expression of emotion is socially approved; sociologists and anthropologists have made clear to us that it depends very much on our social group whether expression of some emotions is socially acceptable or not—grief at loss by death can be strongly expressed in some societies, restrained by ritual in others; aggression—verbal or physical—can be tolerated in some, played down elsewhere; love for others—male or female—can be expressed only within socially defined norms. So again, the result of education of the emotions will be chosen not only in accordance with a general ideal but within the range of permitted emotions for the social, sex, religious, racial group to which the individual belongs.

But without getting involved in this problem of social norms, we note that the educator should not only recognise social attitudes towards behaviour expressing emotions, but consider also the individual's *experience* of emotion. It could be said that there is much in favour of type (4) in emotional education—i.e. one who uses imagination to change the view of the situation and thus change the emotional response to it, so that there would be no need to suppress, or refuse to give expression to the real emotion felt.

Alternatively, where action on a rational basis is possible, and where action might serve to focus attention on practical needs and distract from emotional feelings, then certainly education could try to produce in pupils the habit of concentrating on the objective demands of the situation, and trying to disregard, at least temporarily, personal emotions.

But clearly situations cannot always be dealt with in this latter way; even after rational action there is emotional reaction; there may also be situations in which there is no immediate possibility of action and the individual consequently has no alternative but to face the upsurge of emotions—the television commentators are dealing with the victor, the crowd has turned in that direction, the defeated is alone. Or the emotion may be anger, rejection, loneliness. In such circumstances, it would be useful if education could produce an individual capable of restructuring the situation in imagination—not in compensatory and unrealistic day-dreaming of a different outcome, but viewing it from another point of view, entering into the feelings of other people concerned, looking forward to a more promising future situation or even picturing some undesirable consequences that might have resulted if the situation had really turned out otherwise (the 'sour grapes' approach, only more convincingly done): someone able to avoid prolonging—or even wallowing in—the unpleasant emotional state. More easily, probably, education could encourage the technique of deliberately turning then to imaginary constructions offered by books or similar entertainment in order to change the emotional state; but this could be a less satisfactory solution; it could encourage merely compensatory imagining.

(It must of course be recognised that there are some situations in which no distraction of emotions is possible and indeed in which full acceptance of, and continuation in, distress, grief, regret is the right response. But fortunately these are not numerous; the others, in which changing to another emotion would be helpful, pleasant, constructive, are much more frequent.)

Trying to achieve alternative responses seems the more advisable since it is improbable that education can produce individuals who never feel undesirable emotions (undesirable both from society's point of view and from the individual's); and the solution mentioned earlier, that of complete trust in a benevolent deity, is not one that is possible for all individuals.

Imagining and the improvement of emotional states

Education of the emotions should produce at least individuals who are capable of controlling their actions to an extent acceptable to society. It would be better if, additionally, education could help to lessen conflict between emotion and behaviour and lead to generally happier emotional feeling in those who have been educated. Coping with emotions comes much more easily to some fortunate people than to others; they are of a resurgent temperament which fairly soon presents another focus of attention, even without conscious effort to move to it. But for people of all types, how could education of imagination attempt to help?

In some respects, the solution lies not in imagination but in the real experience provided as part of education. If there is a feeling of achievement in learning (whatever kind of learning is involved), then there is a greater chance of a better emotional state in future: there is a greater ability to resist discouragement—experience of failure can be countered by remembering past success. (Though again, individual differences in level of aspiration complicate the situation.) It is admittedly not always easy to give some children a feeling of achievement; it is also difficult at times to give the feeling of social achievement—to make the individual feel a popular or even an accepted member of a group (one can at times understand well the group's inclination to reject some members). It is also difficult to overcome home conditions which handicap such achievements. But as we are more aware of these problems we may become better at overcoming them and so, indirectly, contributing to the education of favourable emotions.

Apart from feelings of achievement, another kind of experience could contribute to this indirect education of emotion; it is the experience of enjoyment. We saw that for some people pre-sleep imagining may be replaced by recall of happy incidents in the past; and many writers have clearly had immense satisfaction in reviving memories of beauty in things seen, felt, known. The doctrine of making childhood a time of happiness has therefore this additional justification; happiness gives material for future thought which will be satisfying and which may, on occasion, provide the counter-balance to unhappy emotions, to displeasing situations. Some children can derive happiness of this kind indirectly, from books; but all need some direct experience. Again, it is difficult to ensure such pleasure by conscious effort; schools or parents can say: 'Look at this stained glass window' or 'Look at this reproduction of Van Gogh's work' but it is not possible to ensure that the looking gives pleasure or material for reproduction on some future day of boredom or unhappiness. The school cannot ensure the recurrence of memories of the cool grass underfoot on the school playing field, nor the glint of the network of light caught in the swimming pool, nor the joy of perception as a solution falls into place. But the school can provide opportunities for these experiences and other experiences of happiness; it can make the raw materials available; and it can avoid conditions in which such experiences are not possible—or in which the memories are likely to be too unpleasant to contemplate. Achievement and enjoyment thus contribute to future happiness as memories, as part of the self-concept, and as material for imaginative constructions.

The direct use of imagination rather than real experience to improve emotional states would seem to take four forms: the development of the technique of turning attention to other situations when the present situation is unsatisfactory; the development of the technique of re-structuring an actual situation by thinking about it imaginatively; the development of greater imaginative insight into other people's points of view: and the use of imagination in planning.

The first of these is undoubtedly risky; there are, as we have seen, some individuals who spontaneously take refuge in imaginary situations—becoming addicts to television, films, reading or private imagining. Since this occurs spontaneously, it is also less likely that we need to propose it as a technique—though it is possibly a less expensive remedy than the traditional solutions of going tiger-shooting, or on a slow-boat journey, as a cure for emotional distress. If we give access to enjoyable fiction, we have made this resource available to those who can use it: we may remain ready to offer alternative real activities where it seems used to excess.

Re-structuring or re-interpreting a situation in imagination, or turning attention to imaginative planning for future situations is a difficult technique; it needs awareness of one's own thought processes, determination, and a store of relevant and varied experience: with these, other aspects of the situation can be realised and a more sympathetic realisation of the feelings of other people involved in it can be reached. This more objective view may make it easier to fit the situation into the 'continued story' of the individual's existence in a way which does not make it a disaster or a threat to the self-concept. (And of course the more satisfactorily the self-concept has been built up by experience of real achievement, the more likely it is that an imaginative attempt to see a problem situation differently will not be merely compensatory but will produce worthwhile insight.)

Yet to encourage conscious control of thinking is not a straightforward task. To attempt to do so by simple exhortation, by reasoned argument that this is a good thing to do, seems naïve and, on psychoanalytic theories and others, unlikely to succeed. (It seems to be on the same lines as religious exhortations of the past—e.g. to avoid thinking evil thoughts; while such teaching can have some effect, especially on the child who is responsive to verbal communication, it does not seem to have been a particularly successful method; it may have succeeded in establishing standards of value, and producing guilt feelings when behaviour did not reach those standards—which is not a negligible result—but it seems not to have produced many individuals who really did achieve the desired control over evil thoughts.) In modern terms, it might easily boil down into journalistic-type advice about looking on the bright side, avoiding brooding, thinking of something cheerful every day, etc. Training for conscious happiness by thinking encouraging thoughts is not an attractive programme (though Pollyanna made an impact on many youthful readers, and the Coué method had its enthusiasts). Illustration or example may have more effect.

But if education can produce more imaginative understanding of other people, the strength of undesirable or unpleasant emotional reactions may be lessened and fewer problem situations have to be dealt with. Hostility, suspicion, dislike tend to be less strong if the situation can be seen from another position. As we have seen, role-playing techniques seem to have advantages in leading to such insights; similarly films, plays, television programmes can lead to emotional involvement with an unfamiliar point of view. If these are followed by discussions in which spectators or actors become more aware of their own reactions and prejudices, and those of others, it is possible that this insight will transfer to real situations. Perception of the intentions and feelings of the opposition group can lead to less frustration and to perception of more effective ways of reducing or avoiding the opposition. (In some cases, admittedly, clearer perception shows more clearly that there is a conflict of deeply rooted values; and that some people are acting from an appallingly warped emotional state: even so, there may be less furious aggression if this conflict is clearly understood.) A greater general sympathy for other human beings may produce a fuller awareness of the human condition; against this background individual problems can sometimes look less large, and be less emotionally distressing.

The remaining difficulty here is that to choose stories or situations for discussion, and to lead such discussion, demands great ability on the teacher's part. Accounts of some lessons in American schools (which seem to have made more praiseworthy efforts than European schools to deal with this aspect of education) do at times give horrifying examples of superficial discussions, group leaders' failure to perceive the true problem, and some appalling lack of logic in forcing a desired conclusion on the discussions. Still, the abuse of a method is not a good reason for avoiding its use. It is possible too that centralised teaching—e.g. presentation by broadcasts of discussion themes—may lessen the dangers coming from inefficient teachers' choice of material. The discussion method in itself is not new; the old 'moral lessons' which presented a class with a little anecdote or short story and then called for discussion, possibly of a formal question-and-answer kind, were variations of it. The greater scope for the method nowadays comes from the use of sound and pictures, with a variety of actors and other cues in television and film, to make the situation more life-like, and to stimulate imaginative involvement by people who would remain unaffected if words only were used. And 'acting parts' in such moral stories—or in Bible stories—is not a new technique; in the past, as in the present, its effectiveness must depend on teachers' skill. Teachers' skill also is needed to avoid another danger, that of excessive conformity to group standards in discussion; but it is unlikely that individual standards will frequently be much higher than that of the peer group, or that in such cases they will be lowered by discussion sessions.

Finally, in planning: provision of greater real experience and the habit of considering how other people react to situations should make for more satisfactory performance here. Some of the fictional situations discussed may illustrate the weakness of unimaginative or unrealistic planning. If then imagination is used in a more controlled way to foresee the results of plans and so modify them, it is likely that emotional distress of various kinds will be avoided. There could be an additional emphasis on the need to plan for emergencies —to imagine not simply the operation of a plan—an enjoyable prospect—but what could be done if the original plan failed in some way: and this preparation similarly might lessen emotional shock if the situation does not go according to plan. (Some children or adults discover a variant of such planning: having noticed that things never go exactly as imagined in advance, they imagine precisely the situations they do *not* want to happen—thus hoping, by a kind of magic, to prevent their occurrence: but as ill-fortune can take even more forms than imagination, this variant is scarcely to be recommended.)

Education can thus try to influence imagination both directly and indirectly; by directing it towards comprehension of other people's situation, by showing its use as alternative occupation, and by showing the possibility of arriving at a new understanding of the individual's own situation; by providing also real experience of a kind which will contribute to future happiness and confidence as well as to future imaginative constructions. This provision of real experience and opportunity for achievement can be at the same time a provision against the misuse of imagination for excessive compensation or for purely escapist purposes (assuming that life is worth accepting). In some ways education has to be much more concerned with the general experience of the child than with developing detailed exercises of imagination or with specific subject teaching. It has also to be more concerned with these positive contributions than with possible censorship of allegedly undesirable stimulation of imagination.

Educating imagination must be a general process and a gradual one. It is possible that individual lessons in literature or other subjects can make dramatic and important contributions to any one individual's development; a story or poem or painting or piece of music may provide a sudden illumination, give an experience not earlier known; it may in itself be an experience of enjoyment of great importance in future imagining. But the education of imagination is more pervasive and less directly controlled than lessons in literature and other subjects. Imagining is a part of human experience; the school can determine and guide only part of the experience. In cognitive learning, especially in the pro-grammed technique of today, an attempt is made to make learning easier by using clearly defined units; but we lack analogous units of emotion; and we lack controlled methods of instant feedback to emotional responses, reinforcing the 'correct' responses. It is true that in some ordinary situations there is feedback to emotional

expression—expressions of affection, for example, being recipro-
cated. But beyond general approval of emotions that children
express—or disapproval of others—it is impossible to narrow the
focus and take one emotion or one expression of it at a time, or to
adjust precisely the relationship between emotional response by
the learner and immediate reinforcement by the teacher. Indeed
we cannot always know what emotion is being stimulated or
reinforced.

Yet if education can provide the minimum it will have done
much. It may even effect some control of undesirable imagination:
since some imaginative enjoyment—day-dreaming, imaginary companions—arises from a way of life which does not give satisfactory
alternatives in reality, an education which increases real enjoyment
should restrict the search for unreal satisfaction.

Imagining beyond education

Nevertheless though we may set out to foster imagination of an
individually and socially useful kind and to control it where necessary and possible by the intervention of intelligence, it would be
futile to suppose that it is entirely under our control or that imagination should necessarily always be used constructively. We have
said that there are some individuals who seem to have little or no
imaginative ability; we cannot force them to use it widely. For
others in the past, and doubtless in the present and future also, who
discover spontaneously the immense delight that imagining can
give, the situation is different. Imagining continues during all
conscious behaviour: it is not under school control nor is all behaviour consciously directed or governed by social purposes. The
process of thinking is such a remarkable amalgam—a sequence
of images, internal speech, concepts, memories, awareness, sensations
—that imagining must mingle with it. Thinking can to a limited
extent, for limited periods, be directed into more or less objective
fields of attention; but apparently only for limited periods. Human
existence demands sleep, the temporary cessation of normal consciousness and normal thought. To a lesser extent, waking human
existence possibly demands periods of less thought, of lesser control.
Certainly external stimuli do not demand attention all the time;
there are periods when action is not necessary or possible, where
attention is not needed, and yet consciousness continues; and
since the mind cannot always be remembering or thinking constructively or abstractly, it must imagine. If, as recent researches suggest,
dreaming during sleep is essential to health, so imagining during
the waking hours may be, if not essential, at least a normal feature

of mental health. Imagining gives emotional pleasure and such pleasure is to be accepted and enjoyed; as various eminent minds have discovered, we cannot think all the time; it is for the individual to determine which are the appropriate times and amounts of time. For it may be an equal part of the merit of imagination that not only does it help in comprehension of other people and in effective action, but that, giving delight and comfort which are independent of external circumstances, it enables the human being to remain quietly alone in a room.

References

ADAMS, J., 'Day-dreaming', *Journal of Experimental Pedagogy,* ii, 4, (1914).

ALLINGHAM, M., *The Tiger in the Smoke,* Chatto and Windus, 1952.

ALSCHULER, R. and HATTWICK, L. B. W., *Painting and Personality,* Univ. of Chicago Press, 1947.

AMES, L. E., and LEARNED, J., 'Imaginary Companions and Related Phenomena', *Journal of Genetic Psychology.,* lxix, (1946), pp. 147–67.

ANGYAL, A., 'Über die Raumlage vorgestellter Örter', *Archiv für die gesamte Psychologie,* lxxviii, (1930–1).

ARISTOTLE, *The Poetics,* Heinemann, 1936.

ST AUGUSTINE, *Confessiones,* vii, 1, Gaumes Frères, Paris, 1836.

AVELING, F., BARTLETT, F. C., and PEAR, T. H., 'The Relevance of Visual Imagery to the Process of Thinking', *British Journal of Psychology,* xviii (1927–8).

BACON, F., *The Advancement of Learning,* Bk. 2, Oxford Univ. Press, 1966.

BACON, F., *Novum Organum,* Lib. i, Clarendon Press, Oxford, 1878.

BAIN, A., 'Notes and Discussions', *Mind,* v, (1880).

BANDURA, A., and WALTERS, R. H., *Social Learning and Personality Development,* Holt, Rinehart & Winston, 1964.

BARNARD, H. C., *Fénelon on Education,* Camb. Univ. Press, 1966.

BARRON, F., *Creativity and Psychological Health,* D. van Nostrand, 1963.

BARTLETT, F. C., *Remembering,* Camb. Univ. Press, 1932.

BARTLETT, F. C., 'The Functions of Images', *British Journal of Psychology,* xi, (1920–1).

BAUCHARD, P., *The Child Audience,* UNESCO, 1952.

BENDER, L., *A Dynamic Psychopathology of Childhood,* C. C. Thomas, 1954.

BETTELHEIM, B., *The Children of the Dream,* Thames & Hudson, 1969.

BETTS, G. H., *The Distribution and Functions of Mental Imagery,* Teachers College, Columbia Univ., 1909.

BINET, A., *L'Etude Expérimentale de l'Intelligence,* Paris, 1903.

BINET, A., and HENRI, V., 'La psychologie individuelle', *Année psychologique,* ii, (1895–6).

BOSSENCE, R., 'An Island Unto Myself (Sometimes)', *Belfast News-Letter,* (3 Aug. 1967).

BOWYER, L. R., *The Lowenfeld World Technique,* Pergamon, 1970.

BRAITHWAITE, E. R., *To Sir, With Love*, The Bodley Head, 1959.
BRONOWSKI, J., *Imagination and the University*, Univ. of Toronto Press, 1964.
BRONTË, C., *The Professor*, Preface, J. Grant, Edinburgh, 1911.
BROWER, D., 'The Experimental Study of Imagery', *Journal of Genetic Psychology*, xxxvi-vii, (1947).
BRUNER, J. S., OLIVER, R. R., GREENFIELD, P. M., et al., *Studies in Cognitive Growth*, John Wiley & Sons, 1966.
BURGESS, A., 'Television', *The Listener*, 9 March 1967, 335.
BURT, C., 'Capacity and Achievement', *Education*, vol. 130, 3368 (1967), 198–201.
BURT, C., *The Young Delinquent*, Univ. London Press, 1925.

CAMUS, A., *L'Homme Révolté*, Gallimard, 1951, 326.
CATTELL, R. B., *A Guide to Mental Testing*, Univ. London Press, 1936.
CLARK, L. VERDELLE, 'Effect of mental practice on the development of a certain motor skill', *Research Quarterly*, xxxi, (1960), 560–9.
COLERIDGE, S. T., *Literary Remains*, ed. H. W. Coleridge, Pickering, 1936, lecture II.

DAVIDSON, A., and FAY, J., *Phantasy in Childhood*, Routledge & Kegan Paul, 1952.
DEARBORN, G. V., 'A study of imagination', *American Journal of Psychology*, ix, (1897–8).
DEPARTMENTAL COMMITTEE ON CHILDREN AND THE CINEMA: *Report*, H.M.S.O., 1950.
DEPARTMENT OF EDUCATION AND SCIENCE: *Children and Their Primary Schools*, H.M.S.O., 1967, vol. 1.
DESCARTES, R., *Principes de la Philosophie*, ed. Cousin, 1824, 4e, 190.
DESCARTES, R., *Les Passions de l'Ame*, ed. Cousin, 1824, art. 21.
DESCARTES, R., *Meditations*, ed. Cousin, 1824, vi.
DOWNEY, J., 'A Musical Experiment', *American Journal of Psychology*, ix, (1897–8).
DU MAURIER, D., *The Infernal World of Bramwell Brontë*, Gollancz, 1960.

EBBINGHAUS, H., *Grundzüge der Psychologie* (continued by E. Dürr), Veit, 1913.
EISENBERG, A. L., *Children and Radio Programs*, Columbia Univ. Press, 1936
ERICKSON, C. I., 'The Sense of Direction in Mental Imagery', *Psychological Abstracts*, iii, (1929), 2184.
EYSENCK, H. J., 'Some Factors in Appreciation of Poetry', *Character and Personality*, ix, (1940–1).

FEASEY, L., 'Children's Appreciation of Poems', *British Journal of Psychology*, xviii, (1927–8).
FERGUSON, T., *The Young Delinquent in his Social Setting*, Oxford Univ. Press, 1952.
FESHBACH, S., 'The Drive-Reducing Function of Fantasy Behavior',

Motives in Fantasy, Action and Society (ed. J. W. Atkinson), D. van Nostrand, 1958, 160–75.

FESHBACH, S., quoted by BANDURA, A., and WALTERS, R. H., *Social Learning and Personality Development.*

FLEMING, I., *Casino Royale*, Pan Books, 1955.

FLEMING, I., *On Her Majesty's Secret Service*, Pan Books, 1964.

FORMAN, H. J., *Our Movie Made Children*, Macmillan, N. Y., 1933.

FOULDS, G. A., 'Characteristic Projection Test Responses of a Group of Defective Delinquents', *British Journal of Psychology*, xl, 1950.

FREEMAN, J., BUTCHER, H. J., and CHRISTIE, T., *Creativity*, Soc. for Research into Higher Education, London, 1968.

FRIEDMANN, A., 'Über das Minderwertigkeitsgefühl Phantasievoller Kinder', *Zeitschrift für Pädagogische Psychologie*, xxxiii, (1932).

FROEBEL, F., *The Education of Man*, Appleton & Co., 1887, 115, 116, 306.

GALTON, F., 'Visualised Numerals', *Nature*, (1880).

GALTON, F., 'Psychometric Experiments', *Brain*, ii, (1879).

GALTON, F., *Inquiries into Human Faculty*, Macmillan, 1883.

GESELL, A., and ILG, F. L., *Infant and Child in the Culture of Today*, Harper, N.Y., 1943.

GETZELS, J. W., and JACKSON, F. W., *Creativity and Intelligence*, Wiley, London, 1962.

GOLLWITZER, H., *Und führen, wohin du nicht willst*, Fischer Bücherei, 1954.

GORDON, R., 'An investigation into some of the factors that favour the formation of stereotyped images', *British Journal of Psychology*, xxxix, (1949).

GRIFFITHS, R., *Imagination in Early Childhood*, Kegan Paul, Trench, Trubner & Co., 1945.

GRIFFITHS, R., 'A study of imagination in children of five years', Univ. of London, Ph. D. thesis, 1931.

GUILFORD, J. P., 'Progress in the discovery of intellectual factors', *Widening Horizons in Creativity,* (ed. C. W Taylor), chap. 17, J. Wiley & Sons, N.Y., 1964.

GUNN, D. G., 'Factors in the Appreciation of Poetry', *British Journal of Educational Psychology*, xxi, (1951).

HABER, R. N., 'Eidetic Images', *American Scientist*, April 1969.

HADDON, F. A., and LYTTON, H., 'Teaching Approach and the Development of Divergent Thinking Abilities in Primary Schools', *British Journal of Educational Psychology*, xxxviii, 2, (1968), 171.

HALL, G. S., *The Psychology of Adolescence,* Appleton, N.Y., 1914.

HALLORAN, J. D., *The Effects of Mass Communication*, Leicester Univ. Press, 1965.

HALLORAN, J. D., BROWN, R. L., and CHANEY, D. C., *Television and Delinquency*, Leicester Univ. Press, 1970.

HARGREAVES, D. H., *Social Relations in a Secondary School*, Routledge & Kegan Paul, 1967.

HARGREAVES, H. L., 'The "Faculty" of Imagination', *British Journal of Psychology, Monograph Supplement*, x, (1927).

HARRIMAN, P. L., 'Some imaginary companions of older subjects', *Psychological Abstracts*, xi (5178), 1937.

HEIM, A., WATTS, K. P., and SIMMONDS, V., 'The Brook reaction as a test of temperament', *British Journal of Social and Clinical Psychology*, vi, 4, (1967), 304–12.

HIMMELWEIT, H. T., OPPENHEIM, A. N., and VINCE, P., *Television and the Child*, Oxford Univ. Press, 1958.

HOURD, M. L., *The Education of the Poetic Spirit*, Heinemann, 1949.

HUDSON, L., *Frames of Mind*, Methuen, 1968.

HUG, J., 'Test der konstruktiven Phantasie', *La Psychotechnique dans le Monde Moderne*, (1952).

HUME, D., *Essays and Treatises*: vol. 2, 'An Enquiry Concerning Human Understanding', 'A Dissertation on the Passions', Bell & Blackwood, Edinburgh, 1809.

HURLOCK, R. B., and BURSTEIN, M., 'The Imaginary Playmate', *Pedagogical Seminar*, xli, (1932).

INDUSTRIAL FATIGUE RESEARCH BOARD, *A Study in Vocational Guidance*, H.M.S.O., 1926.

I.T.A., *Parents, Children and Television*, H.M.S.O., 1958.

JAMES, W., *Principles of Psychology*, Macmillan & Co., London, 1891, vol. 2, 501.

JERSILD, A. T., MARKEY, F. V., and JERSILD, C. L., 'Children's Fears, Dreams, Wishes, Daydreams, etc.', *Child Development Monographs*, xii, Teachers' College, Columbia, (1933).

KINSEY, A. C., et al., *Sexual Behaviour in the Human Female*, Saunders & Co., 1953.

LANZ-STUPARICH, M., 'Les adolescents et le cinéma: recherches préliminaires', *La Psychotechnique dans le Monde Moderne*, Presses Univ. de France, (1952).

LAZARUS, A. A., and ABRAMOVITZ, A., 'The use of "emotive imagery" in the treatment of children's phobias', *Journal of Mental Science*, cviii, 453, (1962).

LEAROYD, M. W., 'The "Continued Story" ', *American Journal of Psychology*, vii, (1895).

LEY, A., WAUTHIER, M-L., 'Contribution à l'Etude Expérimentale de l'Imagination', *Journal de Psychologie Normale et Pathologique*, xxxv, 1938.

LOCKE, J., *The Conduct of the Understanding*, Clarendon Press, Oxford, 1881.

LOWES, J. L., *The Road to Xanadu*, Houghton Mifflin, Boston, 1930.

LURIA, A. R., *Lecture*, International Congress of Psychology, London, 1969.

LYTTON, A., and COTTON, A. C., 'Divergent Thinking Abilities in Secondary Schools', *British Journal of Educational Psychology*, xxxix, 2, (1969), 188.

MCFARLANE, A. M., 'A study of the influence of the educational geographical film upon the racial attitudes of a group of elementary school children', *British Journal of Educational Psychology*, xv, 3, (1945), 152–3.

MCKELLAR, P., 'Thinking, Remembering and Imagining', *Modern Perspectives in Child Psychiatry*, (ed. J. G. Howells), Oliver & Boyd, 1965.

MACKINNON, A. A., WILSON, S., and MCKELLAR, P., 'Visual Imagery, Perception and Personality', *British Psychological Society Bulletin*, xxii, 75, (1969), 143–4.

MACKINNON, D. W., 'The nature and nurture of creative talent', *American Psychologist*, xvii, (1962), 484–95.

MAGNE, O., and PARKNÄS, L., 'The Learning Effects of Pictures', *British Journal of Educational Psychology*, xxxiii, 3, (1963), 265–75.

MAHLER, W., 'Ersatzhandlungen verschiedener Realitätsgraden', *Psychologische Forschung*, xvii-xviii, (1932–3).

MALEBRANCHE, N., *De la recherche de la vérité*, Bk. 2, Doivin et Cie., Paris, 1938.

MALINOWSKI, B., *Magic, Science and Religion*, Free Press, Chicago, 1948.

MARKEY, F. V., 'Imaginative Behavior of Pre-School Children', *Child Development Monographs*, xviii, Teachers' College, Columbia, (1935).

MEDAWAR, P., 'Scientific Method', *The Listener*, 12 Oct. 1967, 454–5.

MILLER, G. A., GALANTER, E., and PRIBRAM, K. L., *Plans and the Structure of Behavior*, H. Holt & Co., N.Y., 1960.

MILTON, J., *Areopagitica*, A. Murray & Sons, 1868.

MONTESSORI, M., *The Advanced Montessori Method*, Heinemann, 1917, vol. 1, Ch. 9, 256, 275.

MULLINS, C., 'Current Studies of the Personnel Research Laboratory in Creativity' (Appendix), *Widening Horizons in Creativity*, (ed. C. W. Taylor), (1964), 335.

MURRAY, H. A., *The Thematic Apperception Test Manual*, Harvard Univ. Press, 1943.

NATIONAL COMMISSION ON CAUSES AND PREVENTION OF VIOLENCE: *To establish justice, to insure domestic tranquility: Final Report*, U.S.A., 1969.

NIGHTINGALE, F., *Cassandra* (in Strachey, R., *The Cause*, G. Bell & Sons, 1928).

OWEN, D. E. TUDOR, *The Child Vision*, Manchester Univ. Press, 1920.

PEAR, T. H., and KERR, M., 'Unseen Drama and Imagery', *British Journal of Psychology*, xxii, (1931).

PEERS, E. ALLISON, 'Imagery in Imaginative Literature', *Journal of Experimental Pedagogy*, xi, (1913–14).

PETERSON, R.C., THURSTONE, L.L., *Motion Pictures and the Social Attitudes of Children*, Macmillan, N.Y., 1933.

PICKFORD, R. W., 'Imagination and the Nonsense Syllable', *Character and Personality*, vii, (1938).

PITCHER, E. C., and PRELINGER, E., *Children Tell Stories*, International Univ. Press, N.Y., 1963.

PLATO, *The Republic*, trans. Lindsay, Everyman, 1942.

PYTKOWICZ, A. R., WAGNER, N. N., and SARASON, I. G., 'An experimental study of the reduction of hostility through fantasy', *Journal of Personality and Social Psychology*, v, (1967).

RHONDDA, VISCOUNTESS, *This Was My World*, Macmillan, 1933.

RIBOT, TH., *Essay on the Creative Imagination*, trans. A. N. N. Baron, Kegan Paul, Trench, Trubner & Co., 1906.

RIMBAUD, A., 'Les Voyelles', *Oeuvres Complètes*, Gallimard, (1946), 103.

ROUSSEAU, J. J., *Confessions*, Flammarion, Paris, Bk. 1, 8–10, 41–2, 97, 89–90.

ROUSSEAU, J. J., *Emile*, Flammarion, Paris, 1930, Bk. 4, 302.

ROUSSEAU, J. J., *La Nouvelle Héloïse*, Flammarion, Paris, 1938, 2e partie, lettre 37.

SARTRE, J. P., *Les Mots*, Gallimard, 1964.

SARTRE, J. P., *The Psychology of Imagination*, Philosophical Library, N.Y., 1948.

SEASHORE, C. E., *The Psychology of Musical Talent*, Silver, Burdett & Co., 1919.

SHANKS, D. E., 'The scope and aims of the study of prose', Queen's University Education Department Bulletin, iii, Belfast, 1964.

SHUTTLEWORTH, F. K., and MAY, M. A., *The Social Conduct and Attitudes of Movie Fans*, Macmillan, 1933.

SMILANSKY, S., 'Promotion of pre-school culturally deprived children through dramatic play', *American Journal of Orthopsychiatry*, (1965), 201–2.

SMILANSKY, S., *The Effects of Sociodramatic Play on Disadvantaged Pre-School Children*, John Wiley & Sons, N.Y., 1968.

SMITH, T. L., 'The Psychology of Day-Dreams', *American Journal of Psychology*, xv, (1904).

SPEARMAN, C., *The Nature of Intelligence and the Principles of Cognition*, Macmillan, 1927.

SPENCER, H., *An Autobiography*, Williams & Norgate, 1904.

SPENCER, H., 'Moral Education', *Education*, Watts & Co., 1929.

SPENCER, H., *Social Statics*, R. Schalkenbach Foundation, New York, 1954.

SPERBER, A., 'Über den Dianakomplex der Mädchen', *Psychological Abstracts*, xviii, (1944), 1276.

START, K. B., 'Relationship between intelligence and the effect of motor practice on the performance of a motor skill', *Research Quarterly*, xxxi, (1960).

STEPHENSON, W., *Testing School Children*, Longmans, Green & Co., 1949.

STERN, W., and MACDONALD, J., 'Cloud-Pictures: a new method for testing imagination', *Character and Personality*, vi, (1937–8).

STEVENSON, R. L., *Across the Plains*, Chatto & Windus, 1915.

STORA, J., 'Un test d'imagination: le test verbal, 1. J. S.', *Journal de Psychologie Normal et Pathologique*, xxxix–xl, (1946–7).

SUTHERLAND, M. B., 'A note on pre-sleep imagining in 10-year-old children', *Journal of Child Psychology and Psychiatry*, iii, (1962), 111–14.

SVENDSEN, M., 'Children's Imaginary Companions', *Archives of Neurology and Psychiatry*, xxxii, (1934).

SYMONDS, P. M., *Adolescent Fantasy*, Columbia Univ. Press, 1949.

TCHERNIKOVA, N. A., 'Dva ocherka po psikologi literaturnovo tvorchestvo podrostkov', *Izvestia Akademii Pedagogitcheskikh Nauk, R.S.F.S.R.* Moscow, xxxv, (1950).

TERMAN, L. M. et al., *Genetic Studies of Genius*, Stanford Univ. Press, 1926, vol. 1.

TITCHENER, E. B., *Experimental Psychology of the Thought Processes*, Macmillan, 1909.

TROLLOPE, A., *An Autobiography*, Blackwood & Sons, 1883.

VALENTINE, C. W., 'The Function of Images in the Appreciation of Poetry', *British Journal of Psychology*, xiv, (1923–4).

VERNON, M., 'The Development of Imaginative Construction in Children', *British Journal of Psychology*, xxxix, (1948).

VERNON, P. E., 'A cross-cultural study of "creativity tests" with 11-year boys', *New Research in Education*, i, (1967), 135–46.

VYGOTSKI, L. S., *Thought and Language*, trans. Haufmann, E., Vakar, G., MIT Press, 1962.

VYGOTSKI, L. S., *Vo-obrazhenie i tvorchestvo v detskom vozraste*, Moscow, RSFSR, 1930.

WAGMAN, M., 'University Achievement and Daydreaming Behavior', *Journal of Counselling Psychology*, xv, 2, (1968), 196–98.

WALL, W. D., and SIMSON, W. A., 'The effects of cinema attendance on the behaviour of adolescents as seen by their contemporaries', *British Journal of Educational Psychology*, xix, (1949).

WALLACH, M. A., and KOGAN, N., *Modes of Thinking in Young Children*, Holt, Rinehart & Winston, 1965.

WELDON, H., 'Control of Subject Matter in BBC Programmes', Appendix to *Report of the Joint Committee on Censorship of the Theatre*, H.M.S.O., 1967.

WERTHAM, F., *Seduction of the Innocent*, Museum Press, London, 1955.

WHEELER, O., 'An analysis of literary appreciation', *British Journal of Psychology*, xiii, (1923).

WHITE, J. GRAHAM, CALDBECK-MEENAN, J., and MCALLISTER, H., 'The Desensitization of Phobic Anxiety and its Physiological Concomitants', *Papers in Psychology*, Queen's University, Belfast, ii, 1, (1968).

WHITEHORN, K., 'Words Without End', *The Sunday Observer*, (18 May 1969).

WINGFIELD, R. C., 'Bernreuter Personality Ratings of College Students who recall having had imaginary playmates during childhood', *Psychological Abstracts*, xxiii, (1949).

WORDSWORTH, W., *Poems*, 1815, Preface, Macmillan & Co., 1896.

Index

For Product Safety Concerns and Information please contact our EU representative GPSR@taylorandfrancis.com Taylor & Francis Verlag GmbH, Kaufingerstraße 24, 80331 München, Germany

Batch number: 08153780

Printed by Printforce, the Netherlands